THE LOGIC OF EVANGELISM

The Logic of Evangelism

WILLIAM J. ABRAHAM

William B. Eerdmans Publishing Company
Grand Rapids, Michigan / Cambridge, U.K.

© 1989 Wm. B. Eerdmans Publishing Co.

Wm. B. Eerdmans Publishing Co.
255 Jefferson Ave. S.E., Grand Rapids, Mich. 49503 /
P.O. Box 163, Cambridge CB3 9PU U.K.

Printed in the United States of America

11 10 09 08 07 06   15 14 13 12 11 10 9

Library of Congress Cataloging-in-Publication Data

Abraham, William J. (William James), 1947-
    The logic of evangelism / William J. Abraham.
        p.   cm.
    ISBN-10: 0-8028-0433-0 / ISBN-13: 978-0-8028-0433-4
    1. Evangelistic work.   I. Title.
    BV3790.A27   1989
    269'.2—dc19   89-7706
                                                          CIP

www.eerdmans.com

To
James Kennedy
Tullygrawley
Cullybackey

Contents

Acknowledgments

I am extremely grateful to a number of people who gave generous support during the work on this manuscript. A grant from the Lily Foundation enabled me to start on this project in the summer of 1987. Robert Prevost read the manuscript while it was being written and made a number of very valuable suggestions. David Martin and Gregory Jones read the completed manuscript and jointly offered one crucial point of advice, which I have gladly taken. I am especially grateful for the encouragement and support I received informally from my colleagues at Perkins School of Theology. This is not the first manuscript on evangelism they have helped to launch, and I trust it will not be the last. The blemishes that remain despite all this help are entirely mine.

In the end my deepest thanks go to my wife, Muriel, and to my children, Timothy, Siobhan, and Shaun. I would never have completed this work without their good humor and love.

I would like to thank the *Journal for the Academy of Evangelism in Theological Education* for permission to incorporate a revised version of my article, "Church Growth Theory and the Future of Evangelism," which appeared in volume 2 (1986-87), pp. 20-30.

ONE

Evangelism and Modern Theology

One of the undeniable features of modern theology is the scant attention it has given to the topic of evangelism. It is virtually impossible to find a critical, in-depth study of the subject by a major theologian. To be sure, various monographs have appeared on the mission of the church, on the character of the church's ministry, on church growth, and the like. However, there is very little of a really critical disposition that has sought to wrestle with the questions and options open to the modern Christian community with respect to its activities in the field of evangelism. We lack even a sense of what the questions are, where we should turn in order to assemble evidence, what criteria are appropriate in evaluating the possible answers to our queries, and how we might begin to make steady progress on the problems that confront us.

In this book I attempt in a preliminary way to make good on this deficiency. I seek to offer an account of the nature of evangelism and to articulate the implications of that account for the practice of the modern church in the ministry of evangelism. Materially, I shall argue for a very particular way of construing evangelism, which I will defend against the substantial objections that might be laid against it. In the process, I shall outline what the church should do in this field, thereby challenging many of our current procedures. Formally, my intentions cut much deeper than this. I shall also argue a case for taking evangelism radically seriously as a topic of theological inquiry. I consider it nothing short of a disaster that evangelism has been relegated to the fringes of modern critical theology. For too long it has been handed over unceremoniously to those who have little interest in critical reflection and who therefore tend to use the trappings of scholarship as part of a public relations exercise. Hence I plan to delineate the contours of an ongoing research program that could well constitute the beginnings of a new field within the discipline of theology. At the very least I hope to show that there are a wealth of questions that deserve extended attention.

The Rift between Evangelism and Theology

At the outset it would surely be helpful to explore why modern theologians have tended to ignore the issue of evangelism and why we need to discontinue this tendency. By doing so we can begin to spell out the context for this project and indicate its subsequent direction. Thus we can define more carefully what we hope to achieve and indicate in some detail the concerns that have generated the work as a whole. Inevitably our preliminary observations will be impressionistic and suggestive, but they will set us on our way expeditiously by drawing attention to the urgency of our situation. Let us begin with a very brief look at some of the literature on evangelism.

The last substantial monographs on the subject of evangelism appeared over thirty years ago. They are *The Practice of Evangelism*, by Bryan Green (canon of Birmingham Cathedral), published in England in 1951, and *Effective Evangelism*, by George Sweazey (who later became a professor at Princeton Seminary), published in America in 1953.[1] Both books are long on practice and short on critical theological reflection. At their own level they provide a very valuable service, highlighting evangelism as an important part of the church's work and providing much sane advice on how to proceed with integrity in this area.

Since then things have not changed appreciably in terms

---

1. Bryan Green, *The Practice of Evangelism* (London: Hodder and Stoughton, 1951); George E. Sweazey, *Effective Evangelism: The Greatest Work in the World* (New York: Harper and Row, 1953).

of the material available. One best-seller, Coleman's *The Master Plan*, has sought to interact seriously with the ministry of Jesus as a model for evangelism, but the lasting impression one gets from the volume is that it is as much an expression of modern pragmatism as it is a serious appropriation of the ancient Gospels.[2] Most of the remaining literature focuses on various programs for house visitation, personal witnessing, reaching the hard to reach, and the like.[3] The exceptions to this classification fall into three areas. First is the wealth of material on church growth that has been produced by Donald McGavran and his disciples.[4] We shall examine this with some care in due course, but it is worth mentioning here that church growth theorists are themselves thoroughly ambivalent about whether or not their work makes a contribution to the subject of evangelism. In any case, whether or not those committed to church growth are really prepared to subject their proposals to deep critical analysis is a moot question. A good case might be made out that they represent more of a call to arms than a rigorous research operation. The second body of material is provided by the various worldwide conferences on evangelism that have been held in the last half century or so.[5] The volumes produced from these conferences provide much valuable reflection, but, given the

2. Robert E. Coleman, *The Master Plan of Evangelism* (Westwood, N.J.: Revell, 1963).
3. Especially noteworthy is Richard Stoll Armstrong, *Service Evangelism* (Philadelphia: Westminster, 1979). David Watson's *I Believe in Evangelism* (Grand Rapids: Eerdmans; London: Hodder and Stoughton, 1976) is a popular introduction to some crucial questions on evangelism, while Michael Green's *Evangelism in the Early Church* (Grand Rapids: Eerdmans, 1970) is a much used but tendentious reading of the history of evangelism in the patristic period.
4. The classic in the field is still Donald A. McGavran, *Understanding Church Growth* (Grand Rapids: Eerdmans, 1980).
5. One of the earliest of these is *Evangelism*, produced by the International Missionary Council and published in 1938 by Oxford University Press. More recently material has been produced by the World Council of Churches, by various groups of conservative evangelicals, and by the Roman Catholic Church. A useful bibliography is in Rodger Bassham, *Mission Theology: 1948-1975. Years of Worldwide Creative Tension Ecumenical, Evangelical, and Roman Catholic* (Pasadena: William Carey Library, 1979). For a survey of the Eastern Orthodox tradition on evangelism see James J. Stamoolis, *Eastern Orthodox Mission Theology Today* (Maryknoll, N.Y.: Orbis, 1986).

nature of the task, their aim often has been polemical and ecclesiastical rather than critical and academic. Finally, here and there a really solid work of a genuinely critical nature has appeared. David Bohr's *Evangelization in America*[6] is one of the more noteworthy examples. Bohr offers a fascinating synthesis of theology, history, and practical suggestions; his is one of the very few books that could serve as a model for the serious student.

How are we to account for this state of affairs? How are we to explain the paucity of critical discussion about the theory and practice of evangelism as represented by this brief foray into the available literature? Surely it is obvious that there would not have been a Christian community if there had not been any evangelism; nor might there be one in the future. Yet until very recently little attention has been directed to this delicate enterprise. We are probably too close to the situation to provide an entirely satisfactory etiology, but it is worth recording our suggestions and impressions. The explanations we need are multifaceted.

Part of the explanation lies in the fact that Christianity has been a part of the fabric of the West for so long that it has been assumed that Christians do not really need to evangelize. National churches have been in European countries for centuries, while Christianity has been so intertwined with the history of the United States that serious historians often attempt to interpret its ebb and flow as the decline and renewal of its Christian heritage.[7] There has been, therefore, a deep sense of ease about the survival of Christianity in the West. Where evangelism has been taken seriously by the mainline traditions it has been relegated to a position of minor importance. Overall it has failed to fire the imaginations of the leaders of the central ecclesiastical institutions; most of these have been committed pri-

6. David Bohr, *Evangelization in America: Proclamation, Way of Life and The Catholic Church in the United States* (New York: Paulist, 1977). Also noteworthy is the pioneering work of the Latin American theologian Mortimer Arias. See his *Announcing the Reign of God: Evangelization and the Subversive Memory of Jesus* (Philadelphia: Fortress, 1984).

7. See William G. McLoughlin, *Revivals, Awakening, and Reform: An Essay on Religion and Social Change in America 1607 to 1977* (Chicago: University of Chicago Press, 1980).

marily to the maintenance of the institutions and to the handing over of the tradition to those brought up within the confines of the regular life of the church. In such an atmosphere it
is not likely that evangelism will receive much critical attention.
There simply is not in place the kind of intellectual and moral
support to sustain those willing to risk their reputation or their
vocation in such a spiritual and unacademic wasteland.

In addition, the best intellectual efforts of the Christian
community are channeled into fields that either elbow out or
inhibit serious engagement with the topic of evangelism. If evangelism is mentioned at all in the halls of learning it is as a minor
motif within practical theology. At best practical theology is construed as a rag-bag of bits and pieces on how to minister in the
church, with the highest honors going to pastoral care, homilet-
ics, liturgics, and administration; at worst it is the name given
to a topic that no one knows how to define coherently but upon
which anyone is an instant authority. Not many students are
likely to linger long in a critical mood in such an atmosphere.
If they are in earnest about theology they will soon find out
where the real work is done: they will be drawn to historical
study of Scripture, to church history, to philosophy of religion,
to systematic theology, and the like. One should not in the least
scorn this development; in fact, I shall argue that good work in
evangelism depends crucially on sustained and independent research in a whole network of disciplines. My point here is simply that the conventions of the modern academic study of theology militate against serious work in this field. Indeed, given
the way the guild of academic theology operates, it is virtually
impossible for evangelism even to be placed on the agenda of
debate. Evangelism is seen as a sectarian issue that requires the
kind of prior faith commitments that are out of place in a serious academic environment. Some would hold that it depends
on commitments that inevitably will corrupt critical judgment
from the outset.

Within academic theology and religious studies the crucial issues clearly lie elsewhere. Thus, much recent theology has
been deeply concerned about the possibility of the whole theological enterprise. Theologians in the West have been chal-

lenged to defend the very possibility of religious discourse. In addition, we have seen a wave of attacks on the viability of theological claims, stemming from Nietzsche, Marx, Freud, and the penetrating Positivist challenge of the thirties. As a result, no massive vision of the Christian position has really emerged since Barth. Most of our energy has been given to questions of fundamental viability, to considerations of method, and to the problem of translating or adapting traditional material to the modern world. Many of those who were nurtured in the Barthian tradition—Paul van Buren comes to mind—embraced a version of secularism that left little space for anything remotely akin to evangelism in the traditional sense. Indeed many theologians, including those who informed the divisions of the World Council of Churches, openly repudiated any interest in the conventional ministries of the church. The focus shifted to social and political action, and this radical change of emphasis continues with the move from the secular theologies of the sixties to the liberation theologies of the seventies and eighties. Moreover, until very recently the doctrinal commissions sponsored by the Anglican tradition have been devoted less to the content of the Christian message than to questions of its sources and norms.[8] The same can be said of the work done by the corporate theological endeavors sponsored by the United Methodist Church in America.[9] New winds are, of course, blowing, but it is fair to say that the whole ethos and content of twentieth-century theology to date has been incipiently hostile to tackling the fundamental issues raised by those interested in evangelism. This claim is not made in a spirit of chagrin or regret. Each generation has to tackle the issues that catch its imagination and vehemently cry out for its attention. But we do need to be cognizant of the theological context in which we are operating, and we should not be too surprised to find that our efforts are not greeted initially with great enthusiasm. It may well take a

8. See *Christian Believing: The Nature of the Christian Faith and its Expression in Holy Scripture and Creeds, A Report by the Doctrine Commission of the Church of England* (London: SPCK, 1976).
9. See *The Book of Discipline of the United Methodist Church, 1984* (Nashville: The United Methodist Publishing House, 1984).

generation before we can attain the kind of scholarly conversation that is essential in this area.

This will not be easy, for theologians have their own conventions concerning what counts as scholarship in their domain. They expect, for example, that the conversation will be conducted with partners who are already well established as substantial figures in the history of discussion and debate. Clearly this will be very difficult in the initial pursuit in evangelism. The material we have to hand that is explicitly devoted to the topic is not written by those whom modern theologians would generally accept as theological heavyweights. Rather, these authors are often dismissed as second-rate scholars unworthy of sustained attention. In our predicament we have to ferret around in the undergrowth and make a very serious effort to articulate and to examine insights and suggestions that only the very patient will find. Moreover, we cannot turn to the relevant pages in the great theologians of the past and simply look up what they have said about evangelism. For one thing, most of them appear on the surface to have said very little about the subject. For another, those who may have said something significant about it (e.g., John Wesley or Charles Finney) are dismissed summarily from the canon of serious theology simply because they are construed as revivalists or evangelists and therefore necessarily as lightweight scholars.

The reason for our difficulties in this area goes much deeper, however. Even if we were sure that the great theologians had something interesting to say about evangelism, something we should surely assume as true until proven otherwise, we face a perplexing dilemma. We do not know what precisely to define as evangelism, and therefore we are at a loss as to know what to designate as a contribution to a discussion about it. We need at the outset some preliminary conceptual mapmaking. That is why I have given so much time in what follows to delineating the concept of evangelism and to articulating the rival options available to us on this thorny issue. Only after we have done some careful initial work in this area will we be in a position to go back and ransack the history of Christian theology for valuable material on evangelism.

Another crucial factor fostering the climate of disinterest and antipathy is the fact that evangelism has been linked almost exclusively with a particular cluster of schools within modern Christianity, namely with fundamentalism and evangelicalism. Even dictionary definitions of evangelism reflect this, for some confuse evangelism with evangelicalism. This is not accidental, however, for evangelicals have owned evangelism as a distinctive if not exclusive characteristic of their contribution to modern Christianity. Certainly evangelicals deserve great credit for insisting that evangelism cannot be dropped from the activities of the modern church without shedding any theological tears. On the whole, however, they have not expressed their concerns in this fashion; their primary concern has been practice rather than theory. In their theological work they have focused most of their attention to shoring up impossible theories of biblical inspiration and to keeping at bay the acids of modern biblical criticism. This has now reached the point where one of evangelicalism's massive constituencies, the Southern Baptist Convention, is in a process of almost total regression to fundamentalism. This is a tragedy for evangelism. It is highly likely to prevent the Baptist tradition from making the kind of splendid contribution to critical work on evangelism of which it is potentially capable. This shift back into fundamentalism may also rekindle the dying embers of the fundamentalist-modernist controversy, which are still so visible underneath the surface of contemporary theology. In such a climate anyone who seeks to take evangelism seriously will be looked on with considerable suspicion.[10]

All this is not helped by the current image of the evangelist in contemporary society. The best way to highlight this observation is to pause and reflect historically on the lives of evangelists within Protestantism over the last three centuries. The most striking feature of the landscape is the steady decline in the theological abilities of the better-known evangelists over the

10. I have attempted to provide an overview and assessment of modern evangelicalism in William J. Abraham, *The Coming Great Revival: Recovering the Full Evangelical Tradition* (San Francisco: Harper and Row, 1984).

generations. Eighteenth-century evangelists could hold their own in any theological arena. John Wesley is now rightly ranked not just as a strategist but as a theologian who was steeped in the tradition of the patristic period and who made his own distinctive contribution to the debates in his day. Even more significantly, Jonathan Edwards ranks as one of the great theologians of all time, yet he was an active pastor who was intimately involved in the great religious awakening of his time. In the nineteenth century we can detect the beginnings of a major shift. Charles Finney was not incompetent in theology; indeed, he was an astute thinker and, besides helping to found Oberlin College, he left a fascinating corpus of material that has yet to receive the attention it deserves. Yet he also had an impatience with the academy and a large measure of disrespect for the classical traditions and landmark documents of theology, which tended to inhibit any serious interaction with what did not suit his purposes. More important, there is in his work a very pragmatic strain that is anxious to get on with the job so that theology becomes a handmaid of practice rather than an equal partner in dialogue. By the time we come to his successors, D. L. Moody and Billy Sunday, there is no serious theological substance at all. Moody is a fascinating figure who did gather around him at times scholars of considerable distinction, but his theological interests were limited in the extreme.

Things have not improved in the twentieth century. Undoubtedly the best-known evangelist of this period is Billy Graham. A remarkable figure, Graham has won the respect and affection of the church universal. His integrity and sincerity are beyond question. Moreover, he showed remarkable theological insight and courage in helping to forge neoevangelicalism, which he helped to launch in the early part of his careeer as an evangelist. Standard accounts of his work miss this completely. Yet there are obvious limits to his thinking—which he would be the first to acknowledge. He clearly recognizes the importance of critical theology for the health of evangelism over the years, but his own contribution understandably remains underdeveloped.

The new generation of television evangelists are much less

sensitive to critical theology than is Graham.[11] To be sure, they may found universities and colleges, they may appear on stage wrapped in the trappings of degrees, and they may well impress their admirers by offering books of one kind or another—but all these are mere window dressing; they do not represent any serious attempt to reflect deeply about the work in which they are engaged and from which they appear to make a lucrative living. In fact, much of modern mass evangelism has reached such a nadir of public scandal and disorder that one wonders whether the operation represents an evangelistic underworld of spiritual and theological corruption.

No doubt this is a harsh judgment that does a cruel disservice to the honest and self-sacrificial work that many have given to evangelism in this and earlier generations. But one cannot gainsay the fact that there has been a steady decline in the fortunes of evangelism over time. The situation is one of serious crisis for the church in the West. In such circumstances it is not surprising if theologians prefer to pass by on the other side and leave the whole mess to whatever Samaritan may have mercy upon it.

The Need for a Fresh Approach

Such factors as these make intelligible the scarcity of critical reflection on evangelism. The time has surely arrived when we should take a hard look at what evangelism is, reflect seriously on what has gone wrong, and make some suggestions about how it might be pursued with integrity. We need to develop a fresh universe of discourse that will open up a critical conversation on the complex issues that relate to evangelism. There are good reasons why this enterprise should be taken up with enthusiasm and caution.

First, this area deserves to be studied for its own sake. The subject of evangelism raises some very fundamental questions about a variety of issues that are of great importance within the-

---

11. Oral Roberts, Jimmy Swaggert, Jim Bakker, Pat Robertson, and Jerry Falwell readily come to mind at this point.

ology. Reflection on evangelism forces us to wrestle with what the essence of Christianity is and with such topics as conversion, faith, and repentance; it leads us to come to terms with the nature of the kingdom of God and the place of the kingdom in the ministry of Jesus; it leads us to think deeply about the nature of baptism and of Christian initiation; it encourages us to explore the relation between the intellect and the emotions in Christian commitment; it draws us to examine how far the faith of the early centuries can be expressed in the modern world; it makes us tackle anew the nature of apologetics; it makes us focus on how far, if at all, theistic proposals are amenable to rational persuasion. This is just the beginning of the list of topics that can be drawn up; we shall explore more fully on another occasion what exactly needs to be pursued and how they might be held together in a single universe of discourse. My concern here is to alert us to the importance of the topics, which cry out for attention in their own right.

Now, of course, we enter here some well-worn territory: these issues are nothing new in theology. But we are not seeking yet another foray into these questions and the disciplines that attend to them. What we need is the kind of reflection that will take up these matters with one steady eye gazing both descriptively and normatively on the evangelistic activity of the church and the other eye firmly fixed on the relevant data and warrants that any scholar must draw on to deal with them satisfactorily. Not only does this powerfully concentrate the mind on some of these issues, it also brings an angle of vision to these studies which may well yield insights and observations that are otherwise neglected. It is wise not to be too grand about the internal logic of our inquiry, especially at the outset, so we shall not here formalize precisely what kind of study will engage us. Enough has been said to indicate that there is an embryonic field of investigation that deserves attention in its own right.

A further reason for pursuing the topic of evangelism as a separate entity rests on the fact that a significant body of material on this subject is just now beginning to emerge. It is too early to determine *how* significant much of this work will be, but the winds of change are blowing quite strongly in many quarters. In part this has been spawned by experimentation in various kinds of evangelistic activity, in part by those who have set out single-mindedly to study church growth, in part by voices of criticism raised against Western Christianity by advocates of liberation theology, and in part by the astonishing spread of Pentecostalism across the world. We shall explore some of the recent literature in what follows, and it may surprise the reader just how much interesting material is actually available. One has to assemble it from hither and yon, but the exercise is well worth undertaking and the time is now ripe for a critical review of the prevailing options.

The last reason for taking up this study is more debatable but may well be the most pertinent of all. It is highly likely that the modern world will witness a very significant outburst of evangelism as it heads toward a new century. The mood has changed drastically in the last decade. Most modern churches acknowledge that the Western world needs to be evangelized afresh. There may be little or no agreement on what exactly this might mean or on how precisely this ought to be executed, but consensus is emerging that evangelism must become a top priority for the modern church. Thus it is a commonplace of modern sociological study of religion in the West that we have undergone a profound change in the culture since the Enlightenment. We may debate the merits or demerits of secularization, but there is no going back on the thesis that the proportion of the population who take Christianity seriously has shrunk drastically. The evidence in Europe for this is publicly visible in the figures for church attendance and in the intellectual ethos of the media, of politics, and of life generally. The situation in North America is more complex. Recent work by George Gallup, Jr., and his associates reveals that a huge majority of Americans consider themselves Christians. Closer inspection, however, shows that those interested in worthwhile Christian initiation cannot take this seriously. Gallup generously summarizes some of his conclusions in this fashion:

> We boast Christianity as our faith, but many of us have not bothered to learn the basic biblical facts of this religion.

Many of us dutifully attend church, but this act appears to have made us no less likely than our unchurched brethren to engage in unethical behavior.

We say we are Christians, but sometimes we do not show much love toward those who do not share our particular religious perspective. We say we rejoice in the good news that Jesus brought, but we are often strangely reluctant to share the gospel with others. In a typical day the average person stays in front of the TV set nearly 25 times longer than in prayer.

We say we are *believers,* but perhaps we are only *assenters.*[12]

It is small wonder, then, that all segments of modern Christianity are beginning to think seriously on what should be done in this area. This work should not be left to flounder haphazardly on its own. It demands disciplined reflection, and it deserves to receive the best intelligence we can muster.

The Way Ahead

How shall we proceed? Over against those who construe evangelism as the proclamation of the gospel and against those who construe it as church growth, the thesis presented and argued here is that we should construe evangelism as primary initiation into the kingdom of God. We will develop the case for this thesis over the next four chapters. In the first of these we will concentrate on the kingdom of God, and I shall seek to articulate the particular reading of the ministry of Jesus and of the apostolic church that will inform my analysis of initiation. In the second and third chapters I will outline and evaluate the two main accounts of evangelism currently on offer, namely proclamation and church growth. In the fourth chapter I shall lay out the broad contours of what initiation into the kingdom involves, arguing that this approach to evangelism is more illuminating and more helpful than the traditional focus on procla-

12. George Gallup, Jr., and George O'Connell, *Who Do Americans Say That I Am?* (Philadelphia: Westminster, 1986), pp. 88-89.

mation or the more recent emphasis on church growth. In the following two chapters I will explore in some detail the fuller content of my proposal, seeking to spell out the place of conversion, baptism, morality, the creed, the gifts of the Holy Spirit, and the classical spiritual disciplines in initiation. With this in place we shall then seek programmatically to articulate the implications of this conception of evangelism for the practice of evangelism. After that we shall take up two current issues that are liable to be seen as barriers to my proposals, namely the relation between evangelism and modernity and the question of the wider ecumenism.

A word is in order at this stage about the character of this project. It is unusual as regards its subject; that we have already indicated. It is also unusual with respect to its internal structure. At one level it seeks to develop a broad vision for understanding evangelism in the modern world. It argues a specific case normatively as to how evangelism should be understood, and this provides certain crucial clues as to how it should be carried out in practice. This will be developed directly over the next four chapters and indirectly through most of the remaining material. This dimension of the project is therefore fundamentally theological in character as all proposals about evangelism must necessarily be. A further dimension, however, is entirely different in character. Thus at a second level I am proposing that the debate or discussion about evangelism which is sorely needed should proceed in a particular way. Expressed summarily, the debate must not proceed by seeking out or drawing up fresh schemes of evidence by a new breed of specialists, but by bringing to bear on the topic in hand the relevant material from the appropriate disciplines that deal with that topic. This is a very ambitious undertaking, and it is very tempting to give up in despair and turn to more manageable undertakings. Yet this is a logical requirement of the whole operation and therefore utterly indispensable to critical work in this area.

Due to the multidisciplinary nature of the discussion, it will be clear that in developing some of the following proposals, we cannot do full justice to the critical work that has been done or that still needs to be done. Obviously, whole books could be written on some of the subjects that are tackled. Yet it is crucial that the effort be made, and I shall be more than satisfied if I can achieve three things: first, if I can show that it is helpful to conceive of evangelism as initiation into the kingdom of God; second, if I can demonstrate that the debate about evangelism should proceed by bringing to bear on its theory and practice the findings and reflection of a discreet number of disciplines; and third, if I can provoke or inspire other scholars either to provide a better way of pursuing critical reflection on evangelism or to take up and improve on the start I have undertaken here.

Because all this is very important for a proper reading of what is to follow, let me illustrate my main point with reference to the topic of the kingdom of God. This is a pivotal notion for the conception of evangelism that is developed in what follows, yet it is one of the most confused and contested concepts in modern studies of Scripture. What should one do in response to this state of affairs? One can pretend that there is no debate and simply deploy that vision of the kingdom which is most congenial to one's commitments in evangelism. This option is so obviously flawed and self-serving that one does not need to refute it. Second, one can opt for a particular reading of the kingdom, indicating those scholars upon whom one is depending for the ultimate defense of one's position. This is an entirely sensible move, for the sensitive scholar knows that repeatedly we are all dependent on the labors of others in most branches of theology. A third possibility is to review the relevant issues and evidence for oneself, come to a considered opinion on the key issues, and indicate as best one can the grounds for one's decisions. Clearly this is a difficult option for those not acknowledged as specialists in biblical studies, but it does highlight the crucial nature of systematic reflection on the relevant data and warrants.

My own work in this area will fall somewhere between the second and third alternatives. I am in fact relatively confident about the proposals concerning the kingdom of God which I shall incorporate into this project. They have been worked out through attention to the biblical texts, extensive review of the modern debate on the meaning of the kingdom of God, careful reflection on how one should come to conclusions on the issues involved, and acceptence of a considered judgment on the matter. This kind of work shall meet us again and again in the course of our endeavors. Purists will undoubtedly be nervous, and so they should be, for they are the academic conscience of the community; yet, if we are to think comprehensively and coherently about evangelism we cannot be intimidated by their scrupulousness; someone must take the risk, gather up the relevant evidence, and boldly strike out with specific proposals in this area. This is common in theology, so we should not be unduly perturbed.

Lastly, it is worth emphasizing at the outset that I aim to be both irenic and ecumenical in the deliberations that follow. It would be naive to think that I have not been deeply influenced and shaped by the traditions in which I have been nurtured in both faith and logic. Informed readers will be able to pick up the theological and intellectual breezes that have filled the sails and carried me on the ensuing voyage. They may even spot here and there a dangerous waterspout or its effects. Yet my intention is not to serve the interests or agenda of any particular party or denomination within modern Christendom. I still have much to learn from all the great traditions that have been inspired by the gospel of Jesus Christ across the centuries in a myriad of cultures. It is only in recent years that I have discovered the treasures of the Eastern Orthodox Church, and I still have not begun to assimilate the profoundly rich heritage of the black churches in America. In a host of areas I am merely a beginner who is crawling toward light and intelligibility. If I can advance the developing conversation on how that faith which has nurtured the lives of the saints might appropriately be transmitted across the generations and from believer to unbeliever, then I shall be more than satisfied.

TWO

The Gospel

A ny considered attempt to develop a coherent concept of evangelism that will be serviceable in the present must begin with eschatology. Whatever evangelism may be, it is at least intimately related to the gospel of the reign of God that was inaugurated in the life, death, and resurrection of Jesus of Nazareth. Any vision of evangelism that ignores the kingdom of God, or relegates it to a position of secondary importance, or fails to wrestle thoroughly with its content is destined at the outset to fail. This is so because the kingdom of God is absolutely central to the ministry of Jesus and to the mission of the disciples that launched the Christian movement into history. What is not at stake here is the prevalence of the idea of the kingdom of God in the biblical writings, although that could be argued persuasively.[1] What is at stake is the fundamental theological horizon within which both Jesus and his followers conceive and carry out the first, and paradigmatic, evangelistic action of the church. This cannot be the last word but rather must be the first word on evangelism.

The Debate about Eschatology

Immediately we are confronted with a dilemma. It is precisely the eschatological framework of early Christianity that is the

---

1. The classic case for this is still John Bright, *The Kingdom of God* (Nashville: Abingdon, 1953).

great stumbling block to belief and commitment in the modern world. The world of eschatology is not our world; it is a strange universe of divine intervention and angelic activity, of Messiah and Son of Man, of woes and resurrections, of cosmic battles with powers of evil, of vindications and judgments, of the end of time and history. If evangelism is concerned with contemporary commitment to Christianity (and only the uninformed can deny this), then we seem set on a collision course from the very beginning. We are calling forth a universe of discourse that is alien and immediately irrelevant. It should not therefore surprise us that our first thoughts on evangelism do not naturally turn in the direction of the kingdom. They turn to aspects of our current practice such as crusades or television evangelists; or they are directed to times of past glory, like the great revivals of the eighteenth century; or they focus on the expansion of the church and research on church growth; or they are taken up with the phenomenology of religious experience as represented by the conversions of Paul and Augustine. To be sure, no one is going to claim abruptly that we should ignore the concept of the kingdom of God, but we are not naturally going to gravitate toward it as the fundamental starting-point or horizon of our reflections.

This same stumbling block, however, is the cornerstone for the building we shall seek to erect. Evangelism should be housed very firmly within the dynamic rule of God on earth. This will provide fresh conceptuality for grasping its fundamental nature and new inspiration for its practice. To achieve this we need to articulate our understanding of the kingdom of God. More particularly, we must tread our way through the thicket of scholarship on this notion in order to identify the primary blocks required for the initial stages of our edifice. We do not need to get everything in place at this point, for we can add material as we proceed, but we must at least get the foundation straight.

Until recently the term *eschatology* had a broad meaning. It applied to those doctrines that were concerned with the ultimate destiny of the cosmos. Materially it focused on the last things, that is, it developed a kind of linear vision of the death of the individual person, the intermediate state, the return of Christ, the general resurrection, the last judgment, heaven and hell, and so on. Thus understood, it had a secure place at the end of those theologies that sought to expound a comprehensive vision of life from its beginning to its end. This treatment of eschatology has fallen on hard times of late in the West. Outside those narrow circles that still seek to work out timetables of the end, doctrines of the last things tend to be an archaic residue from earlier generations. Talk of judgment and vindication, of heaven and hell, perhaps even of life after death—all these lack serious content; outside the odd moment of crisis when circumstances force us to face up to our finitude they fail to carry much conviction or excite our imaginations. The last thing we desire when we think of them is to be offered a religious insurance policy to cover the contingencies.

When the early Christians began evangelizing they may well have shared some of our sense of embarrassment. They were undoubtedly interested in eschatology; some may even have been obsessed with it. Yet the last thing that would have been in their minds was that eschatology was merely a matter of things yet to come and that their first responsibility was to buy celestial fire insurance. For them eschatology had to do with events that had recently transpired in their midst; it was intimately related to their experiences of God. It was not just a matter of some future hope that lay out there on the horizon of history and from which they then made certain inferences about a change in life-style. Eschatology was something that had already dawned and had brought a whole new direction and power into their lives. God had moved decisively to establish his reign; the events of the new age were already under way; the kingdom had come already in Jesus Christ; they now experienced the fullness of the Holy Spirit in their personal lives, in their corporate worship, and in their service to the world; and they eagerly looked forward to the full dawning of the consummation of God's final act when at long last his purposes for the cosmos would be realized.

It is obvious from these cursory remarks about the coming of the reign of God that if we are to make any sense of eschatology we need to stand back for a moment and identify at least three essential assumptions. First, we must assume that God is a transcendent agent who has created the world for certain intentions and purposes. Without this assumption it will make no sense whatsoever to speak of God making promises and then fulfilling them, of God entertaining certain plans for creation, and of God acting both in history and at the end of all history to bring those plans into being. In fact, to speak of the rule of God or the reign of God or the kingdom of God is fundamentally to speak of the action of God in history—and it is difficult to begin to get purchase on this discourse without trading on the idea of God as an agent analogous to the personal agents we know in experience and through which we learn the logic of language about agency. Second, we must assume that God has acted in the life of the people of Israel, making himself known through events in history and through his word to the prophets. This is not a formal claim about the concept of God assumed in talk about the reign of God but a material claim about what God has in fact done to pave the way for the coming of the kingdom in the life of Jesus of Nazareth. In this case talk about the rule of God makes little or no sense outside the traditions of Israel that, taken as a whole, provide the particular conceptual cradle and the more precise content of the specific claims about God's action that are at the heart of the Christian gospel. Third, we must assume here that eschatological claims about the kingdom of God involve irreducibly a futuristic dimension that defies adequate depiction. Expressed negatively, the coming of the kingdom of God and all the activity of God associated with this cannot be exhausted by a description of events that are on the plane of history either in the present or in the future. Expressed positively, the coming of the rule of God is consummated by the end of history as we know it; it incorporates a mysterious taking up of the earth and of history into a radically transformed plane of existence that is presently beyond our capacity to imagine or to describe satisfactorily.

Clearly, all three of these assumptions demand further analysis, and they very naturally cry out for careful attention in their own right. My claim here is simply that without these assumptions it would be impossible to make much sense of the modern debate about the coming of the rule of God. The main protagonists in the debate argue from within these assumptions. They assume the basic rudiments of theism, that is, that God exists and that God acts to fulfill certain intentions; they presuppose that God's reign is first articulated and promised in the traditions of Israel; and they propose that someday, somehow, history will come to an end and this present life will be incorporated into the ultimate purposes of God. The debate concerns two fundamental matters. On the one side it is a historical dispute about what Jesus and his earliest followers believed and taught about the coming of the rule of God; on the other it is theological discussion about how and in what form the earliest Christian traditions about the kingdom can be appropriated today. It is extremely difficult to determine how far these two issues can be kept logically or psychologically distinct. For the moment our primary interest is in the first of these debates.

The fundamental options for the modern scholar have not really changed since the emergence of three main positions that have developed over the last two generations.[2] As is well known, the gauntlet was first thrown down by the pioneering work of Johannes Weiss and Albert Schweitzer. On their reading of the evidence, the kingdom of God was an entirely future, cataclysmic event that Jesus expected would happen almost immediately. This expectation of the coming rule of God was absolutely at the heart of Jesus' message and life. Clearly, it did not happen; hence Jesus must remain an alien figure to all those who want to be ruthlessly honest about what really happened in his ministry. These scholars derived their primary evidence for this proposal from a general theory about the meaning of the kingdom of God and related ideas in first-century Judaism, and from the varied texts in the Gospels that speak of the coming rule of God. The second main option, which arose in reaction to this dramatic account of the coming of the kingdom, took

2. Useful reviews of the literature can be located in Norman Perrin, *Jesus and the Language of the Kingdom* (Philadelphia: Fortress, 1976), and George Eldon Ladd, *Jesus and the Kingdom* (Waco, Tex.: Word, 1964).

a very different line and argued that the kingdom had already come in Jesus' life and ministry. One of the leading champions of this view was C. H. Dodd, who coined the phrase *realized eschatology* to describe the fact that the kingdom had really and definitively come in Jesus. Those who held this position construed references to a future coming of the kingdom as merely an accommodation of language. In reality the eternally present realm of God had come into history in the life of Jesus. These scholars found their chief evidence in those traditions that spoke of the kingdom as already present. The third alternative, as might be expected, was a synthesis of these two positions, which sought to do justice to both the present and the future coming of the kingdom of God. The basic move in this tradition was to argue that the kingdom of God is a dynamic reality that is anticipated in history before it is fully made manifest at the end of history. Thus justice is said to be done to both the present and future dimensions of the reign of God.[3]

As might be expected, the debate on the merits of these rival proposals is intense among historians of early Christianity. It has engaged some of the best minds in modern theology and spawned an impressive body of literature, though no consensus has emerged. In fact, it is unlikely that scholars will ever agree upon a solution to the problems facing them in this domain. The issues raised are tangled and numerous; sensitive and contested philosophical and theological considerations impinge on the materials of the debate; and there is no denying that the outcome is self-involving in the extreme. To look for consensus in such circumstances is utopian and unrealistic. Yet decisions must be made, for agnosticism represents a failure of intellectual nerve. For our purposes it will be sufficient to indicate the general direction of our thinking on the kingdom of God. We do not need to get everything straight at this point. What we need to articulate is the basic stance that we take on the rule of God; we shall soon see that this is more than enough to launch us on our quest for an adequate and healthy conception of evangelism.

3. For a sustained analysis along these lines see Ladd, *Jesus and the Kingdom*.

The perceptive reader will have noticed by now that I favor some version of the third option. This represents, as I see it, the most compelling analysis of the relevant evidence.[4] What we need to do now is articulate as succinctly as possible the central ingredients in the vision of the kingdom, which will inform the account of evangelism that is to follow.

The Kingdom as Already Here

When Jesus and the early church spoke of the kingdom of God, they were to a great degree on familiar territory. The idea of the kingdom or reign of God had been developing in various directions among the people of Israel for generations. It was especially prominent among the prophets and among the writers of the apocalyptic tracts that circulated within Judaism. The prophets spoke of God as the king both of Israel and of all the earth. God was the king over Israel in a special way, having visited Israel in Egypt and made them a distinct people, and having entered into a covenant with them over the years. God gave them the land of promise and established them, but over time the people refused to submit to God's rule, thereby facing discipline and judgment. In the course of their dealing with God there developed a hope that one day God would act in a decisive way to establish his rule. This hope was taken up and expanded by the apocalyptic writers, who extended it to embrace a final, cosmic transformation of the whole of creation. Central to the hope that was nourished in Israel was the expectation of a special agent of God who

4. The most illuminating account of the issues that I have encountered is in the work of G. B. Caird. See *The Apostolic Age* (London: Duckworth, 1955), chap. 12; *Jesus and the Jewish Nation* (New York: Oxford University Press, n.d.); "Eschatology and Politics: Some Misconceptions," in Johnston R. McKay and James F. Miller, eds., *Biblical Studies: Essays in Honor of William Barclay* (Philadelphia: Westminster, 1976), pp. 72-86; *The Language and Imagery of the Bible* (London: Duckworth, 1980), chap. 14. A valuable review of the biblical material can be found in G. R. Beasley-Murray, *Jesus and the Kingdom of God* (Grand Rapids: Eerdmans, 1986). Also valuable is A. L. Moore, *The Parousia in the New Testament* (Leiden: E. J. Brill, 1966). For a very different view see Lloyd Gaston, *No Stone on Another: Studies in the Significance of the Fall of Jerusalem in the Synoptic Gospels* (Leiden: E. J. Brill, 1970).

would have a crucial role in God's activity in the end times. These writers deployed a variety of images to describe the Lord's anointed, with a considerable diversity of opinion as to what precisely the Messiah would actually do.

When John the Baptist appeared on the scene in Galilee, he spoke in a context that was laden with eschatological expectancy. He announced the arrival of the Coming One and called the people of Israel to baptism and repentance. Jesus endorsed John's ministry and began a ministry of his own, which eventually led to his death at the hands of the authorities. In the traditions that enshrine the earliest witness to his activity we find ample evidence for the claim that Jesus and the disciples who gathered around him were convinced that the reign of God had already dawned. Then as now this remains one of the most contested proposals that has appeared in the history of religion. The issues at stake are so consequential for the deepest cosmic and theological questions that humankind has ever faced that it is ludicrous to think that one can adopt any position without it being fiercely contested. From the outset Jesus evoked a response that ran all the way from studied hostility and angry opposition through indifference, confusion, and bewilderment to joyful gratitude and wholehearted commitment. One is reminded of Hobbes's remark that if "two plus two equals four" were a matter of political significance then we could be sure that a party would be formed to contest the truth of this claim.

The witness of the evangelists to Jesus is that the dynamic rule of God has appeared in Jesus' life. In narrating his story they indicate that both his teaching and his deeds were saturated by the rule of God appearing now in history. Taken together these constitute the fundamental loci in the Gospels for the conviction that God has moved dramatically in history to inaugurate his rule.

In other words, Jesus' teachings, as enshrined in Scripture, bear witness to the dawning of the kingdom of God in the present. Mark's summary of the preaching of Jesus (1:15) insists that the kingdom of God has arrived. The exorcisms Jesus practiced also suggest that the kingdom is now present (Matt. 12:28; Luke 11:20). John the Baptist saw the miracles and healings as witnesses that he who was to come is here now (Matt. 11:5-6; Luke 7:22-23). In John's own ministry the kingdom was powerfully operative, even though Jesus' arrival was so significant to John that he considered the least in the kingdom to be greater than he was (Matt. 11:11; Luke 7:28). The eyes that see what the first disciples witnessed are blessed, for many prophets and righteous men longed to see and hear what they saw and heard (Matt. 13:16-17; Luke 10:23-24). In his account of Jesus' visit to Nazareth, Luke proclaims that the great day of Jubilee and liberation has been inaugurated (4:16-30). Moreover, although there are no cast-iron proofs or physical signs of the kingdom, it is now within reach of those exposed to Jesus; one can now experience its saving power (17:21). It is powerfully breaking out into the world and violent men are strongly attacking it (Matt. 11:12; Luke 16:16). Those who are within the circle of Jesus' disciples have been given the secret of the kingdom; they have been given access to the news of the in-breaking of the kingdom in the words and deeds of Jesus (Mark 4:11-12).

The content of the parables of Jesus provides very striking witness to the presence of the kingdom of God in history, a fact that is now commonly recognized. Thus Jesus' action as an exorcist is compared to that of a strong man who has entered the palace of the enemy, disarms him, and plunders his goods (Mark 3:27; Matt. 11:29; Luke 11:22). A variety of comparisons suggest that the kingdom is already here and that the blessing of salvation is currently available. Hence the kingdom is said to be similar to a treasure hidden in a field, which leads the finder to sell all he has to procure it; it is also like a pearl of great price that the enthusiastic collector takes drastic steps to obtain (Matt. 13:44-46). That the kingdom has already dawned is also suggested by the imagery of feasting. The table of banqueting is already laid out and the invitations have been given. Those unwilling to show up for the first course will not get to eat the splendid meal that has been prepared (Matt. 22:1-14; Luke 14:16-24). Moreover, the shepherd is out looking for the sheep that has been lost in the wilderness and the widow is rejoicing over the coin that has been found (Luke 15:4-10). The prodigal son and his elder brother are both invited now to attend the feast that their waiting father has prepared (Luke 15:11-32). The wedding guests are to cease their fasting (Mark 2:19-20); there is now new wine that cannot be contained by the old wineskins, for the new cloth that Jesus represents cannot be sown into the old clothes (Mark 2:21-22). The ruler of the kingdom is like an extravagant employer who offers the last to be called the same sovereign goodness that he has given to the first (Matt. 20:1-16) so that tax-gatherers and prostitutes are entering the kingdom of God ahead of those who think they have first rights to its privileges (Matt. 21:31). Those released from debt must, on pain of judgment, show the same kind of mercy as has already been displayed toward them (Matt. 18:23-35). Especially prominent is the use of agricultural imagery. The kingdom is like a grain of mustard seed that starts out very small but ends up being surprisingly big (Mark 4:30-32; Matt. 13:31-32; Luke 13:18-19). Or it is like seed that has been planted by the farmer who then departs to other work, leaving it to grow secretly until it is ready for harvesting (Mark 4:26-29). Proclaiming the word of the kingdom is compared to a sower who manages to gain an extremely rich harvest even though most of the seed is lost (Mark 4:1-9; Matt. 13:1-9; Luke 8:4-8). The kingdom is like wheat sown in a field; an enemy sows the same field with tares so that both now grow together until the harvest (Matt. 13:24-30). Other imagery is used as well: even now the dragnet has been cast into the sea and fish of every kind have been drawn ashore in it; in due course there will be a sorting of the good from the bad. God's kingdom is at work in history as truly as his judgment will manifest it (Matt. 13:47-50).

As I have suggested, we need to understand the deeds of Jesus in the context of the dawning of the rule of God. Thus the miracles and exorcisms described in the tradition represent the dawning of the new age in the present. They are not just manifestations of a sympathetic compassion for humanity; in the tradition the healings are linked intimately with the proclamation of the kingdom. As Michael Grant nicely summarizes the matter,

> the medically curative and philanthropic aspects of Jesus' healings were secondary to his main intention, which was

to signify that the Reign of God had begun. Such signs were not only "symbols" of what was happening or about to happen, but also at the same time they were *actual component parts* of these happenings. They are symbolic or sacramental acts that point beyond themselves to some further meaning and not only announce but also help to effect what they symbolize: effectual signs which cause what they signify. And so Jesus' cures, too, were not only symbolic seals of his mission but at the same time actual victories in the battle that had already been joined against the forces of evil.[5]

What is particularly striking in Jesus' ministry is the authority and scope of his activity as manifested in his miracles and his exorcisms.[6] It is entirely natural to see here the power of God breaking into history in a unique way and to interpret it as a pledge of the full eschatological kingdom that is yet to dawn. Some of the miracles (e.g., those related to sight) properly can be construed as acted parables that call the observers to open their eyes and see the radical significance of what is now made manifest in Jesus' ministry. All in all, the events associated with Jesus and his disciples, as portrayed in the tradition, display the saving power of the kingdom as now operative and even resident in history.

The Kingdom as Yet to Come

While it is true that the kingdom has already come, it is also true that it yet remains to come in the future. Thus the disciples are taught to petition God: "Thy kingdom come" (Matt. 6:9-13; Luke 11:2-4). The beatitudes are shot through with a future hope of full satisfaction in the kingdom of God (Matt. 5:3-12; Luke 6:20-23). Moreover, Jesus looks forward to a future day when many will come from east and west and sit at table with Abraham in the kingdom of heaven (Matt. 8:11). Various sayings about entry into the kingdom clearly imply a future com-

---

5. Michael Grant, *Jesus* (New York: Scribner's, 1977), p. 34.
6. See Ladd, *Jesus and the Kingdom*, pp. 149-50.

ing of the kingdom that is yet to be realized. So not everyone who mouths "Lord, Lord" will enter the kingdom of God (Matt. 7:21); and those who are rich are going to find it difficult to enter (Mark 10:25). Many of the entry sayings could apply to either a present entry or a future entry; but in many cases present entry would seem to signify participation in the kingdom that will arrive in its fullness at the judgment.[7]

Equally many of the parables, while speaking of the present reality of the kingdom, indicate that its coming has future dimensions that have not yet been realized. Thus those that depend on the agricultural imagery of sowing often present a picture of the kingdom as something that has been started now but will be fully manifest only in the future. The parable of the wheat and the tares clearly implies the coming of an ultimate day of judgment, as does the parable of the dragnet. A few parables seem to speak more directly of a coming kingdom. So the coming of the kingdom is compared to a burglar who shows up unexpectedly (Matt. 24:43-44); it is seen as an event that catches people off guard like foolish maidens who do not have enough oil for their lamps as they await the arrival of the bridegroom (Matt. 25:1-13); it is depicted as similar to the arrival of a master who has returned to find out how well his servants have used their talents in his absence (Matt. 25:14-30); it is also construed as a great final day of judgment when the shepherd will finally separate the sheep from the goats (Matt. 25:31-46).

One of the most important passages that speaks of the kingdom of God as a future event is that commonly referred to as the Olivet discourse. All three Synoptic Gospels refer to an apocalyptic consummation when the Son of Man will come in glory to gather his elect (Mark 13:1-36; Matt. 24:1-51; Luke 21:5-36). This event is described as a theophany that will shake the natural order and result in the judgment and the setting up of the perfect kingdom of God. It is to be preceded by the appearance of an evil personage and a terrible time of tribulation, which Luke explicitly depicts as a siege of Jerusalem and a his-

7. Beasley-Murray, *Jesus and the Kingdom of God*, p. 175.

torical judgment upon the Jewish nation. Moderns for the most part find this material repellent, for we are not used to the literary genre in which it is expressed. What is remarkable about it, however, is the restraint exercised in the content. Readers are warned again and again to beware of those who would lead them astray by insisting that they are the actual embodiment of the event referred to in the prophecy; very little information is given with regard to exact chronological details; in fact, only the Father knows the time of the final hour. It appears, then, that events in history, in particular the fall of Jerusalem, are linked intimately to the final coming of the Son of Man in glory. The natural reading of this material therefore has been to see in this tradition the great stumbling block to a responsible and honest appropriation of eschatology in the modern world. Read plainly, the texts appear to speak of an early end to history, something that the inexorable march of events has shattered as patently false. Here we certainly have a future kingdom with a vengeance; there is no mistaking the future dimensions of this coming of the kingdom, yet the kingdom is predicted as just around the corner in time, and every schoolchild knows that is nonsense. Contrary to this widely held opinion, however, this material can bear an entirely different interpretation which, if well founded, provides a vital clue to a healthy reading of the relation between the initial and ultimate comings of the kingdom of God.

Two pieces of background information, one historical and the other linguistic, are crucial at this point. On the historical side, we need to see the whole of Jesus' ministry as a mission to Israel that is firmly rooted in history and in the prophetic traditions. In Jesus, Israel faced a crisis of obedience in which she had to decide to follow either the road of national repentance or the road to national ruin. John the Baptist had already insisted on this and Jesus set his own message firmly within this context. Expressed bluntly, if Jerusalem abandoned God in the person of his messenger then God would abandon her to her enemies. It is this horizon that makes sense of Jesus' repeated warnings to Jerusalem, most of which are couched in language that is drawn from the prophecies of Jeremiah and

Ezekiel. It also accounts for the urgent missionary tour conducted by his disciples in the middle of his ministry.

On the linguistic side, it was common in the prophetic and apocalyptic traditions of Judaism to use eschatological language in bold and creative ways.[8] Much eschatological language had as its primary referent the end of the world, a natural result since those who used it believed that the world had a beginning in the past and would have an end in the future. However, eschatological language was also used metaphorically to refer to events here and now even though it was well known that these events were not in any literal sense the end of history or the end of time. Modern usage of eschatological discourse can illustrate what we mean here. People often describe ordinary events of history or of experience in eschatological categories, using such terms as heaven, hell, purgatory, limbo, and paradise. In such instances only the most wooden literalist would object to such usage; we all instinctively know that the language of eschatology is being used metaphorically. Likewise, prophets such as Jeremiah and Joel used language drawn from the beginning and end of history to describe events in history that were times of decisive crisis for Israel. Thus an expression like "the day of the Lord" can be given both a short- and long-range application. It can refer to a great day of judgment at the end or to a great day of judgment ahead in history but prior to the end. Indeed the two can be set side by side in a dramatic way to bring out the fact that the present events in history anticipate or foreshadow the climactic events of vindication and judgment that are anticipated at the consummation of history. What God is doing now in history or what he is about to do in history is a foretaste of what he will do eventually at the end of history. Thus the future has already been realized in the present.

In light of these considerations, we can make sense of the Olivet discourse. Mark's version begins with a question about the destruction of the temple. Read on a pedestrian level, it looks as if Mark has tacked on to the end of his answer the answer to another question, namely, When is the world going to end? As it stands the chapter is self-contra-

8. See Caird, *Language and Imagery of the Bible*, pp. 256-60.

dictory: on the one hand, Jesus knows that the Son of Man will come within a generation; on the other hand, no one knows when the end will come, for only God is privy to such information. From the vantage point laid out above, however, these features of the text are entirely intelligible. The fundamental point is that the disaster to Jerusalem will come within the lifetime of the present generation, and when it comes the reader is to see in it the coming of the Son of Man to whom God has given the judgment of the nations. The point about the contradiction is this: when construed as an event in history, the day of the Lord would come in a generation; in its full literal reality the time of the day of the Lord is known only to God. The two are laid side by side not just for reasons of psychological impact but because what God is doing now in history is in line with what he will do in the ultimate fulfillment of his purposes.

It is worth pausing to note that the description of the events of Pentecost fit this pattern. Thus after the dramatic coming of the Holy Spirit—which is made manifest in a profound awareness of God, in speaking in tongues, and in a bold proclaiming of the mighty works of God—Peter's sermon interprets these phenomena as a fulfillment of the prophecy of Joel. The prophecy begins prosaically enough with talk of an outpouring of the Spirit that will lead various groups to dream dreams, see visions, and so on. But it ends with dramatic apocalyptic language:

> And I will show wonders in the heaven above,
> and signs in the earth beneath,
> blood, and fire, and vapor of smoke;
> the sun shall be turned into darkness
> and the moon into blood,
> before the day of the Lord comes,
> the great and manifest day. (Acts 2:19-20)

Clearly nobody objected to Peter's irrelevant application of Scripture, for convention allowed the use of apocalyptic language to bring out the full significance of what had just happened. God had acted to fulfill prophecy and the events referred to embodied a real foretaste of what God would do in the great and manifest day of the Lord.

If all of this is at all plausible, then it is clear that the scriptural references to the future are not the embarrassment that scholars often thought them to be. Aside from evoking a profound sense of hope for the accomplishment of God's purposes for creation and history, they dramatically highlight the fact that God is now actively engaged in history in the events associated with Jesus. He was there anticipating his future actions. God established his reign on earth in the life, death, and resurrection of Jesus. This activity did not cease with the resurrection and ascension of Jesus but continued in the ministry of his disciples, in the outpouring of the Holy Spirit, in the formation of the Christian community, in the fall of Jerusalem, in the missionary activity of the early Christians, and the like. God's rule has indeed begun in earnest; it is currently within the grasp of all who will reach out and receive it, and it will be brought to perfection in the great and manifest day of the Lord. God's kingdom has come in the past; it is here in the present; it will come in the future. All three tenses are required if we are to begin to do justice to its inner complexity and dynamic. We live now suspended between the times. God's kingdom has come and all creation is invited to share in the blessings of salvation; God's kingdom is yet to come and all creation is invited to strain toward the final consummation of God's justice and love with eager anticipation.

The Kingdom and Divine Action

We can now satisfactorily dispatch several important matters that hover in the neighborhood. First, it is not surprising that the coming of the kingdom remains hidden or that the events associated with it are open to contrary interpretations. God's action in history is often indirect. He works within and through nations, and he achieves his purposes through events like the crucifixion of Jesus or the fall of Jerusalem or the summons of a group of fishermen. Even dramatic actions like miracles and exorcisms, although in a sense they constitute signs of his presence, do not coerce assent. It is perfectly possible to be exposed to such events and remain totally bewildered and confused by their appearance or to be tempted to explain their occurrence in terms of the piety and power of their agent or in terms of demonic activity (Acts 3:12; Mark 3:30). Nor are they the only locus of divine action, as if the coming of the rule of God merely involves occasional intervention here and there in a display of theological fireworks. God works mysteriously as well as openly in the establishment of his rule so that to demand prepackaged signs and wonders is to miss the possibility of his action here and now in the mundane events of history. In order to read the coming of the kingdom of God in history we need discernment of heart and spirit; we need the ability to hear what God is saying to us through them and to be prepared to reorient our lives in the light of them. We also often need access to a word of prophecy that on the basis of divine revelation makes known the actions and intentions of God that are being realized in history. Hence it is entirely appropriate to speak of the hidden character of the coming of the kingdom in the present.

It is also appropriate to apply the language of the kingdom in various contexts. In the modern debate about eschatology much has been made of the failure of nineteenth-century liberalism when it spoke of the coming of the kingdom in terms of the moral transformation of individuals and society in the wake of the impact of Jesus and his teaching. The common orthodoxy on this position is that it has been smashed once and for all by Weiss and Schweitzer. Likewise, one frequently hears complaints about the attempts by modern existentialist theologians to appropriate the language of eschatology by reducing it to the crisis that the individual must face when confronted with the word of God in Jesus or in the kerygma about Jesus. The former position appears to miss the full force of the eschatology enshrined in the traditions about Jesus, while the latter seems to dehistoricize eschatology by lifting it completely out of history into a numinous realm of subjective experience. We seem to be between a rock and a hard place.

A more plausible way to read both traditions is to see them as embodying entirely legitimate extensions of the language of eschatology. The coming of the rule of God does indeed mean a profound crisis for the individual. It calls for a death to the old life and a resurrection to a new life in the Spirit; it involves a radical reworking of one's self-understanding and a decisive turning from a life of idolatry to one of service to one's neighbor. In such circumstances it is entirely natural to speak of being born again and of entering into eternal life here and now. The Son of Man has come to take up his abode in one of God's little ones—so let there now be rejoicing in heaven in anticipation of the ultimate destiny of those who have accepted God's reign. Moreover, since God is vitally involved with the course of history, nineteenth-century European liberals as well as their evangelical opponents in North America were entirely correct to look for the coming of the rule of God in the social and moral transformation of society. God is active providentially in all of history to establish his kingdom: his intentions regarding justice, peace, and love cannot be confined in principle to the inner lives of the pious and to the final events of history; they embrace all of creation and all of history. Hence they embrace events now in every particular history, and it is a failure of both faith and logic not to look and to work for the coming of God's rule in society. Where both liberal and existentialist theologies have erred is not so much in what they have affirmed but in what they have denied. Working out of incomplete and inadequate accounts of eschatology, they have tended to confine God's coming to their favorite hunting grounds for divine action. They have lost sight of the sophisticated link between present and future that is at the heart of eschatology and thus they tended to collapse the whole of eschatology into the present. By restoring the inner logic of God's action as it embraces past, present, and future, we can build on their insights without embracing their costly errors. God's reign has begun; he has come in Jesus to bring judgment and liberation; he comes repeatedly in history in salvation and discipline; his rule is within reach of both individuals and nations; we can now enter into its penultimate inauguration as we strive toward its full and final consummation. Yet there is more to come; what we experience now is a foretaste and foreshadowing of those ultimate acts of God that will bring history to its teleological denouement at the great and manifest day of the Lord, which is beyond literal description.

Holding fast to the subtleties of eschatological language also helps us to understand why so many are led astray down false paths of date setting and speculation. In modern times much of this stems from the craving for national and personal security in the midst of social chaos and political turmoil. Surely it is no accident that people turn to apocalyptic teaching when they are desperate to hear a word of assurance about the final destiny of the world and of history. Those who are scared about the future of the late, great planet earth will gladly turn to those who promise to unlock the mysteries of the future by charting the geography and chronology of the last days. Apocalyptic literature was created to speak in a powerful way and with a dramatic seriousness that would match the sense of hopelessness and terror that can easily grip a generation in the midst of a profound crisis. But those who fail to put apocalyptic and eschatological literature into its setting in the ancient world invariably read it as if the writers had minds as literalistic as the readers' own. They treat this kind of material as if it were on a par with the proceedings of the stock exchange. Thus it is not surprising that they go astray and lead the gullible pious in their train.

The causes of misunderstanding in the ancient world itself lie in other directions. First, it is easy to be misled when an author or speaker switches from a more literal to a more metaphorical use of eschatological discourse, especially when he puts penultimate events in history alongside the ultimate events that will occur when God will usher in the great and final hour of all history. Second, it is well-nigh impossible to keep the eager sense of delight and hope that correlates with the experience of the coming of God's rule here and now from welling up into premature anticipation. This is especially so when one senses that all of creation is in travail to realize its ultimate divine destiny and that the powers of evil are liable to break out repeatedly in a last-ditch effort to thwart the purposes of God. Such a hastening of the end is common in both secular and sacred eschatologies that see history heading for a final realization of its purposes. Finally, it would be amazing if the early church did not at times move in this direction. The intellectual challenge posed by the events surrounding Jesus was staggering in the extreme. On the one hand the church had the oral traditions about Jesus transmitted by disciples, who were convinced that Jesus was the supreme agent of God sent to redeem Israel and the world. On the other hand it had the ancient traditions of prophecy that provided the conceptual tools out of which it sought to make intelligible sense of Jesus' ministry and of the disciples' experiences of the Holy Spirit. The traditions that articulated the hopes of Israel were varied and complex; particular patterns of divine action and promise were clearly discernible. Yet the word of prophecy was not itself a simple blueprint for God's action in history and at the end of time. As Meyer has suggested, prophetic knowledge is not precise determinate knowledge, "as if [it] were a kind of empirical-knowlege-by-anticipation but with symbolic frills and trimmings."[9] Hence the correlation between prophetic word and event is ambiguous. The event interprets the word as the word interprets the event.

> The ambiguity is denied equally by the fundamentalist's simplistic affirmations of fulfillment and the rationalist's simplistic discernment of mistakes. If God speaks in prophecy, he speaks in the history that follows on history and it is history, history grasped within the perspective of faith, that does what the prophet cannot do—namely, decipher prophetic symbol, translating image into event, schematic sequence into actual sequence, and symbolic time into real time.[10]

To be sure, the members and leaders of the early Christian community were not operating as autonomous agents seeking to patch together such information as they had about Jesus into the oral and written traditions of Judaism. They were convinced that God continued to be in their midst guiding them and speaking to them. But even so it would be incredible if some did not

9. Ben F. Meyer, *The Aims of Jesus* (London: SCM, 1979), p. 246.
10. Ibid., p. 247.

fully grasp what was going on and hastily identified the events currently happening with those that lay as yet in the mind and hands of God. Such events as the resurrection of Jesus and the outpouring of the Spirit would have been enough to send most minds saturated in the hopes and promises of Israel into believing that the end of the world could well be just around the next corner of history.[11]

The Kingdom and the Spread of the Gospel

These events were also enough to provide the early community with its primary motivation for evangelism. Christianity began as a kind of renewal within Judaism. This is entirely in keeping with the eschatological setting that we outlined above. The gospel was for the Jews first, because from the outset they were destined to have a universal role in the redemption of the world. Jesus' ministry was directed almost entirely—if not exclusively—to Israel, for he came to fulfill the promises to her and to usher in the new age that was to radiate out from her. Even certain prophecies spoke of the Gentiles flocking to Israel to witness and to experience the salvation of God (Micah 4:1-2). Thus, the kingdom that Jesus inaugurated began in Israel and was constituted by the restoration of Israel, symbolized in the calling of the twelve. It was fitting, therefore, as well as psychologically compelling, that the first acts of evangelism should be directed to Jerusalem and to Jewish listeners.

What is especially striking is the way in which the gospel of the kingdom initially spread. It did not spread because of a carefully designed program of evangelism; nor did it start because the early disciples meditated on the Great Commission and felt that they had better obey it to assuage their feelings of guilt. The church did not begin its evangelistic activity because

---

11. Caird expresses the matter succinctly: "It is perhaps plausible that the early Christians were so deeply conscious of having experienced in Christ, in his resurrection, and in the coming of the Spirit, the fulfilment of the Old Testament promises that occasionally, especially in times of apocalyptic crisis, they felt the frontiers of the future close in upon them." See "Eschatology and Politics: Some Misconceptions," pp. 85-86.

it was terrified about the prospects that faced those who died without hearing about Christ; the Christian movement was not initiated by a band of professional evangelists eager to sign up a public relations firm and get the show on the road. Rather, the gospel spread and the church grew because the sovereign hand of God was in the midst of the community that found itself surrounded by people who were puzzled and intrigued by what they saw happening. The overwhelming impression created by the traditions witnessing to the early evangelistic activity of the disciples is that the Holy Spirit was present in the community, bringing in the reign of God and inspiring the disciples to speak boldly of the mighty acts of salvation that God had wrought through the life, death, and resurrection of Jesus. The signs and wonders associated with the ministry of Jesus and to which Jesus introduced his disciples continued in the early community. The first converts gathered around the disciples and met together in the temple and in their homes for teaching, prayer, praise, fellowship, mutual care, and the breaking of bread (Acts 2:42). They proclaimed the word about Jesus boldly, and when martyrdom and persecution drove them out of Jerusalem they continued to wait upon the guidance of God and gossiped the good news of the kingdom to those who would listen. In other words, evangelism was rooted in a corporate experience of the rule of God that provided not only the psychological strength and support that was clearly needed in a hostile environment but that also signified the active presence of God in their midst.

We have now come full circle. We began by suggesting that whatever evangelism may be, it is intimately related to eschatology. But eschatology is not just an esoteric theory about the last things. Within the Christian tradition it is also an account of the dramatic action of God in history in which God begins to realize those intentions that will be accomplished completely when he brings history to a close and establishes a new heaven and a new earth. Eschatology is a vision of the coming of the kingdom of God that was initiated in Jesus of Nazareth, was experienced and cherished by the community that arose after his death and resurrection, and is now within the grasp of those who will repent and receive the gift of the Holy Spirit; yet it remains to come in all its glory and fullness. If this vision is correct then there is good news for the world; there is indeed a gospel worth sharing. Moreover, evangelism is an activity of the followers of Jesus that should be rooted and grounded in this dynamic, mysterious, numinous reality of the rule of God in history. We have not defined exactly what evangelism is as yet but, whatever it is, it must draw its fundamental content and inspiration from the early community that gave birth to its initial efforts in this domain and from the same God who inaugurated his rule through the coming of Jesus Christ into the world. Evangelism is at the very least a continuation of vital elements in the work of the early apostles, prophets, and martyrs who found themselves dramatically caught up in the reign of God in the world.

THREE

Proclamation

Since the coming of the rule of God was absolutely central to the ministry of Jesus and to the teaching of the early church, we might naturally construe evangelism as first and foremost the proclamation of the arrival of that kingdom on earth. Indeed, the traditional view of the ministry of evangelism has embraced this position in its conception of its work. In this chapter I shall examine the adequacy of this position, and argue that it is vulnerable to very serious criticism and is unlikely to survive attempts to correct it.

As we embark on this task, it is worth remembering that our notion of evangelism, although the word has an ancient and honorable pedigree, is a relatively modern one. In the eighteenth century, for example, no one would have thought of referring to John Wesley or George Whitefield as an evangelist. In the nineteenth century similar pastors would have been known in most quarters as "revivalists," the common designation for itinerant preachers. In fact, *evangelism,* like its conceptual cousin *evangelization,* came into prominence only in the late nineteenth century. For arbitrary reasons the latter term got lost and has now surfaced in ecumenical circles as an alternative to *evangelism.* Somehow there is less stigma attached to the term *evangelization,* even though usage from the late nineteenth century to today makes it virtually impossible to separate these terms in meaning. Of course, one can always stipulate a difference of meaning between them, but this does not alter the fact that historically the two mean much the same thing. People prefer the word *evangelization* because it gives them more freedom to change the meaning of the term and because it cuts them loose from the negative associations of the word *evangelism*. In my view nothing much hangs on the distinction.

The Link between Evangelism and Proclamation

The prevailing conception of evangelism in Western Christianity ties it intimately to the proclamation of the Christian gospel. Most Christians, if asked to define *evangelism*, would naturally construe it as the announcing or communicating or proclaiming of the Christian message to those outside the Christian faith. Dictionary definitions in both Britain and North America bear this out. *Webster's Third International Dictionary* defines evangelism as "the proclamation of the gospel; especially the presentation of the gospel to individuals by such methods as preaching, teaching, and personal or visitation programs." According to the *Oxford English Dictionary,* evangelism is "the preaching or promulgation of the gospel." Likewise an evangelist is defined as an itinerant preacher who proclaims the Christian message wherever he or she will receive a hearing. And evangelization is defined as the "action or work of preaching the gospel." Other sources refer to "instructing in the gospel," "converting people to Christianity," "bringing under the influence of the gospel," and the like. However, the prevailing impression is that evangelism is basically the preaching of the Christian message to those who will hear. And this is underscored by the conventional image of the evangelist as an itinerant Christian worker who preaches the gospel and calls people to commitment to Jesus Christ as Savior and Lord.

The etymology and semantic associations of the word *evangelism* help to underscore this view. The Greek verb from which *evangelism* is derived, *euangelizomai,* means "to bring or announce good news," and the Greek from which we get our word *gospel, euangelion,* means simply "good news." It is only natural, then, that *evangelism* and *evangelist* should come to be heavily associated with announcing and proclaiming the gospel. Evangelical Christians in the West and Orthodox Christians in the East have for the most part favored this view of evangelism. Thus the Lausanne Covenant says that

> to evangelise is to spread the good news that Jesus Christ died for our sins and was raised from the dead according to the Scriptures, and that as the reigning Lord he now offers the forgiveness of sins and the liberating gift of the Spirit to all who repent and believe.[1]

Metropolitan Mar Osthathios distinguishes between evangelism and mission in this fashion: "Evangelism is the spreading of the good news by proclamation, whereas mission is the outflow of the love of God in and through our life, word and deed."[2]

The close link between evangelism and proclamation surely helps to explain one of the most puzzling features of the usage of the term *evangelism* from the second until the nineteenth century, namely, its use to refer to the writers of the four Gospels. If the early evangelists were those who traveled abroad to communicate the good news of the gospel, and if that good news was intimately linked to the Gospels about Jesus, it would be very natural also to call the writers of the Gospels "evangelists." What is less explicable is the speed with which this usage caught on and the extent to which it overshadowed the earlier usage, which has been recaptured in the twentieth century. Little attention seems to have been given to this question, but we may never be in a position to provide a comprehensive analysis of the astonishing loss of the earlier usage for most of the church's history. It is utterly remarkable that it has been recovered and spread so quickly into common parlance.

At least three factors are at work in this fascinating revolution in linguistic usage. One is the determined efforts of evangelical Christians to search out the biblical background to modern terms and to reinstate as best they can the original meanings into contemporary usage. This desire is fueled by a variety of theological concerns that range from a deep reverence for the

---

1. John Stott, *The Lausanne Covenant: An Exposition and Commentary* (Minneapolis: World Wide Publications, 1975), p. 20.
2. Metropolitan Mar Osthathios, "Worship, Mission, Unity — These Three," *International Review of Missions* 65 (1976): 39.

biblical text to a desire to provide clean, clear-cut definitions of key terms in their theological discourse. Another factor is the impact of C. H. Dodd's famous and widely adopted attempt to show that the early church made a definite distinction between preaching and teaching.[3] Drawing on the speeches in Acts as the primary source for the content of the primitive Christian kerygma, Dodd argued that the proclamation of the early church was a distinct act within the activities of the first Christians. The content of the preaching fundamentally focused on a brief recital of the birth, death, burial, resurrection, exaltation, and return of Jesus set in the context of the fulfillment of Old Testament prophecies. This act of preaching was followed up by acts of teaching, which focused on ethical instruction and exhortation derived to a great extent from Jewish antecedents and shaped by the evolutionary development of the early church as it awaited the return of Christ. Dodd himself did not apply this to questions about the meaning of evangelism, but his widespread influence helped to reinforce the distinction between proclamation and teaching and thus aided in the restoration of the older conception of evangelism. But undoubtedly the most significant factor in this restoration has been the outburst of activity by professional evangelists in the modern world. With the development of radio and television and its use by Christian preachers there could be no stopping the universal dissemination of that usage, which has now become second nature to both believer and unbeliever.

This does not mean that everyone has been comfortable with this conception of evangelism. As we shall see, those committed to the study of church growth have pressed for a different understanding, and where theologians have taken the time to attend to evangelism they have produced a welter of alternatives. But the standard modern conception of evangelism has stood the test of time exceptionally well, and even those who want to depart from it tend to ride on its coattails. Thus the attempts to see evangelism as witnessing or as the active pres-

---

3. C. H. Dodd, *The Apostolic Preaching and its Developments* (New York: Harper and Row, 1936).

ence of Christians in the world or as the spreading abroad of the sacraments are still tied to the concept of proclamation. In all of these cases the link to evangelism is preserved by the assumption that these acts proclaim the Christian message by action rather than by word. Thus the sacraments of baptism and eucharist proclaim the Lord's death, acts of service and kindness proclaim the love of God for his creatures, and acts of personal witnessing, whether verbal or nonverbal, achieve the same aim. We might say that in these cases *proclaim* is being used metaphorically or analogically; it is therefore parasitic on a primary or original use that related evangelism to the verbal proclamation of the gospel. Thus, to deepen or enrich our conception of evangelism will take more than a few verbal shuffles and more than a shift from the literal to the metaphorical to bring about the necessary changes.

The Case for Proclamation

But do we need to enrich our conception of evangelism? Is not the recovery of the original conception and its reinstatement into our theological vocabulary a major advance in clarity and an implicit call to exercise a responsible ministry in this area? There are surely excellent reasons for a positive response to this question. Certainly there is here a very clear conception of evangelism. To be sure, we need to emphasize that by "proclamation of the gospel" we mean the *verbal* proclamation, in order to prevent evangelism from sliding into a thoroughly vague notion that stands for everything and anything that the church does in witness and service. Once we allow the latter to happen we lose sight of those distinct activities that distinguish evangelism from other activities in which the church engages, which in the long run destroys any deep sense of accountability in this area. If evangelism refers to everything the church does, then it is extremely difficult to identify; hence it is well-nigh impossible to think specifically and carefully about the evangelistic ministry of the church. If everything is evangelism then nothing is evangelism; and we should be surprised if anyone in the church takes it very seriously. Defining *evangelism* as the verbal proclamation of the gospel provides a clear, manageable concept that is rooted in the early history of the word and that calls the church to excellence in communicating the Christian gospel to those who are prepared to listen.

Moreover, nothing in this definition precludes the church from engaging in other laudable and urgent tasks. Thus commitment to evangelism as traditionally understood does not rule out the possibility of undertaking liturgical, medical, educational, social, and any other kind of activities that Christians consider to be imperative in the modern world. Of course, in reaching decisions about the various options open to it, the church, like any other human institution, must at times make judgments about the use of scarce resources. Conceiving evangelism as the verbal proclamation of the gospel does not, however, predetermine what conclusions should be reached at any particular moment in its history. All sorts of factors, both theological and nontheological, will come into play at this point. To be sure, it may well be that those who are committed to the prevailing conception of evangelism have crusaded for evangelism as the primary and possibly even exclusive obligation of the church in its service. But this does nothing to undermine the legitimacy of the standard definition; it simply shows that some who hold to this vision of evangelism have other commitments that decide the issue of one's obligations in the Christian community. Indeed, by being circumspect about its conception of evangelism, the church paves the way for clear and responsible decisions about all its obligations. The church identifies clearly those activities that are not evangelism and is called to responsible obedience in these areas.

Furthermore, it is becoming increasingly clear that the ongoing debate between those committed to evangelism on the one side and those committed to social action on the other is really a carryover from the futile fundamentalist-modernist controversy that rocked North American Christianity at the turn of the century. It would be naive to think that this debate is entirely over or that there do not still exist Christian thinkers who continue to be impaled on the horns of the false alternatives that have been canvassed for too long; but those most eager to press the conception of evangelism outlined above have gladly accepted that there exist a host of tasks for the church to perform and that commitment to evangelism in no way undermines the need for social service and acts of justice and mercy. The Lausanne Covenant makes this very clear.

> Although reconciliation with man is not reconciliation with God, nor is social action evangelism, nor is political liberation salvation, nevertheless we affirm that evangelism and socio-political involvement are both part of our Christian duty. For both are necessary expressions of our doctrines of God and man, our love for our neighbour and our obedience to Jesus Christ.[4]

From the other side, Emilio Castro, general secretary of the World Council of Churches, states quite bluntly that "no Christian solidarity with the poor can exist which does not point to the totality of the kingdom promises, including the invitation to personal faith and witness."[5]

Equally important, nothing in this definition of evangelism would preclude the possibility of adequate incorporation of new Christians into the life of the church. From within this vision, evangelism will be conducted in such a way that new converts will be suitably instructed, brought to participate in the appropriate rites of initiation, and established in the privileges and responsibilities of membership in the church. But such activities will be considered extra-evangelistic and will be called something other than evangelism, such as catechesis, initial instruction, initiation, nurture, and so on. Strictly speaking, those responsible for evangelism are not accountable for such activities. The task of the evangelist is to proclaim the gospel, to announce the good news of the kingdom, and to communicate the message to as many as possible; others, such as teachers, priests, pastors, and the like, are to be responsible for the work of instruction within the church. This does not mean that evangelism is to be sepa-

---

4. *The Lausanne Covenant*, p. 25.
5. Emilio Castro, *Sent Free: Mission and Unity in the Perspective of the Kingdom* (Grand Rapids: Eerdmans, 1985), p. 101.

rated from these activities. The issue is one of logical distinction, not empirical separation. Evangelists are responsible for the proclamation of the gospel; others are responsible for initiation into the community and for Christian nurture. Ideally both work together amicably, coordinating their activity to ensure that those who respond to the Christian message are instructed in the faith and incorporated into the community.

Many find this conception of evangelism attractive because it relieves the pressure to evaluate evangelism in terms of results. Whether or not people respond is not really the concern of the evangelist. The results are left entirely in the hands of God. Hence there is no need for manipulation, nor for anxious concern if no one responds. What matters is that the gospel be appropriately presented. The message should be heralded boldly and clearly, and it should remain true to the fundamental content of the gospel. Thus it focuses on what God has done in Christ, on the offers of forgiveness and the gift of the Holy Spirit, and on the need for repentance. If what is preached is something other than the content of the gospel, say, a string of stories about religious experiences or a promise of health and wealth in return for personal and financial commitment, then evangelism has not occurred. Nor has evangelism taken place if the evangelist has failed to obtain a hearing or if he or she has been unable to communicate the message properly. In either case the criteria of success have absolutely nothing to do with the statistics of response. And this, it will be argued, liberates the evangelist from bondage to numbers and from the temptation to tailor the message to make response easier or less costly. Additionally, some will point out that it leaves the hearer entirely free to accept or reject the Christian message with dignity and it leaves God to work graciously in the hearts of the hearer without undue interference from those human agents whom he has called to the ministry of evangelism.

Furthermore, this conception of evangelism fits nicely with the office of evangelist as it was established in the early church and renewed in the last century or so. God calls certain people within the church to be evangelists and over time equips them with the appropriate gifts and graces to fill this office. When established churches refuse to acknowledge such persons, God does not cease to call them; he simply sets them to work outside the boundaries of the conventional ecclesiastical institutions. Moreover, it is normal to find them moving from one place to another; their task is to travel to the ends of the earth to proclaim the gospel. They cannot therefore take it upon themselves to instruct, baptize, equip, nurture, direct, and counsel those who accept the good news of the gospel. This work must be left to others, and thus other offices are appointed in the church to carry on these crucial ministries. This does not mean that those committed to the office of pastor or teacher do not proclaim the gospel; nor that one hears the gospel only once in his or her lifetime. On the contrary, the gospel is constantly taught and proclaimed in word and sacrament, for this is what shapes Christian identity and forms Christian character over time. What is at issue here is not the means of Christian nurture but the means of effective outreach to the world. Both require the proclamation of the gospel, but the latter is distinctive enough to need the services of those who are set apart for this particular task. Scripture, the history of the church, and the religious experiences of those called to this work combine to make a weighty case for conceiving evangelism as the verbal proclamation of the gospel.

We must concede that this latter argument runs the risk of making evangelism the responsibility of the chosen few who are called to exercise this ministry. At a popular level, many committed to evangelism are fearful of this possibility. They see evangelism as the responsibility of every Christian and will be very reluctant to deploy an argument that might undercut the efforts that have been made in the last generation to take evangelism out of the hands of the clergy and restore it to the laity. Furthermore, experiences in places like China over the last two decades show what can be achieved when ordinary Christians are released to evangelize their neighbors. Besides, Christianity first flourished because Christians simply gossiped the gospel among their friends and acquaintances. To turn the clock back on all this would be disastrous, they believe.

However, the implications of this argument are less alarming than suggested here. For one thing, evangelists do not have to be recruited from the ranks of the clergy; it is perfectly possible that many of those called to evangelism will be and will remain among the laity. Thus, the number of people gifted in this way could be enormous. Might it be that the church does not find such people in her ranks because she either refuses to take evangelism seriously or because she refuses to acknowledge that such evangelists might exist as one of God's gifts to the ministry of the whole church? It could well be the case that every local church has a number of people who are especially gifted in the ministry of evangelism. Some might work in one particular area and some might itinerate in the traditional manner—either way, this does not destroy the fundamental conception of evangelism that is at stake here. A second and more compelling point is that construing evangelism in this way does not at all rule out the privilege that every Christian has to bear verbal witness to the gospel. Common sense makes it clear that ordinary Christians are perfectly free to communicate the Christian message to those who will give it a hearing, and history shows that this can be a highly effective means of evangelism. Moreover, we can easily see why verbal witness should be called evangelism, for such activity fits the definition under review. On this view anyone who proclaims or communicates the essentials of the gospel is an evangelist. That some may have a special calling to engage in this kind of activity as a vocation in no way undermines the call of all Christians to share the gospel with others.

The Case against Proclamation

Much can be said in favor of the standard conception of evangelism that has developed afresh over the last century. However, a weighty case can be made out against it, and my own suspicion is that it needs drastic revision if we are to see the development of a healthy ministry of evangelism in the modern church. There are several reasons for challenging the traditional vision of evangelism that currently prevails in many quarters.

We can begin by noting that the contemporary vision of

the evangelist and of evangelism involves a selective reduction of the activities that one usually associates with the work of the evangelists in the early church. It is tempting initially to conclude that we face here the same problem that we encounter in the search for the so-called historical Jesus. In our search for the historical evangelists of the early church we gaze into the well of history and see the pale reflections of our own faces staring back at us. Thus we think of the early evangelists as itinerant Protestant ministers, preaching evangelistic sermons that focus on the individual's need to respond to the message of salvation. But this is a far cry from what meets us in the scanty evidence available. For example, what do we find in Scripture about Philip? There are two references. The later text (Acts 21) describes him as an evangelist whose four daughters prophesied, whose home was open to the prophet Agabus, and who gave a message from the Holy Spirit to Paul. The earlier material (Acts 8) is even more revealing. Philip was driven from Jerusalem by persecution and went to a city of Samaria where he proclaimed the Christ. While there he was involved in a ministry of miracles, healing, and exorcism. He appears to have participated in the baptism of those who became believers, and he spent time with Simon, a local magician. We are also informed that he was whisked off by supernatural guidance to instruct an Ethiopian civil servant in the meaning of the Old Testament, to tell him about Jesus, and to baptize him on the spot. Thus to reduce his work to that of the proclamation of the gospel is a gross reduction of the varied activities in which Philip was engaged.

The case becomes more complicated if we appeal to the early apostles and Paul as paradigms of evangelism. Whether we can do so is, of course, debatable, for nowhere are they officially designated as evangelists, and all will agree that they had a unique role in the establishment of the Christian community in its foundational phase. But again the point to note is that they did much more than travel from place to place to preach the gospel. In addition, they taught, argued their case about Jesus Christ, gave guidance, were involved in healings, exhorted, and the like. In other words, they were involved in laying the foundations of Christian faith and practice; they were not content to spread the word as assiduously as time and talent would permit. They were keen to see that those who responded became part of a community, and it is difficult to see how this would be possible without a fair amount of instruction and teaching.

Recent responses to Dodd's attempt to set up a sharp distinction between preaching and teaching in the early church support this concern. Critics now widely acknowledge that Dodd's view is an artificial division of labor that is not borne out by the evidence. Worley points out, for example, that teaching in the early church was not restricted to believers but was aimed at anyone who listened.[6] Furthermore, such teaching occurred in a variety of places, ranging from Temple and synagogue to hilltops, villages, houses, lakes, and boats. Where preaching and teaching are conjoined, teaching often comes before preaching, suggesting that the words are used interchangeably. Moreover, there is little evidence to suggest that the teaching mentioned was ethical instruction, moral exhortation, or catechetical instruction directed at believers only. All this is in keeping with the Jewish antecedents of early Christianity, where teaching and preaching were interchangeable practices in the local synagogues. Both involved exhortation, instruction, and edification and could be carried on in house study groups, schools, the Temple courtyard, and in settings where propaganda and proselytizing were appropriate.

It is in fact very difficult to say what an evangelist really was in the early church. Paul exhorted Timothy to do the work of an evangelist (2 Tim. 4:5), which suggests that to be an evangelist was less an office and more a function of his work or a specific kind of ministry, for we know that Timothy was also a pastor and teacher. Evangelists appear in the list of gifts given by God to the church for equipping the saints for the work of ministry (Eph. 4:11). Here they are set between a rock and a hard place, nestling between apostles and prophets on the one side and pastors and teachers on the other. It is tempting to read this passage as saying that evangelists are a particular of-

---

6. Robert C. Worley, *Preaching and Teaching in the Earliest Church* (Philadelphia: Westminster, 1967), pp. 35-36.

fice in the church, but this is by no means certain, for the context suggests that the gifts mentioned here may have been shared in varying degrees by the whole church. Even if evangelists do constitute an office it is not entirely clear what they do. Does their work follow chronologically that of apostle and prophet and come before that of pastor and teacher? If it does, their role would appear to be redundant, for surely the apostles have already preached the good news of the gospel. Or does "apostles" refer here to the founding agents of the early church who are the guardians of the traditions about Jesus, meaning that evangelists do similar work to that of apostles without enjoying their special position as the initial builders of the church? Or are all the offices mentioned here meant to be part of the local church with each performing distinct and exclusive activities? It is extremely difficult to say exactly what an evangelist was in the Ephesian community and, even if we could, it would be precarious to build a case on this isolated reference.

In these circumstances it is not surprising that those committed to the conventional view of the evangelist have in recent times been keen to appeal to the so-called Great Commission (Matt. 28:18-20) as a crucial paradigm for evangelistic activity. David Barrett, for example, has been careful to distinguish evangelization from conversion, baptism, church growth, and christianization.[7] He suggests, moreover, that Christian missionary endeavor since the apostolic era has been fundamentally inspired by the Great Commission. Anyone familiar with the attempts to garner support for evangelism in modern Protestantism will know how frequently the Great Commission is appealed to as a description of evangelism. What is most striking about this is the stark contradiction between the content of the Great Commission and the conventional understanding of evangelism. Even a superficial reading of the text shows that

7. David Barrett, *World Christian Encyclopedia* (Oxford: Oxford University Press, 1982), p. 119. In a fascinating later study Barrett begins by trying to confine evangelism to proclamation, but in the end he does not sustain this analysis. See his *Evangelize! A Historical Survey of the Concept* (Birmingham, Ala.: New Hope, 1987), esp. chap. 22.

the emphasis falls not on proclamation but on making disciples, on baptizing, and on teaching. Thus when modern television preachers appeal to their viewers for money by describing their work as that of an evangelist and by citing the Great Commission as a warrant for giving financial support, they are talking literal nonsense. There is simply no way in which sermons preached on television or on radio can fulfill the minimum requirements laid out in Matthew 28, for baptism cannot be performed through television, not to mention the difficulty of making disciples or teaching them through these media. What we have in this instance is a primary appeal to the conventional understanding of evangelism: if evangelism is merely communicating a message then of course it can be carried out through television; but this is not evangelism as implicitly described in Matthew. Rarely is it noticed that these two understandings of evangelism are radically different.

In this critique of the conventional understanding of evangelism I have sought to show that it is difficult to argue that evangelists confined themselves to the proclamation of the gospel. This can be seen from the early church to the modern world. Those in the history of the church whom we today would undoubtedly refer to as evangelists do not at all fit the standard definition of their work. While references to evangelists in the patristic period are scant, one extended reference in Eusebius is interesting for its description of the work of an evangelist. Speaking of the second century he says, "There were still many evangelists of the Word eager to use their inspired zeal after the example of the apostles for the increase and building up of the divine Word."[8] More significantly, he writes:

> Very many of the disciples of that age whose hearts had been ravished by the divine Word with a burning love of philosophy [i.e., Christianity] first fulfilled the command of the Saviour and divided their goods among the needy. Then they set out on long journeys, doing the work of evangelists, eagerly striving to preach Christ to those who had never heard the word of faith, and to deliver to them the

8. Eusebius, *Ecclesiastical History* 5.10.2.

holy gospels. In foreign lands they simply laid the foundations of the faith. That done they appointed others as shepherds, entrusting them with the care of the new growth, while they themselves proceeded with the grace and cooperation of God to other countries and other places.[9]

Surely we would be putting a strain on this tantalizing passage by reading it as if the evangelists mentioned merely preached the gospel and then moved on. They must have been involved in an initial work of building and instruction; otherwise it is hard to claim that they laid the foundations of the faith. It is also difficult to believe that they did not baptize and ground the young converts in the faith before entrusting them to the care of local pastors. Presumably the pastors came from the ranks of the converts themselves, which also suggests that there was much more involved than the proclamation of the gospel. Proclamation is clearly crucial, and for that reason it is singled out, but this is by no means all that the evangelist does.

An even more compelling example comes not from the second century but from the eighteenth, in the work of John Wesley. The conventional picture of Wesley as an evangelist is that of an itinerant preacher, proclaiming the good news of the gospel in the marketplaces of the British Isles. This is a thoroughly inaccurate view, though, for Wesley was especially intent on not only proclaiming the gospel but seeing that those who responded were converted, established in the faith, incorporated into class meetings, and related to the local parish churches. In fact, Wesley met in conference with his helpers twice to discuss the issue of whether they would preach in places where there were no societies. In 1745 they decided to preach wherever they had opportunity, regardless of the existence of societies to take care of those who were interested. In 1748 they overturned this decision and refused to preach where they could not care for those who responded positively.[10] We can, of course, avoid the implications of this by suggesting that

9. Ibid., 3.37.2.
10. See the *Minutes of the Methodist Conferences* (London: John Mason, 1862), p. 39.

Wesley was more than an evangelist; he was, let us say, a great teacher or an effective church planter. Or we can argue that Wesley was an exceptionally good evangelist because he kept evangelism in close touch with other ministries of the church. Technically speaking, these are feasible options. More attractive, however, is the argument that limiting evangelism to the mere proclamation of the gospel is artificial; rather, we should begin to enrich our conception of evangelism by expanding it to embrace crucial elements of Christian initiation.

It is in fact extremely difficult to stop the work of the evangelist from spilling over into other kinds of activity beyond proclamation. Consider the use of altar calls. Even the modern Calvinist R. T. Kendall has argued that one may legitimately use them at the end of evangelistic services.[11] Since altar calls are almost a surrogate for baptism, the evangelist who uses them is engaged in much more than proclamation.[12] There is clearly the attempt to move into a phase of Christian initiation. This is even more marked in parachurch organizations like Campus Crusade for Christ, which works among modern university students. The concern to make disciples rather than record personal decisions has led to the point where some converts know very little about life in the local Christian church. They are recruited, initiated into the Christian faith, trained in discipleship, and sent out to minister. Evangelism has spilled over into initiation; it has not been confined to proclaiming the gospel.

Perhaps the most telling example of this is seen in recent developments in crusade evangelism. Michael Cassidy, himself a convert from Billy Graham's Harringay Crusade in 1954, has been a staunch defender of the standard vision of evangelism as the spreading of the gospel message, and has been involved in crusade evangelism in South Africa. He is well aware of the problems associated with crusade evangelism. What is especially interesting is his proposed remedy for some of the problems.[13] At

11. R. T. Kendall, *Stand Up and Be Counted: Calling for Public Confession of Faith* (Grand Rapids: Zondervan, 1984).
12. See below, p. 131.
13. Michael Cassidy, "Limitations of Mass Evangelism and its Potentialities," *International Review of Missions* **74** (1976): 202-15.

heart it involves a drastic expansion of the work of those involved in evangelism to include congregational analysis and evaluation, teaching about church growth, the implementation of programs for structural renewal, discipleship training, and the retrieval of nominal members of the churches involved. Only after these have taken place do we have public rallies for proclamation, which are to be followed by a phase that involves working through the sociopolitical implications of the gospel both generally and specifically. However, the issue at stake here is not the merits or limitations of crusade evangelism;[14] rather, it is the fact that it is increasingly difficult to limit evangelism to proclamation. In theory we may define it as the verbal proclamation of the gospel, and we may insist that it should be evaluated in terms of the content of the message rather than in terms of consequences, but in practice it is difficult to keep this line intact. On the one hand, we begin to fill out the concept of evangelism by saying that the objectives, aims, and consequences of evangelism include persuasion, bringing people to obedience to Jesus Christ, incorporating converts into the church, and calling them to responsible service in the world. On the other hand, when we then begin to build these objectives into evangelistic work the net result is a vast expansion of activity, all of which is supported by the call to evangelize.

Suppose, however, that we ignore these criticisms, or that we develop appropriate dexterity in theory and practice to take them into account. Does this still leave the traditional view intact? Can we still continue to construe evangelism as proclamation and be satisfied? I suggest at least three further reasons why we cannnot remain satisfied.

First, continuing to define evangelism as proclamation alone involves a radical transformation of the practice of evangelism, lifting it out of its original setting and landing it in the middle of the twentieth-century church as we know it in the West, especially in Protestantism. In the early church one could be relatively sure that the verbal proclamation of the gospel

14. For an interesting defense of mass evangelism see James S. Stewart, "Evangelism: A Question of Method," *The Expository Times* 63 (1951-52): 353-54.

would be intimately linked to the Christian community and to the other ministries of the church that are essential to the rebirth and growth of the new believer. For the early Christians it would have been unthinkable to have evangelism without community and community without evangelism. Thus, instruction in the faith and initiation into the community would have been entirely normal and natural for those who were contacted with the message of the gospel. It is precisely these elements that we cannot take for granted in the modern Western world. Since the middle of the nineteenth century evangelism has, for the most part, been cut loose from local Christian communities. Given the quest for autonomy, given the cult of individualism that is everywhere around us, given the drastic changes in communication, and given the deep antipathy there is to community and tradition, it is well-nigh impossible to link evangelism in an organic way with life in the body of Christ. To continue to construe evangelism as verbal proclamation is to ignore the radically changed sociological and ecclesiastical situation in which we have to work and to cling to the wrong kind of verbal continuity with the past.

This subtle argument for the most part trades on the drastically changed circumstances in which the church must work. On one side are the changes that are internal to the church. Here religion has become a private affair severed from its roots in tradition and community. Evangelism has been relegated to the fringes of the church or cast out of it altogether. This process began with Wesley and Whitefield in the eighteenth century; it was further developed by Charles Finney and his imitators in the early part of the nineteenth century; it was perfected by D. L. Moody and Billy Sunday in the last half of the nineteenth century; it has been tempered and qualified by Billy Graham in the last generation; and it has now received a whole new lease on life with the arrival of the so-called television evangelists. On the other side are changes external to the church, like the development of radio and television, the creation and perfecting of advertising and marketing techniques, and the radical individualism of modern society. All these enhance the kind of evangelism where the evangelist is seen as the communicator of the gospel message. In such circumstances, efforts will, of course, be made to tie evangelism back into the church and to incorporate converts into the life of the community, but these are unlikely to lead to the changes that are essential if we are to come close to what appears to have been the case in the evangelism of the early church. We need a radical shift of perspective that will work for a deeper continuity with the early church and will take us far beyond our sharing a conception of evangelism that limits it to verbal proclamation. In fact, to cling to this definition of evangelism will help perpetuate precisely the kind of problems that have brought evangelism to such a position of low estate in the economy of the church.

The second objection also trades on assumptions about the history of evangelism in the modern world. It is surely clear to the observant student that much of the evangelistic preaching of the last two hundred years in the West has failed to deal seriously with the eschatological content and reality of the gospel as outlined in the preceding chapter. Evangelistic preaching for the most part has failed to focus on the coming of the reign of God in Jesus Christ. At the risk of making hasty generalizations, what we need is a sharp reminder of some crucial shifts in the landscape of history. Again the eighteenth century is a watershed period. Both Jonathan Edwards and John Wesley were deeply committed to the coming of the rule of God on earth as well as in heaven. So also was Charles Finney a century later. Yet in them we can detect a shift away from a focus on the reality of the kingdom as it comes in Christ and in the operations of the Holy Spirit to a focus on the religious affections and on personal religious experience. This is entirely understandable. When the kingdom of God appears on earth it calls for drastic renewal of our personal lives. Edwards, Wesley, and their followers saw this and developed the implications of it with a vengeance. Edwards, whose vision of God in his intrinsic beauty and glory represents one of the lasting achievements of Western theology, made the crucial change when he developed a keen interest in the morphology of conversion, and when he decided to locate true religion in the affections. This anthropocentric turn has been the undoing of modern evangelism. Over the years it has led to a fierce concentration on the response of the individual, as we can see in the primary focus of Wesley's standard sermons. In the mind and hands of Charles Finney it led to a focus on the kind of techniques that will bring about conversion and personal renewal, even though Finney has a fine record in his fight for the transformation of society. Once the latter element drops out, as it does toward the end of the last century, there is little left but a message of sin and salvation that has relegated eschatology to the last days of history, as we can see happening in the fragile theology of D. L. Moody. Modern evangelists for the most part inherit this anthropocentric emphasis. Although valiant efforts have been made to recover the original focus on Christ and his kingdom as the center of proclamation, it is still filtered through the lenses of soteriology. Thus Christ's death as an atonement for sin becomes in many quarters the heart of the message, and the whole drama of the coming of the rule of God in his birth and incarnation, in his life and ministry, in his death and resurrection, in his ascension and the coming of the Holy Spirit, and in his continued presence in the worship and ministry of the church are all treated as a kind of scaffolding or backcloth to the salvation of the individual sinner.

The impression one receives from the New Testament is very different from this. There the content of the message is tied intimately to the good news of the kingdom of God. And this in itself goes a long way toward explaining the focus on proclamation in evangelism. What makes proclamation evangelism is not the act of proclamation *per se* but the message being proclaimed: the coming rule of God. Surely this deserves to be announced and made known. Constituted as it is by the events that are intimately related to Jesus of Nazareth, it is logically necessary that the good news of the kingdom take the form of an announcement about this slice of history. Without this announcement people will not know about its arrival, nor will they have a clear view of what it means for the kingdom of God to come now in the present or in the future. The failure to incorporate this crucial element of the New Testament witness into the basic message of the gospel is one of the worst features of modern evangelism. The irony is that the contemporary focus on evangelism as verbal proclamation has not at all remedied this fault.

The third reason for challenging this conception of evangelism is closely related. Our modern notions of communication and proclamation, shaped as they are by the Protestant pulpit and the mass media, fail to convey a dynamic element that is essential to the proclamation of the early church. We speak here of the numinous reality of the Holy Spirit that is present in the lives of those who announce the coming of the kingdom. This is not just a matter of getting the word out to all who will listen, using any means of communication that comes to hand. It is a matter of the power of the living God, unveiling himself to the minds and hearts of the listener as the gospel is taught and made known. Paul expresses this by insisting that he spoke at Corinth in "demonstration of the Spirit and of power" (1 Cor. 2:4). Elsewhere he refers explicitly to the power of signs and wonders (Rom. 15:19); whatever we make of this, it shows very clearly that his evangelistic activity was overshadowed by the power of the Holy Spirit. The issue at stake here is nicely captured by a report from the Orthodox Consultation on Confessing Christ through the Liturgical Life of the Church Today:

> Proclamation should not be taken only in the narrow sense of an informative preaching of the Truth but above all of incorporating man into the mystical union with God. At every step of the liturgy we encounter the word of God. The saving events of the Divine economy, although chronologically belonging to the past, through the Holy Spirit's action transcend time's limitation, become really present, and the faithful in the here and now live that which historically belongs to the past, and to the eschaton. In the liturgy we do not have a simple memorial but a living reality. It is an Epiclectic contemporization and consecration. A continuous Parousia, a real Presence of Christ emerges liturgically.[15]

The issue here is the dynamic presence of the kingdom of God that Christians encounter in worship, which is also present in

15. "Reports from the Orthodox Consultation on Confessing Christ through the Liturgical Life of the Church Today," *International Review of Missions* 75 (1975): 418.

the proclamation of the kingdom to those yet to participate in its reality. Thus, it is precarious to construe as evangelism the mere spreading of the word of the gospel, for this omits a vital, mysterious dimension that is central to the experience of the church.

An Attempt to Rework the Proclamation Model

Despite the objections that I have leveled against the conventional view of evangelism, there are bound to be those who will suggest that the way ahead is not to abandon it, but to cleanse and purify it. Suppose, for example, we retrieve the primary focus on the kingdom of God, and suppose we put the kingdom back into the heart of the church's message of the gospel. Would this not be an adequate response to some of the difficulties identified heretofore? This appears to be the fundamental move proposed by David Lowes Watson in his work on evangelism. His suggestions deserve careful consideration before we close this chapter on proclamation.

In certain respects Watson is a traditionalist in his thinking about evangelism. Thus he defines evangelism as "the verbal presentation of the gospel by proclamation and testimony."[16] As such it is to be distinguished but not separated from other ministries of the church. So it differs from works of obedience to which it calls believers.[17] This does not mean that the latter are unimportant or secondary, for both word and deed should receive equal—but distinct—emphasis in the ministry of the church "as it pursues the messianic mission of God in the world."[18] Keeping the two distinct prevents the message from being subjected to impossible criteria of efficacy, and it prevents the messengers from seeking to fulfill impossible ideals of worldly reform. Evangelism also differs from the recruiting of church members: "Evangelism and

16. David Lowes Watson, "Towards a Social Evangelism," *Perkins Journal* 34 (1981): 41.
17. David Lowes Watson, "Evangelism: A Disciplinary Approach," *International Bulletin of Missionary Research* 7 (1983): 6.
18. Ibid.

membership recruitment are much more effectively implemented when they are regarded as quite distinct features of
ministry, and each given an intentional emphasis in the life
and work of the church."[19] This is familiar territory and a natural consequence of the standard definition of evangelism.
Moreover, it allows Watson to press for evangelism as a distinct area of study within practical theology.

Watson, however, is clearly dissatisfied with much traditional evangelism, and he shares our complaint that "a great
deal of evangelism is patently deficient in the substance of the
New Testament message."[20] More particularly, "the church as
evangelist must plumb the depths of the Christian tradition with
the specific objective of honing the essentials of its message
against the panorama of human history."[21] Were it to do so satisfactorily, it would result in two distinct forms of evangelism, the
prophetic and the personal, each constituted by the provision
of information and by the call to repentance and conversion. In
each case the message will focus on the coming of the rule of
God, and ideally it will be accompanied by the presence of the
Holy Spirit working preveniently to bring people to decision.

Personal evangelism, as might be expected, takes place
when Christians share their faith with others, entering into dialogue and conversation to make known the evangel. The information shared in personal contacts and encounters is fundamentally historical. It involves telling the evangel in its
essentials as "the reality of God's salvation in the life, death, and
resurrection of Jesus Christ."[22] It is crucial to see this material
as information, for the power of the gospel lies in its very his-
toricity. "The lostness of humankind in sin was at once exposed
and remedied in the man of Nazareth, crucified, dead, and
buried when Pilate still governed."[23] In addition, the personal

19. David Lowes Watson, "The Church as Journalist: Evangelism in the
Context of the Local Church in the United States," *International Review of Missions* 72 (1983): 71.
20. Watson, "Evangelism: A Disciplinary Approach," p. 7.
21. Ibid.
22. Ibid., p. 8.
23. Ibid.

evangelist shares what is happening in his or her own life, while the Holy Spirit draws and invites the listener to salvation. In turn, this leads to the invitation to repentance and discipleship. This should be given spontaneously, trusting that the Holy Spirit provides both the opportunity and the means of response. Again we are on traditional terrain, although the emphasis on evangelism as something that takes place outside the confines of church buildings is more marked than one often finds in the field as a whole. The prevailing ethos among those who stress proclamation tends to tie it more to the professional evangelist working in local churches or public meeting places. Also notable in Watson's analysis is a certain reserve about apologetics. Apologetics may be important, but its rightful place belongs to a subsequent exercise in Christian growth and understanding and not to evangelism proper.

Watson is more radical and original in his proposals about prophetic evangelism—that is, Christians communicating the message that announces the New Age of Jesus Christ. The church declares the presence of the risen Christ in the power of the Holy Spirit, affirming the promise of God's coming rule, and calling on all to repent and be reconciled to God. More particularly, to engage in prophetic evangelism is to tell persons at every level of worldly power that God's sovereignty over the whole of creation is to be restored to its fullness. To do this effectively, one needs certain skills, namely, discernment and interpretation. The prophetic evangelist must be able to seek out the signs of the New Age in human history and existence, must be able to interpret them in the light of God's coming rule, and must then be able to communicate them as good news to as many as possible. Especially important within this is the need to interpret the signs of God's social grace.

> There is much to censure in a world of oppressive systems and imbalanced wealth and power, but the message of the evangel is that the world stands judged, not from afar by an apathetic God, but by a sympathetic God whose light comes into the world unrecognised. The prophetic message is to point to that light for those with eyes to see.

It is to give the routine and the commonplace new meaning. It is to announce, over and over again, the presence of God's salvation in the very midst of the world.[24]

The place to do this is from within the local church. Those working in prophetic evangelism are to seek out, identify, and make known the signs of the coming rule of God already present in the world that form the context of the local congregation. They are to announce the presence of such signs to everyone, regardless of response, calling persons, societies, and nations to repentance and conversion. They declare that there is hope for the world, for God's kingdom is to come on earth, as in heaven. So the call to repentance is not just a call to ethical accountability.

It is primarily a call to eschatological expectancy for those with ears to hear, to an active waiting in hopeful anticipation, with a warning that the time is short. It is not that injustice, oppression, suffering, hatred, and indifference are wrong. They are out of date.[25]

It is important to pause and note the full theological freight that Watson has placed on board his account of evangelism. It involves an extension, or at least an application, of the language of salvation to society. In traditional theologies of evangelism much has been made of the *ordo salutis* as a perspective through which to understand the process of individual salvation. Thus the individual moves through such phases as repentance, faith, regeneration, justification, the internal witness of the Holy Spirit, sanctification, glorification, and the like. Watson insists that grace is at work not only in the life of the individual but also in the world; the signs of it are already discernible for those with eyes to see and ears to hear. In other words, just as persons are convicted of sin, repent, are reconciled to God, and then grow in grace, so does the rest of creation. Watson spells out very clearly what this means for evangelism.

24. Ibid., p. 7.
25. Ibid.

It calls us to accept God's grace, not only in persons, but in societies and systems. It calls us to be prophets, not only against injustice and oppression, but for the working out of God's salvation in the world. It means the question of power, not merely as that of identifying its abuse, but also of its redemption by God for the New Age. And more, it means being ready to accept this redemption when it actually occurs. This enlargement of our evangelistic vision must have as full a message for systems as for individuals. Communities, cities, nations, conglomerates, must not only be analysed as sinful, but must be called to repentance, and can be expected to repent. Their salvation, along with that of individuals, is to be nurtured and brought to fulfillment by the love and grace of God.[26]

The final descriptive point to be made in our outline of Watson's position relates to his favored analogy for the evangelist. Given his stress on communicating the gospel over against persuading people to believe it, it should not surprise us that he finds it helpful to see the evangelist as a journalist. Since our planet is being made ready for the fullness of the kingdom, the signs are already around us; thus, the task of the evangelist is to be that of the journalist telling a good story.[27] The journalist, enabled by Christian insights to discern what God is doing in the world, defines and interprets the good news of the coming kingdom already present in the midst of history. He or she then circulates the message on a regular basis, ensuring that it reaches as many people as possible in the local community. Every available medium is to be used: tracts, church newsletters, tape recorders, radio, telephones, television, photography, and the like. God's work of salvation in local communities is to be discerned in history, reported on faithfully, and circulated consistently by the local congregation.

All this adds up to a fascinating revision of the traditional understanding of evangelism that, although still programmatic

26. David Lowes Watson, "Prophetic Evangelism: The Good News Of Global Grace," in Theodore Runyon, ed., *Wesleyan Theology Today: A Bicentennial Theological Consultation* (Nashville: Kingswood Books, 1985), p. 222.
27. Watson, "Church as Journalist," p. 64.

in character, represents one of the more original contributions to evangelism in recent years. It involves a determined attempt to recover the eschatological perspective of the early church, and it insists that evangelism be rooted in the life of the local Christian congregation. Moreover, it is interesting that Watson does not in the least want to downplay the significance of discipleship. To be sure, he seems to favor an open door policy on membership of the church, for he holds that anything less than this will mean that we shall have to engage in the questionable activity of judging the motives of those who wish to join.[28] However, his extended study of the class meeting system in early Methodism and his creative suggestions on how this might be suitably refurbished and used in the modern church make it abundantly clear that he has little time for cheap grace and superficial commitment.[29] In spite of all this, I doubt that his proposal will really solve the fundamental problems that face us in evangelism in the modern world.

No doubt some will be quick to point out that the margin of error in discerning the signs of the kingdom in history is very great. Watson is well aware that doing so presupposes a deep exposure to Christ and to the tradition of the church, for it is within this context in part that one is given the skills to discern God's action in the world. He is also sensitive to the possibility that we will be prone to read our own political and ideological agendas into our scripts of the signs of the coming rule of God. The modern church in the West has its fair share of ideologues of both the left and the right announcing their political convictions in the name of the rule of God. So he is not at all naive about this operation. Moreover, he would be quick to reject scripts such as a premillennialist reading, which he sees as fundamentally a false and hyperliteralist view of the New Testament, one that provides a very different reading of history from that which he proposes. He is surely entitled to deploy this argument in rebuttal to those who think that his position opens

---

28. Ibid., p. 71.
29. See David Lowes Watson, *Accountable Discipleship* (Nashville: Discipleship Resources, 1985); *The Early Methodist Class Meeting* (Nashville: Discipleship Resources, 1985).

the door to a pessimistic reading of history that portrays the present age as a time of antichrists, tribulations, famine, warfare, and the like. Watson's position lends no support to such eschatological speculations.

Yet we must note that discerning the coming of the rule of God in the events of Belfast or Beruit or Birmingham or Berlin or Boston or Ballygobackwards is precarious in the extreme. There are two reasons why this is necessarily so. First, it is not at all clear that the kind of concepts that have been forged to discern the activity of God in the life of the individual can be carried over to the process of history. Watson does not really develop his view with sufficient thoroughness; where he does, as in the case of justification, he is not very convincing. He is not very clear, for example, on how he is going to apply the concept of the witness of the Holy Spirit, and the other concepts associated with the *ordo salutis*, to the social order. If he cannot do so, his position is in danger of complete collapse. Second, Watson appears to omit one crucial ingredient in any attempt to discern the hand of God in history, namely, the need for the prophet who has access to the intentions and purposes of God through revelation. Unless God speaks, it is surely going to be extremely difficult to say exactly what God is doing in history. Human skill, spiritual insight, access to the canon of Scripture, and reflection on the tradition of the church are necessary but not sufficient conditions for reading the activity of God in the world with the kind of certainty that is essential to Watson's program. This is not to say that God is not at work in history, nor is it to take back the claim that the kingdom has been inaugurated in Jesus of Nazareth, nor is it to stop Christians from interpreting their personal and local history in terms of the kingdom of God. It is simply to exercise the kind of intellectual and spiritual modesty that becomes those who as yet see through a glass darkly. At the very least Watson needs to say a lot more about how Christians are to read the hand of God in history and get it right. Without this his concept of prophetic evangelism does not really get off the ground.

Even were he to succeed in this, his position is still in jeopardy. Suppose we could with certainty discern the actions of God in contemporary history; should these be part of the content of the Christian message in evangelism? Surely not. At the very best they represent reasons for believing that the kingdom is coming in history rather than being an integral part of the announcement of the coming of the kingdom of God in Jesus of Nazareth. The early Christian traditions address this issue in an interesting fashion. Luke, for example, tells us that John the Baptist sent his disciples to inquire if Jesus was the one who was to come (7:18-19). Jesus' answer—that they are to tell John that the blind receive their sight, that the lame walk, that lepers are cleansed, that the deaf hear, that the dead are raised up, and that the poor have the good news preached to them—is a recitation of signs of the coming rule of God in the world. Yet nowhere does he offer these signs as the content of the proclamation of the kingdom. Likewise Paul's ministry, as we have already seen, was accompanied by such signs and wonders, yet he resolutely refused to make them the content of the gospel message (1 Cor. 1). Paul's message focuses very specifically on the cross of Christ, and he rejects the Jewish demand to focus on signs of any kind. (Unfortunately we cannot here address the issue of how the proclaimer of the kingdom became the proclaimed.) Both the Gospels and Paul clearly teach that the gospel message has a narrow focus on Christ and his work. This cannot be accidental. Moreover, it is carefully distinguished from the signs of his coming. Where these are identified, they seem to involve miracles of healings, exorcisms, and the like rather than the action of God in either the life of the individual or in history. If this is the case, then the emphasis on the impact of the gospel on the individual, which is central to Watson's proposals for personal evangelism, and the emphasis on the signs of God's grace in history, which constitutes his vision of prophetic evangelism, are a major distraction from the fundamental and more narrowly focused content of the gospel of the kingdom.

Conclusion

All in all, then, Watson's intriguing attempt to work within the boundaries of the conventional definition of evangelism does not succeed. It represents a valiant effort to retrieve the eschato-logical dimension of the gospel, but it leads us down some pre-carious pathways that are unlikely to get evangelism back on track. Nor does it adequately address the varied objections that have been leveled against the conventional understanding of evangelism when it focuses so narrowly on proclamation. The issue is not just that of getting the message straight, difficult as that may be. Also at stake is the recovery of the full implica-tions of the Great Commission as applied to evangelism. And also at issue is the appropriation of what evangelism has actu-ally meant in the early church and in history, not judged by the etymology of the word *evangelism* and its rather occasional use in Scripture, but by what evangelists have actually done in both proclaiming the gospel and establishing new converts in the kingdom of God. Above all, what is important is to combat the isolation of evangelism from the full ministry of the church and to rescue it from the shallow anthropocentrism and individual-ism into which it has tumbled in the last two centuries. This does not mean that we abandon the crucial significance of proc-lamation in evangelism, but it does mean that we enrich our conception of evangelism to include the vital first phases of initiation into the kingdom of God.

F O U R

Church Growth

If evangelism is not adequately represented by the activity of proclamation, perhaps it can be rescued by construing it as the planting of local churches. This is exactly the proposal currently espoused by some of the leading writers on the subject. More especially, it is championed by a group of scholars who have founded a school of mission that is committed to church growth as the heartbeat of the life of the church. In this chapter I shall offer a general assessment of their contribution to the field of evangelism.

My grand design is clearly beset with difficulties, however. Most noticeably, and perhaps notoriously, there is bound to be a kind of hang-glider effect throughout. We are attempting to hover above a vast body of material and controversy and arrive at a broad judgment about its merits. Our judgments cannot, therefore, be rigorously formal. We are seeking to weigh a series of considerations that cut across our standard academic disciplines; we are working with probabilities that cannot always be pried apart and examined separately; most important, we are depending on what John Henry Newman once graphically described as the ultimately silent effect of arguments and conclusions on our minds.[1] Yet we do need at times to take stock of a whole tradition of thought and run the risk that this involves. It is imperative that we do this here with respect to church

1. John Henry Newman, *An Essay in Aid of a Grammar of Assent* (Notre Dame: University of Notre Dame Press, 1979), p. 240.

growth theory as we seek to lay the foundations for further academic work in the field of evangelism.

Evangelism and Church Growth

Clearly, evangelism and church growth are not exactly identical. However, they are intimately connected in at least three ways. First, evangelism ideally should lead to the numerical growth of the church. It is odd to think of evangelism taking place without the presence of those who respond positively to the message of the gospel and who then join the Christian community. Even those who insist that evangelism be construed exclusively as proclamation accept that the growth of the church will be a natural consequence of evangelism. So we expect there to be some kind of causal relation between evangelism and church growth. Second, many today think of evangelism fundamentally in terms of the growth of the church. In part this stems from the impact of the work of Donald McGavran and his disciples. Although church growth theorists are for the most part careful to distinguish between church growth and evangelism, those who take their bearings in evangelism from this tradition do not always notice the distinction. Enough confusion exists to allow many to treat evangelism as church growth without making a critical examination. Thus, seminars, lectures, and workshops on church growth are seen as contributions to reflection in the field of evangelism. Finally, exponents of the church growth tradition characteristically have been driven to reject the conventional understanding of evangelism and develop their own. They have pressed indirectly for a significant reorientation of perspective on evangelism. Peter Wagner, for example, has vigorously argued that we should understand evangelism to include Christian presence, Christian proclamation, and the persuading of people to join a local body of Christians.[2] More recently John Wimber has pressed for the inclusion of a "power encounter" with the Holy Spirit as a cru-

2. C. Peter Wagner, *Strategies for Church Growth* (Ventura, Calif.: Regal Books, 1987), pp. 113-31.

cial element in authentic evangelism.[3] So recent work on church growth is a very significant contribution to the whole debate about the character of evangelism.

The relevant material on the subject can be found in the body of literature associated with and in part inspired by Donald McGavran.[4] However, before we assess the proposals of the church growth tradition we need to bear in mind several salient points. First, church growth theory is not a unified whole. As we shall see, in fact, an intriguing internal tension exists in the tradition as it is currently developing. Of special interest to us here is that this tension relates to the way in which the New Testament material on eschatology is appropriated. Before we examine that, however, we shall focus on the mainstream proposals that are readily identified by concentrating on the work of McGavran and the scholars who work most closely with him.

It is also crucial to realize that church growth theory is less a set of specific suggestions about evangelistic practice and more a program of research. McGavran's primary concern in developing the discipline of church growth was to initiate the serious study of those factors that affect the numerical strength of the church. He set out to ransack the available empirical data in order to assemble hypotheses about those factors that are relevant to the growth of the church. Ideally, one conducts this sort of research using all the tools at one's disposal from such disciplines as history, sociology, anthropology, and the like, as well as on-the-spot investigation of the church under scrutiny. The driving force, then, is prolonged, thorough, exacting research, which cuts through the fog of confusion and asks searching questions about growth and decline regardless of consequences. Only after one has conducted this research can one develop specific proposals. Out of the research directed at particular churches in their unique contexts and circumstances it

3. John Wimber with Kevin Springer, *Power Evangelism* (San Francisco: Harper and Row, 1986).
4. A valuable bibliography related to church growth can be found in Charles Edward Van Engen, *The Growth of the True Church* (Amsterdam: Rodopi, 1981), pp. 518-37.

is hoped that particular programs of evangelism leading to the growth of the church will suggest themselves.

This is well illustrated in the fascinating shift in strategy that church growth advocates have worked out in the light of studies of church growth in North America. In the seventies the style in personal evangelism was unashamedly aggressive. James Kennedy and his associates led the way in teaching that the best way to evangelize was to confront people with their finitude and guilt, present a simple gospel message about sin and salvation, and then move in for decision.[5] Two questions were at the heart of this: "Have you come to a place in your spiritual life where you could say you know for certain that if you were to die today you would go to heaven?" and "Suppose that you were to die today and stand before God and he were to say to you, 'Why should I let you into my heaven?' what would you say?"[6] Although this approach is exceptionally fruitful when presented to those with a nominal Christian background, many Christians find it much too aggressive. Kennedy expected this kind of evaluation but pressed on because of his conservative theological convictions and because this approach actually worked. Church growth advocates, while perfectly open to Kennedy's proposals, approach evangelism from a different angle. They seek initially to establish why people join local churches. They have found that most do so not because of television, or radio, or letters of invitation, or newspaper advertisements, and the like, but because of contacts they already have with people who are inside the church. Approximately 80 percent of church members join a church due to existing networks of contacts with church members. In other words, friendship is one of the keys to church growth. In the light of this a program has been developed to focus on friendship as a crucial factor in evangelism.

This does not mean, however, that the church growth tradition does not have specific proposals that are deemed relevant to virtually any situation. Over the years church growth advo-

---

5. D. James Kennedy, *Evangelism Explosion* (Wheaton: Tyndale, 1977).
6. Ibid., pp. 17-18.

cates have inferred a number of material principles from their research. At this level empirical research merges with normative convictions to produce strategies for action. Thus it has been argued that those who want to see the church grow should concentrate resources on receptive populations, should work to develop homogeneous communities of believers, should seek to bring unbelievers into the early stages of discipleship and leave the task of perfecting Christians to others appointed to this work, should develop the kind of leaders that will best enhance church growth, and so on. In short, a significant body of material proposals that are to direct evangelistic strategy emerges. In this domain empirical and theological considerations are welded together to produce specific suggestions for the future of evangelism. We shall mention these in the course of our assessment.

Any evaluation of the modern church growth tradition must begin with a thoroughly positive recognition of the contribution it has made to the revitalization of the debate about evangelism in the modern church. No doubt some have found the writings of Donald McGavran and his associates to be so polemical in tone and so conservative in content that they would gladly forget the issues raised by church growth theorists. However, McGavran and his associates are far too astute ecclesiastically and much too well organized politically for this to count for much. Over the years, despite a shaky start, they have managed to keep their concerns and their agenda before the whole church and to do this so effectively that they must be the envy of many an ecclesiastical iconoclast determined to secure attention for his or her cause. This does not in itself constitute a criticism of the church growth tradition. Evangelism has for a long time been something of a political football within the church, and it very naturally provokes controversy. So one cannot but admire the tenacity and courage of those who are prepared to advance bold claims, take on the opposition without hesitation, and get on with the job. Moreover, most academic disciplines have been established and sustained by the development of rival schools of theory and practice that in the contest to outwit each other have spawned a substantial body of literature and animated discussion. This is inevitable if not essential for the field of evangelism, so we can be grateful to church growth protagonists for their lively contribution to the modern debate. Their proposals have deservedly become an effective catalyst that has already provoked a valuable body of material.

Therefore we should acknowledge at the outset that several aspects of the literature are exceptionally refreshing. Three deserve mention. First is the aggressive, iconoclastic spirit that is determined to get at the facts. We surely need to know not only where the church is growing and declining but why it is doing so. Moreover, in pursuing such matters we need to make use of all the relevant empirical and quasi-empirical disciplines that will gather and assess the relevant data and warrants. To be sure, the relevant disciplines, such as anthropology, communications, sociology, psychology, statistical studies, history, and the like, are often marked by extensive internal disputes regarding their findings, their methodologies, and their underlying conceptualities. However, this in no way undermines our need to unearth the relevant information. Nor does it dispose of the formal requirement that appropriate scientific procedures be used to get at whatever truth is available. Like colleagues in other branches of theology we have to make use of whatever tools are at our disposal rather than turn our backs on the issues that have to be addressed. In this context it is worth noting that perhaps without realizing it church growth theorists have helped a whole generation to appropriate an important dimension of the Enlightenment.

Second, we should welcome the attempt to put pioneer evangelism back on the map of the church's missionary endeavors. The primary issue here is not how we are going to define or quantify the number of "unreached peoples."[7] Ralph Winter may or may not be correct about this.[8] What matters is that on even the most conservative estimates there is a large

---

7. This issue is helpfully discussed in *Reaching the Unreached: The Old-New Challenge,* ed. Harvie M. Conn (Phillipsburg, N.J.: Presbyterian and Reformed, 1984).

8. See his "Unreached Peoples: What are They and Where are They?", in ibid., pp. 44-60.

configuration of groups who have yet to be reached with the gospel and the modern church must resolutely face up to its responsibilities in this domain. Furthermore, we can surely be grateful that church growth advocates have insisted that this work be done with cultural, moral, and spiritual sensitivity. Again we need not stop and work out the details of what this involves, for the deep questions about, say, the relation of Christianity to other religions cannot be resolved at the stroke of a pen. What matters is that we gladly acknowledge the significance and integrity of cultural diversity in the spread and expression of the gospel and yet do this without losing sight of the enormity of the task that still needs to be completed.

Finally, we should accept unreservedly the avowed intention of church growth specialists to wrestle with the varied and complex theological issues that their work has precipitated. Thus they have sought to engage in a many-sided debate on such matters as the nature of the church, the relation between personal evangelism and social action, the meaning and implication of the Great Commission, the relation between evangelism and the kingdom of God, and the like. Clearly these issues are vital to any extended account of the nature of evangelism. In a field that by definition must be oriented toward the practical life of the church these questions are bound to evoke controversy and polemic—but in the long run the conceptual and theological problems they involve cannot be shelved indefinitely. We can be grateful, therefore, that some of these have now been explicitly identified by church growth protagonists.

Problems in the Church Growth Position

The overall impression created by a careful reading of church growth literature, however, is far from satisfactory. The issue is not that there is a problem here and a difficulty there that can be resolved by tinkering with isolated elements of the system. What is at stake is something much more subtle and profound. Some might even want to say that we are confronted here with a disease that is difficult to identify and name but that is clearly evidenced by a wide variety of primary and secondary symptoms.

Initially one can try to redescribe the individual symptoms and maybe even explain them away as growing pains that will disappear over time. However, together they stubbornly refuse to disappear under scrutiny and the drastic remedies that have to be prescribed bear all the appearance of endangering the life of the patient.

The fundamental tension I am seeking to identify here can best be summed up in this fashion: despite disclaimers to the contrary, a set of significant tensions exists between the requirements and character of authentic evangelism and the principles and policies of the church growth tradition. Let me begin by laying out two secondary concerns of an impressionistic character before we move on to more specific matters.

An initial cause for concern is the fierce pragmatism of the movement. In itself there is nothing at all wrong with a healthy commitment to develop policies and practices in evangelism that really do achieve intentionally adopted goals. What is at issue is the way this spirit begins to corrupt various aspects of evangelism. As we saw earlier, recent church growth research has revealed that the vast majority of people in America came into the church through friendship and kinship relationships. Consequently evangelism "strategy" has shifted from the more confrontational style of something like Evangelism Explosion to an emphasis on using friendship as a vital means of outreach. However, the obvious danger that lurks in this is not sufficiently recognized. Unless we are very careful such delicate matters as friendship and love will be turned into one more utilitarian means or tool to increase the statistics of church membership.[9] Before we know what is happening sacred human relationships will have lost their integrity and the distinctive character of Christian love will have been eroded by an evangelistic orientation that construes them not as ends in themselves but as means to an end.

Moreover, the pragmatism underlying church growth may well have led growth theorists into a false confidence if not into outright pretension concerning what they have achieved. Thus

9. This is the distinct impression given by the recently released film, "Who Cares About Love?"

on the ecclesiastical front, McGavran has recently averred that various books that resulted from degrees pursued at the School of World Mission "touched with the magic wand of church growth a new set of pastors, missionaries, national leaders, mission executives, and professors of mission."[10] One might dismiss this as youthful exuberance were it not for two current factors that add fuel to the fire. One is our bewitchment with superstars and celebrities in the history of evangelism and in the modern church. Many a pastor yearns to build even a modest empire and therefore falls prey to the almost irresistible temptation to emphasize size and numerical growth and to put into practice programs to achieve them. Thus there develops a new canon of saints and heroes whose primary credentials are their ability to produce external results. The other factor to be noted here is the sobering truth that some mainline churches in America and Europe are in a fit of panic about their future and their hard-pressed bureaucrats are liable to turn to anything that will reverse their numerical decline. In such circumstances there is a real danger that the deeper theological and spiritual issues intimately related to evangelism will be set aside in the push to find a magic wand to increase church membership.

This is all the more likely to happen if one believes that church growth research is a new science that makes available hitherto unknown secrets about the growth of the church. This is certainly the impression created by protagonists of church growth. Thus we are offered a dazzling array of neologisms, we are encouraged to pursue various subdisciplines such as anthropology and communications theory, and we are liable to be told that our criticism of church growth may really stem from a refusal to avoid the new insights of fresh intellectual breakthroughs that are on a par with Marx or Freud. Obviously we all want to be on the side of the intellectual angels, but it is unrealistic to think that we have here anything amounting to a new science.[11]

10. "Church Growth Movement," in Walter A. Elwell, ed., *Evangelical Dictionary of Theology* (Grand Rapids: Baker, 1984), p. 202.
11. See Peter Wagner, *Church Growth and the Whole Gospel* (San Francisco: Harper and Row, 1981), pp. 75-77.

Rather, what we have is a group of diverse studies that are loosely connected in some way with church growth. Such studies are extremely valuable for certain purposes, but they do not at all add up to a coherent intellectual discipline of even the softest variety. As we seek to pursue the development of a fresh field of inquiry within practical theology it is extremely important that our claims be advanced with appropriate caution. The drive to get things done both within and without the academy must not stampede us into hasty intellectual claims about what has been achieved.

A second symptom suggesting that things have gone astray in the structure of church growth theory is the subsidiary role that is given to theological considerations in evangelism. I have already acknowledged that we can be grateful to church growth theorists for the fact that they have raised some crucial theological issues related to evangelism. My point here, however, relates to the *kind* of issues they have raised and their inability to reach any kind of consensus on them. The most striking illustration of the former point can be found in McGavran's *Understanding Church Growth*.[12] The theological issues that McGavran considers really significant are those that will somehow undergird his pursuit of the growth of the church. Thus the only categories that really catch his attention are those of a search theology or a harvest theology, and his primary concern is to ask the simplistic question of whether or not God wills it.[13] This in turn determines his use of biblical material, as he selectively concentrates on those passages that will support the so-called harvest theology. It is only natural, therefore, that he gives a rather tendentious place and reading to the commissioning of the disciples in Matthew 28:18-20. All this betrays a serious lack of theological balance and a lamentable failure to come to terms with the host of theological concepts within

12. Donald McGavran, *Understanding Church Growth* (Grand Rapids: Eerdmans, 1980).

13. Ibid., pp. 26ff. The whole of Part I of this volume is supposed to be devoted to theological considerations. In reality they receive very scant attention. It is also worth noting that McGavran does not conceive theological considerations as foundational; this coveted position is given to sociological considerations, as indicated by the title of Part IV.

and without the biblical corpus that clearly impinge on the nature and practice of evangelism.

This situation has not improved with the passage of time. Despite various promissory notes and an extensive body of books and articles, the fundamental issues that need to be addressed remain unresolved. Some questions have been pursued with care, perhaps most notably in the field of ecclesiology with the publication of Van Engen's rather ponderous *The Growth of the True Church*.[14] Overall, however, the situation looks something like this. First, the most serious criticisms of the tradition have tended to be either ignored or answered in a rather *ad hoc* fashion.[15] The most glaring example of this is the failure to answer the penetrating objections raised to standard church growth exegesis of the Great Commission.[16] Yet without the standard reading of this text with its artificial distinction between various kinds of discipling and its forced separating of teaching from discipling, a vital element in church growth theology is bereft of significant warrants.

Second, it is rather obvious that competing and even conflicting doctrinal traditions have been able to embrace church growth theory without shedding any theological tears. Thus church growth theory appears decked out in a variety of doctrinal costumes from the polemical, anticonciliar evangelicalism of Donald McGavran to the austere, revisionist Calvinism of Arthur Glasser.[17] We can graft our theology of church growth onto the restrained dispensationalism of George Peters[18] or we can marry it to the radically revised Pentecostalism of John Wim-

---

14. See note 4.

15. The latter is well illustrated by Peter Wagner's response to criticisms of the homogeneous unit principle in *Church Growth and the Whole Gospel*, chap. 9.

16. An excellent analysis of this issue can be found in David J. Bosch, "The Structure of Mission: An Exposition of Matthew 28:16-21," in Wilbert R. Shenk, ed., *Exploring Church Growth* (Grand Rapids: Eerdmans, 1983), pp. 218-48. A penetrating review of the exegetical foundations of mission can be found in Donald Senior, C.P., and Carol Stuhlmueller, C.P., *The Biblical Foundations for Mission* (Maryknoll: Orbis, 1983).

17. See esp. his "Church Growth and Theology," in A. R. Tippett, ed., *God, Man, and Church Growth* (Grand Rapids: Eerdmans, 1973), pp. 52-68.

18. George Peters, *A Theology of Church Growth* (Grand Rapids: Zondervan, 1981).

ber[19] or Paul Cho.[20] We may integrate it into the psychological hedonism of Robert Schuller[21] or the prosperity and success in life of Robert Tilton.[22] In fact, we may forget about theology altogether and translate church growth into a set of public relations and management skills that we can sell to those who are severely tempted to domesticate the Holy Spirit in the structures and requirements of a prosaic profession. All in all, the result of twenty years of work is not some renewed vision of mission, nor a penetrating challenge to the secularism of a barren church, nor a revitalized clergy devoted to the rescue and saving of lost sheep under the sovereign rule of the Good Shepherd. What we have is considerable theological disarray, shallowness, or indifference, a fostering of false hopes concerning what can be achieved by research and programing, and a rather conspicuous failure to face up to the radical demands of the Christian gospel. As this last point takes us to the primary symptoms of disease in the church growth tradition, let us pursue it with some care.

As we approach this issue let me state that I share the church growth tradition's concern to link evangelism in an intimate way with the development of local churches. Thus, rather than tie evangelism both conceptually and practically to proclamation in the exclusive way that has been common since the late nineteenth century, it is much wiser to conceive evangelism in such a manner that it can naturally incorporate within it the persuading of people to become Christians and to take their place as responsible members in the body of Christ.[23]

19. Wimber and Springer, *Power Evangelism*.

20. Paul Cho, *More than Numbers* (Waco: Word, 1984).

21. Van Engen refers to Schuller as "one of the major figures in the American Church Growth Movement and one of its principal teachers and theorists." See *Growth of the True Church*, p. 471.

22. Robert Tilton is pastor of the Word of Faith church in Dallas and is one of the leading exponents of the gospel of health and wealth.

23. I follow here the definition found in Donald A. McGavran and Winfred C. Arn, *Ten Steps for Church Growth* (San Francisco: Harper and Row, 1977), p. 51. This definition needs to be set alongside McGavran's definitions and descriptions of evangelism in his "Essential Evangelism," in Donald McGavran, ed., *Eye of the Storm: The Great Debate in Mission* (Waco: Word, 1972), pp. 56-66. There he says that "evangelism is activity undertaken with the intent of communicating the good news" (p. 64), that "evangelism is seeking and saving

Clearly, therefore, church growth falls under the auspices of evangelism as I understand it. Furthermore, it is useful to distinguish between two kinds of questions that will confront us if we think clearly about church growth. The first are conceptual questions that seek to identify what we consider to be the church and what we consider to be growth. The second are empirical and practical questions about how growth can be causally or efficaciously brought about. For the purposes of this book I am happy to conceptualize growth in external, statistical terms. That is, I set aside the kind of growth Costas identifies as reflective, organic, and incarnational.[24] What I wish to argue is that both our conception of numerical growth and our practical operations to achieve this end must, logically speaking, be governed by the kind of crucial theological concepts that are either ignored or hopelessly diluted in the church growth tradition.

The Erosion of Initiation into the Kingdom

We can approach this matter usefully by recalling that becoming a Christian is a complex and radical affair. This is powerfully brought home to us when we bear in mind the fundamental concepts and analogies that have been deployed since the earliest days to capture what happens when we come to Christ. Thus it is said that we are born again, that we have been fully justified or acquitted before God, and that we have been raised from death to life. We are like someone who has been awakened out of a deep sleep, we are converted from darkness to light, and we have experienced the firstfruits of the age to come. We have been adopted into the family of God, we have entered into the new covenant, and we have become members of the body of Christ. We have been incorporated into the kingdom of God, we have been initially sanctified and set aside for the service of God

---

sinners" (p. 66), and that "evangelism is actually grafting multitudes of wild olive branches into the Divine Tree" (p. 66).

24. Orlando Costas, *Christ Outside the Gate: Mission Beyond Christendom* (Maryknoll: Orbis, 1982), p. 47.

to the world, and we have become bond-slaves of Jesus Christ. We have repented of our sins, we have been enlightened and convicted by the Holy Spirit, and we have come to trust not in ourselves or our merits but in the mercy and grace of God. We have been saved from our sins, we have been reconciled to God through the death of Jesus Christ, and we have been given the internal witness of the Holy Spirit. We have been set free to love God, we have been sent forth to love our neighbor as ourselves, and we have been equipped to stand up against the forces of evil that would hold us in bondage. We have been baptized and filled with the Holy Spirit, we have been baptized with water, and we have tested the powers of the age to come.

In offering this catalogue of descriptions my primary concern is to draw attention to the complexity of Christian initiation into the body of Christ. I am not, therefore, insisting that every convert be explicitly aware either consciously or conceptually of all that is going on when one becomes a Christian. Nor am I insisting that every evangelist deploy all the concepts and analogies outlined here.[25] My aim is to highlight the profound significance of what it is to accept Jesus Christ as Savior and Lord and to insist that crucial elements are captured here that constitute initiation into the church. Without these elements our conception of the church is impoverished and inadequate; attempts to increase the size of the church that fail to take these into account are necessarily shallow and superficial. In other words, what we have here is a rhetoric of interlocking convictions, commitments, covenants, emotions, affections, and experiences that form the matrix of Christian initiation.

What is disconcerting about church growth theory is that in various ways it blunts the whole thrust of this point. Thus church growth theorists give little or no attention to what it is to be incorporated and grounded in the kingdom of God, for example. Their focus is on membership of the church, an emphasis that is of course both salutary and correct. But surely one cannot become a genuine member of the church without being

25. John Wesley, e.g., tended to focus on justification and new birth — but for him these were the tip of a complex theological iceberg.

incorporated in a substantial way into the dynamic realm of God's sovereign rule, with all the privileges and obligations that this involves. The establishing and grounding of people in God's kingdom is surely an element of evangelism. There must be genuine initiation rather than superficial initiation; firm and adequate foundations must be laid in the lives of new converts before we can talk intelligibly about going on to Christian nurture, spiritual formation, Christian perfection, or whatever else we want to call it. Yet church growth theorists give only scant attention to this since their primary interest is in the external features of church membership.[26] The results are only too predictable: if we take this route we are sowing the seeds for the emergence of a Pascal or a Kierkegaard who must launch a fresh attack on Christendom for its bogus Christianity.[27]

It is important not to be distracted at this point by the genuine concern of church growth theorists to abandon the individualism of the West with its emphasis on isolated conversions. We can fully endorse the view that we can speak coherently of group conversion or multi-individual decisions, and we surely need to construe conversion as both social and personal in nature.[28] The issue is not what we really mean by conversion, but what we mean by genuine initiation into Christ, into his kingdom, and into his church. Conversion is but one dimension of this complex process, and so the honors and demands of the latter cannot be captured by expanding conversion to cover groups rather than just individuals.

This failure to acknowledge the comprehensive and radical character of Christian initiation bedevils the policies and prac-

---

26. The idea of the kingdom of God is tacked on as an afterthought in Peter Wagner's *Church Growth and the Whole Gospel*.

27. This is not idle speculation. C. René Padilla has gone so far as to claim that the harm caused by the emphasis on numerical growth in the Third World "is incalculable." See C. René Padilla, *Mission Between the Times* (Grand Rapids: Eerdmans, 1985), p. 101.

28. J. Wascom Pickett's treatment of this issue is especially sensitive. See his *Christian Mass Movements in India* (New York: Abingdon, 1933) and *Christ's Way to India's Heart* (New York: Friendship, 1938). Pickett displays a concern about the dangers of group conversions that one does not generally find in modern church growth literature.

tices of church growth advocates in the field of evangelism. Their focus on numerical church growth systematically distorts the whole ethos of our evangelistic endeavors and misdirects the way in which we conceptualize and resolve the problems facing us. I can think of several examples. First, the legitimate attempt to respond to the particularity and integrity of cultural diversity becomes, through use of the homogeneous unit principle, a subtle way of ignoring the radical demands of the gospel with regard to repentance from social and corporate sin; it is also a means of riding roughshod over the radically inclusive character of the people of God. The way in which church growth theorists introduce and discuss the matter, given the history and continued prevalence of racism in America, is astonishing. They seem to have no sense of how the advocacy of such a principle will almost inevitably be used to keep the social status quo in place, and they make no attempt to explore and explicate other options, which is necessary if the deep problems related to racism and cultural diversity are to be resolved. Church growth theorists are not so much wrong in some sort of absolute way; they are somewhat blind, insensitive, and unrealistic. Second, the legitimate desire to draw some kind of division of labor between evangelists and church planters on the one side and pastors and church teachers on the other leads to an artificial division between level 1 and level 2 discipling and thereby begins to undercut the rich, demanding conception of discipleship to be found in the New Testament. Third, the entirely laudable desire to give the young convert space to breath both morally and spiritually leads to a limiting of the Holy Spirit to working in the inner conscience of the hearer,[29] and causes one to forget that the call to repentance as found in John the Baptist, Jesus, and Paul is alarmingly specific in its content.[30] Fourth, the insistence that evangelism is a vital obligation and necessity laid upon the church leads to a cooking of the books in advance by

29. See Wagner, *Church Growth and the Whole Gospel,* pp. 142-43. If the Holy Spirit can work in the life of the hearer, surely he can work in the life of the speaker. It is thoroughly artificial to construe the work of the Holy Spirit in this fashion.

30. See Luke 3:10-14 for a biblical example.

suggesting that the issue of priorities be couched in terms of the so-called evangelistic mandate versus the so-called cultural mandate. Given the obvious significance of eternity over against time and a few other theological platitudes, it will not be difficult to show that evangelism takes precedence over all else the church does.[31] But this totally ignores the primary horizon of the kingdom of God, a horizon within which evangelism, social action, pastoral care, and all else the church does must ultimately be set. Fifth, understandable caution concerning the involvement of the church in political issues leads to a tendency to adopt the common falsehood that society can only be changed through changing individuals; it leads to a soft-peddling of the reality of injustice and oppression; it nurtures a sense of ease in Zion that should not exist; and it fosters a persistent neglect of the voice of the Holy Spirit speaking to us in the conscience of the church at large—such as happened with the slavery issue in an earlier generation. Finally, a refreshing openness to the liveliness, the theological insights, and the significant innovations in ministry developed within Pentecostalism and its offspring leads to the treating of signs and wonders, or the gracious intervention of God in the world, as one more scheme of evangelism or one "more powerful spiritual instrument"[32] to be incorporated in the practical resource-kit of the church growth specialist.

Power Evangelism

Reference to Pentecostalism leads into an obvious and important rebuttal to my fundamental objection to the church growth tradition. My basic objection is that insufficient attention is being paid to the eschatological content and context of evangelism. Against this it will be averred that the work of John Wimber represents someone from within the tradition who has sought to interact with the eschatological dimensions of the gospel. Indeed both he and Peter Wagner have tried to take seriously the reality of the coming rule of God here and now. Hence,

31. See Wagner, *Church Growth and the Whole Gospel*, pp. 99-101.
32. This is the language of Peter Wagner in his foreword to John Wimber's *Power Evangelism*, p. ix.

they say, the church growth tradition has paid attention to this issue. Let us pursue this line of inquiry with some care.

Wimber's writings and work in evangelism represent a very significant development within the church growth tradition. Although making no pretensions to being a scholar, Wimber has sought to come to an understanding of evangelism that is rooted in the eschatological teaching of the New Testament. He has set his ministry of evangelism firmly in the tension between the present and future coming of the kingdom and is in the process of building a whole denomination that seeks to make manifest the present power of the kingdom. That power is present in the mystical awareness of the Spirit in worship, in the presence of healings and exorcisms, in the operation of words of knowledge and guidance, in boldness in proclaiming the gospel, and in the development of kinship groups and small units of effective pastoral care. This has led to an approach to evangelism that focuses less on program and traditional training and more on the direct guidance of the Holy Spirit in revelation. In his own ministry Wimber seems to have shifted from the more typical church growth adviser to one who finds himself in the midst of the kind of awakening that has occurred again and again in the history of Protestantism. Thus he has become a significant figure in charismatic circles both within and without mainline Christianity. His writings represent a distillation and revision of the basic material that has emerged in Pentecostal and neo-Pentecostal groups over the last generation. What is striking and original is the refreshingly casual style of his ministry, the honesty and candor that confronts the skeptical observer of his activity, the way in which he has been able to avoid the sectarianism and sensationalism of much modern Pentecostalism, and the extent to which he has earned the respect of the established churches.

It is not yet possible to offer a comprehensive account and evaluation of Wimber's contribution to modern evangelism. All the evidence is not yet in and that which we do have is only partially available in the public domain.[33] Moreover, his work

33. That which is available is *Power Evangelism* and John Wimber and Kevin Springer, *Power Healing* (London: Hodder and Stoughton, 1987).

raises some deep theological questions that we cannot resolve here. What matters at this juncture, however, is that even a preliminary survey of his activity and writings poses some searching questions for the church growth tradition, which those on the inside of the movement may be reluctant to acknowledge. It is no accident that some in the church growth tradition choose to ignore his work entirely; some have informally expressed the fear that his proposals threaten to derail the whole church growth position as conventionally developed.

We agree that there is a clear link between the church growth tradition and the work and reflection of Wimber. For example, he noticed that there seemed to be a direct connection between church growth and phenomena like healing and exorcism in studies emanating from the Third World. Wimber explored his observations by asking whether these might have serious implications for evangelism in the West. If a Pentecostal approach to evangelism worked elsewhere, why should it not work in a secular society that needs to be encountered in signs and wonders by the reality of God? In a real sense, therefore, he was asking church growth type questions and seeking church growth type answers. What we must press, however, is whether his preliminary and somewhat *ad hoc* conclusions are really compatible with the general orientation of the church growth tradition. That they are not is suggested by the following considerations.

First, Wimber's reflections and experience have led him to place a very strong emphasis on eschatology, which is not just a complement to standard church growth theology insofar as it exists but is a marked contrast to most others in the tradition. Some, like McGavran and Hunter, pay little or no attention to it at all. The notable exception is Wagner, but his treatment of the kingdom is a passing phase in the development of his thinking as a whole. He deals with it because his critics have censured him for not heeding it, but then it appears it is back to business as usual. For Wimber the kingdom constitutes the basis of thinking on evangelism. It provides the fundamental categories for his ministry and without it he would be at a loss to make sense of his work.

Second, this leads to a much more demanding conception of discipleship than is the norm in church growth thinking. Wimber eschews the distinction between various levels of discipleship one finds in McGavran. His clear desire is to see evangelism lead to the development of active saints who are equipped with the gifts of ministry and who are assiduously assaulting the forces of evil in the world. There is no handing over of this task to others as something that belongs to a later phase of perfecting or of Christian nurture. The whole approach to discipleship is much more substantial than is usual in the church growth tradition.

Last, as already indicated, Wimber's strategy completely subordinates planning and programs to the direct guidance of the Holy Spirit in the church. This is a radical reversal of emphasis and priorities. Of course, he is not opposed to careful planning and reflection in evangelism. What is at issue is the secondary role these play compared to the emphasis on supernatural guidance that pervades his thinking and practice. The standard approach of the church growth strategist is to focus on the mundane, naturalistic factors that lead to numerical increase in membership. There is a great reticence to speak of God acting directly in the manner envisaged and taught by Wimber. To be sure, the presence of the Holy Spirit will be invoked in traditional church growth activity, but the manner of the Spirit's working is conceived along traditional, non-Pentecostal lines. Wimber stresses the direct action of the Spirit as absolutely vital to an adequate ministry of evangelism. The contrast here could be a matter of theological reticence or understandable caution on the part of church growth theorists, for it is obvious that if they endorse Wimber's kind of radical theology they will cease to appeal to those segments of Western Christianity to which they hope to be of service in evangelism. But this is a debatable explanation. At the very best it appears that the signs and wonders embraced by Wimber as integral to evangelism are treated as an optional extra that can be set aside at will. If one's theology allows for or fosters this kind of ministry, well and good. If not, there are plenty of human resources available and backed up by research that can be used to increase church membership figures. In other words, signs, wonders, words of revelation, and the like do not have any normative status. For Wimber, however, they constitute effective and appropriate evangelism—and therein lies a profound contrast between his work and that which is associated with the standard teachers of the church growth tradition. It is of little help, therefore, to appeal to Wimber in order to counter my central objection to church growth theory. His work represents a profound challenge to the fundamental orientation of McGavran and his disciples.

In any case, it is unlikely that many will seek to lean upon Wimber's suggestions as a rebuttal to my argument. His proposals are at best too controversial in their content and at worst too ambiguous in their implications to carry much weight in the discussion at present. For some his whole approach to evangelism may be considered too embarrassing to deserve mention, much less critical analysis. For better or worse, however, Wimber and what he represents constitute a significant development in modern evangelism since the rise of Pentecostalism. Those committed to objective and comprehensive evaluation of the available options cannot ignore him. It is sufficient for our purposes to note that Wimber and his associates have sought to interact as best they can with the eschatological dimension of the gospel. It is clear that others in the church growth tradition are moving in that direction.[34] As yet, however, they have not adequately conceptualized the implications that this has for evangelism.

Conclusion

Where, then, does all this leave us? As I pointed out at the beginning, nothing but good can come from extensive interaction with the church growth tradition. We have here a body of fascinating material that has raised some crucial questions about the nature and practice of evangelism. We ignore this at our in-

---

34. See Eddie Gibbs, *I Believe in Church Growth* (Grand Rapids: Eerdmans, 1981), pp. 43-70.

tellectual peril. Moreover, it is obvious that the study and practice of evangelism can never quite be the same given the iconoclastic spirit that has propelled church growth theory on to the printed page, into the public eye, and into the churches. However, the flaws in the fundamental structure cannot be ignored. Those committed to faithfulness and excellence in the field of evangelism must therefore ensure that other options are expounded and critically examined and that the serious problems identified in church growth theory be resolved. No doubt some will find it helpful to stay within the fundamental boundaries of the church growth position and seek to amend its ways as best they can. The idea of church growth is itself clearly flexible enough for it to be an umbrella concept harboring a variety of conflicting opinions and proposals. In my view it is important that some pursue this whole option, for only in this fashion will the full insights and fatal flaws of the tradition finally be identified. As with any other body of ideas, explanations, and insights there is no substitute for the patient, costly, fallible, and even controversial working through of one's hunches and convictions to their limits.

For my part, I prefer at this stage to work more cautiously and modestly. Evangelism, however we define it, is bounded by a series of questions that require the collection and use of a wide variety of data and warrants if they are to be properly addressed. We find ourselves like rabbits let loose in a large field, and we are going to have to dig a lot of tunnels if we are to get around it safely. Moreover, the tunnels we dig will need at some stage to be connected if we are to avoid some of the traps and snares that will be set for us. At this juncture I am content to insist that one tunnel that badly needs to be dug is that one which opens up to us the complex character of initiation into Christ, into his kingdom, and into his church. We also need to work out the implications of this for our understanding and practice of evangelism.

F I V E

Initiation

Evangelism in the early church was rooted in the eschatological activity of God, which was inaugurated in the life,
death, and resurrection of Jesus of Nazareth and continued in
the acts of the Holy Spirit. Given what God had done in and
through Christ and the Holy Spirit, it was only natural that
Christians should proclaim the mighty acts of God in salvation
and liberation, and that they should found communities committed to celebrating all that God had done. They were propelled by a wellspring of joy and love that was at once irre-
pressible and contagious.

An Explanation of Our Varied Definitions of Evangelism

It is not at all surprising, therefore, that when modern theologians and Christian activists formalize their thinking on evangelism they focus on either proclamation or the planting of
churches as the heart of the matter. To be sure, both of these
are inspired in part by epochal movements in the past life of
the church. Thus the sixteenth-century Reformers' emphasis on
the proclamation of the word encouraged the church to limit
evangelism to acts of proclamation.[1] Indeed, the propensity to
derive a vision of evangelism from word studies in the Scriptures is itself a cardinal feature of certain streams of the Refor-

---

1. An illustration of this is Henry Snyder Gehman, "You are an Evangelist," *The Princeton Seminary Bulletin* 52 (1958): 10-16.

mation tradition. Equally, the proposal to press on beyond proclamation to the planting of local churches is very congruent with the great missionary movements of the nineteenth century, where one of the primary aims was to establish local churches across the face of the earth. One can very naturally construe the modern church growth tradition as an attempt to fulfill the goal to evangelize the world in a generation, a sentiment that was central to the Student Volunteer Movement, out of which Donald McGavran emerged.

Yet both these attempts to characterize the essence of evangelism represent an obvious feature of the coming of the reign of God in Jesus Christ. God's action in Jesus surely cries out to be proclaimed to the whole creation in joy and celebration. If the church did not proclaim the good news of the kingdom, then the very stones would take it upon themselves to do so (Luke 19:40). Equally, the kingdom cries out to be established in a vibrant institution that is committed to letting God reign in its own life and in the world. In fact, the messianic community constitutes part of the messianic rule—there must be an Israel in which God rules. This is not just an afterthought that is to be tacked on to acts of proclamation as a happy accident; it is essential to the coming of the rule of God on earth. So it is not surprising that scholars and evangelists should develop both proclamation and church planting as the core activity in evangelism.

There are, however, three other conceptions of evangelism available to us. For the sake of completeness we should mention them. First, evangelism is often construed as converting people to Christianity. The traditional term for much of this activity is "soul-winning." The unbeliever is presented with the facts of the gospel; he or she is then led through repentance and faith to a personal commitment to Christ, which is marked by an experience of assurance instilled by the Holy Spirit. The paradigm text for this tradition is in the Gospel of John, where Jesus informs Nicodemus that he must be born anew if he is to see the kingdom of God (chap. 3). Revival meetings, which were institutionalized in nineteenth-century American Protestantism, are an exemplary historical embodiment of this tradition. A second conception of evangelism is that of witness. The crux of this view is the sharing of one's faith or testimony on a one-to-one basis with an unbeliever. Clearly this has affinities with the model of proclamation, for the primary focus is on the verbal sharing of one's faith. It differs, however, in two respects. First, there is a strong tendency to make experience the essential content of what is shared; hence testimonies are often the hallmark of evangelism in this mode. Second, there is a constant temptation to broaden the concept of witness to embrace anything done to bear witness; hence it is easily extended to cover acts of love, mercy, and justice carried out by the individual Christian or by the church. In this light it is perhaps not surprising that there has been an intense debate between those who stress personal evangelism and those who stress acts of compassion as the heart of the mission of the church; the two share a common root that makes them cousins. Interestingly, both appeal in their popular rhetoric to the mandate in Acts to be witnesses in Jerusalem, in Judaea, in Samaria, and to the end of the earth (1:8). The third conception of evangelism makes much of the idea of discipleship. Lamenting the gross inadequacy of recording decisions without any serious follow-up and instruction, some have insisted that the essence of evangelism lies in making disciples who are not only brought to a decision to follow Christ but are also taught to be disciples. The young disciple is instructed in the fundamentals of faith and piety, with the goal of being the kind of person who can make disciples of others. This model of evangelism is especially prominent within parachurch organizations that have developed in student circles.[2]

These three ways of construing evangelism grow naturally out of the coming of the rule of God on earth. It is to be expected that the coming of God's rule has radical, transforming effects on the lives of individuals. The language of conversion and new birth is entirely appropriate as an attempt to capture this. However, it is not surprising that those converted should want to witness to their experience of God's love and

2. A good statement of this approach can be found in Robert E. Coleman, *The Master Plan of Evangelism* (Old Tappan, N.J.: Revell, 1964).

grace manifest in their initiation into God's kingdom. And it is also not surprising that they carry out their witness both in terms of verbal testimony to what God has done in their lives and in deeds of mercy, compassion, and justice. Finally, it is obvious that entering the kingdom of God does involve the process of becoming a disciple, that is, a lifelong learner who needs to be grounded in the basic dimensions of Christian life and witness.

Thus, we have here a convenient and useful explanation for the development of all five competing conceptions of evangelism. Each of them focuses on an important dimension of the coming of the rule of God and erects it into the essence of evangelism. Given what the coming of the rule of God involves, it is not at all unusual that those committed to its spread throughout the world should pick one of these elements and identify it as the heart of evangelism. The human yearnings for simplicity of conception and for economy of action no doubt reinforce the drive to focus on a single aspect of the reign of God as the crucial factor.

A New Definition of Evangelism

Despite the current confusion over evangelism and the tendency toward reductionism that each of the above-mentioned views represents we have available to us a way out—an immediate solution. My proposal is very simple at this point. We can best improve our thinking on evangelism by conceiving it as that set of intentional activities which is governed by the goal of initiating people into the kingdom of God for the first time. What I want to do now is to present the fundamental content of this claim and answer some obvious objections that will be brought against it.

We can begin with a formal definition. The *Oxford English Dictionary* defines *initiate* in this way:

> to admit a person with proper introductory rites or forms
> into some society or office, or to knowledge of or partici-
> pation in some principles or observances, especially of a
> secret or occult character; hence more generally to intro-

duce into acquaintance with something, to instruct in the elements of any subject or practice.

We can detect here both a narrower and a broader meaning of initiation. Narrowly conceived, initiation is an act or set of acts that admits one to a secret society.[3] Clearly, there is nothing of the occult about initiation into the kingdom of God, and, insofar as it involves anything secret, it is an open secret to be shared with the world rather than kept hidden under lock and key. So this is not of much help. More broadly, initiation is an act or set of acts that admits one into a society, a set of principles, a body of knowledge, a way of living, and the like. This second conception of initiation is most serviceable as a way of understanding the concept of evangelism. To initiate someone into the kingdom of God is to admit that person into the eschatological rule of God through appropriate instruction, experiences, rites, and forms.

It is crucial to grasp at the outset that the activity or experience or institution into which one is initiated determines the material character of the initiation under review. For example, to initiate someone into an academic discipline will differ radically from initiation into a secret society like the Masonic Order, or from initiation into a specialist profession like surgery. In each situation certain features are shared in common. Particular traditions will be handed over, special principles will be taught, determinate capacities and experiences will be fostered, certain ceremonies will be held, and so on. What these are and how they are carried out will be governed by that into which the person is being initiated. They will differ drastically from one domain to another. Hence initiation into the kingdom of God will have its own internal grammar, its own internal structure, constraints, and logic. It is crucial that we acknowledge the uniqueness of that logic; if not, the result will be confusion and

---

3. C. J. Bleeker suggests that secrecy is an element of initiation, but this is an exaggeration. See his "Introductory Remarks on the Significance of Initiaition," in C. J. Bleeker, ed., *Initiation* (Leiden: E. J. Brill, 1965), p. 16. A fascinating general analysis of initiation in the history of religion can be found in Mircea Eliade, *Rites and Symbols of Initiation* (New York: Harper and Row, 1958).

misunderstanding. In other words, the nature of the coming of the rule of God sets its own unique agenda concerning what is characteristic of initiation into the rule of God. It is therefore seriously misleading to confuse initiation into the kingdom of God with initiation into something other than or less than that reality. Moreover, the unique character of the rule of God and how it has come into history shapes and informs from beginning to end how initiation is to be carried out.

What I am proposing here should not, therefore, be confused with Christian initiation as generally understood in the church at large and as discussed extensively in modern liturgical studies. Much overlaps, as we shall see, but the two are not the same. Recent scholars have provided a fascinating body of material charting the fortunes of Christian initiation across space and time. Diachronic studies have shown how over a period of six hundred years the unified rites of initiation, developed in the patristic period and identified in and around baptism, confirmation, and admittance to the eucharist, were split apart into isolated moments and rites that then began to disintegrate in the modern era. In addition, synchronic studies on the nature of initiation in the contemporary church have highlighted the great diversity of patterns of initiation that currently exist.[4] Thus we can identify the following divergent models of initiation. The Eastern Orthodox Church still preserves the unity of the patristic rites and practices, at least in theory. The Roman Catholic Church and the central Reformation churches, that is, the Lutheran, Presbyterian, and Anglican bodies, basically hold to a two-stage process focusing on infant baptism and confirmation climaxed by admittance to the eucharist. The Anabaptist traditions practice fundamentally a single stage centering on conscious conversion and baptism. Finally, the Pentecostal tradi-

4. The following are very helpful on the history of Christian initiation: Aidan Kavanagh, et al., *Made, Not Born* (Notre Dame: University of Notre Dame Press, 1976); Hugh M. Riley, *Christian Initiation* (Washington, D.C.: The Catholic Universtiy of America Press, 1974); Geoffrey Wainwright, "The Baptismal Eucharist before Nicea: An Essay in Liturgical History," *Studia Liturgica* 4 (1965): 9-36; idem, "The Rites and Ceremonies of Christian Initiation," *Studia Liturgica* 10 (1974): 2-24; idem, *Christian Initiation* (London: Lutterworth, 1970).

tions use a two-stage process stretching from conversion to an experience of baptism by the Holy Spirit accompanied by baptism in water and the laying on of hands. Such studies are a very valuable contribution to the discussion about evangelism, but in my judgment they begin at the wrong starting point. By construing Christian initiation as initiation into the church, they ignore what is logically prior to this, namely, initiation into the kingdom of God. Hence it is not surprising that they concentrate on the various external rites that lead to initiation into the church and tend to construe the theological issues at stake in terms of how and where God is supposed to act in the various human acts that are carried out in the process of initiation. The debate about whether the Holy Spirit comes in baptism or in confirmation illustrates this admirably.

A Change of Focus

What I am proposing calls for a fundamental reorientation in our thinking about Christian initiation. We begin by asking what it is to be initiated into the rule of God, which has been inaugurated in Jesus of Nazareth and in the work of the Holy Spirit at Pentecost and thereafter. From within this horizon we then proceed to articulate what it is to be initiated into the community of the kingdom, that is, the church. Logically speaking, this takes the primary focus away from external admittance into a particular organization and relocates it in the sweep of God's action in Christ and in the Holy Spirit. Our eyes are not then initially on ourselves, on the ecclesiastical community to which we belong, or on whatever we have to do, either as agent or recipient, to become part of the appropriate body; they are firmly fixed on what God has done in Christ, and on what the Holy Spirit continues to do now. We shift from an anthropocentric horizon, where the focus is on what we do or on what is done to us in certain rites and ceremonies, in various acts of catechesis, and the like; we move from this to a theocentric horizon where the focus is on the majestic and awesome activity of a trinitarian God whose actions on our behalf stagger our imagination and dissolve into impenetrable mystery. It is extraordinarily difficult to capture this conceptually and even more demanding to sustain it across the generations, but in itself this shift of horizon should radically alter the whole temper and ethos of our evangelistic ministries. I can think of nothing more important or more decisive in charting the contours of a healthy vision of evangelism than this shift of focus.

Shortly I shall suggest that initiation into the kingdom of God, from the point of view of the person being initiated, involves not just a corporate aspect represented by baptism but at least five other dimensions that can very naturally be distinguished from admittance to baptism. Before we turn to that, however, it would be fruitful to review what the coming of the rule of God has at times meant in the history of the church. We could do so by recreating the history of the beginnings of the Christian movement at Pentecost, but as this would take us into contested debates that are beyond resolution here, we will work from something closer to hand. I have in mind the intriguing accounts of renewal and awakening, particularly within Protestantism, that have from time to time done so much to rekindle and fuel the evangelistic imperative of the Christian gospel. I select the example almost at random.

Between the years 1914 and 1925 the number of Christians on the island of Nias off the west coast of Sumatra increased from eighteen thousand to sixty-five thousand, with another twenty-three thousand persons under instruction.[5] This remarkable growth after years of very modest developments did not happen because of some great scheme of evangelism. It began very quietly when the missionaries of the *Rheinische Missionsgesellschaft* called together the local leaders of the Christian community to review fifty years of work in the region. Out of this jubilee assessment and celebration various meetings were held in homes to seek God and to find ways to remove the defects that had been identified. Some of these meetings were devoted to preparation for a special celebration of the eucharist. In time these meetings were thronged

---

5. For details on this episode see E. Kriele, "The Nias Revival, the Story of a Spiritual Awakening," *International Review of Missions* 16 (1927): 91-102.

with people and they became the catalyst for a work of the Holy Spirit that had enduring results.

People became profoundly aware of God. They were overwhelmed with a sense of God's majesty and their own sinfulness. They thirsted to hear the gospel, and they eagerly spent time confessing their sins to their pastors. They were flooded with joy, so much so that they could not but share their faith with others. They made significant reparation for the wrongs they had committed. They insisted on doubling and then trebling the number of services that were held. They met every Friday for fellowship and catechetical instruction, and they devoured any Christian literature they could find. They offered themselves for service in the Christian community to the extent that the number of evangelists increased from six in 1916 to one hundred in 1925.

This brief catalogue of events cannot begin to do justice to what happened in Nias, but it is typical in the profound sense of the presence of God that is the mark of periods of genuine awakening. My aim in mentioning this incident is not to offer a model of how evangelism should be conducted, nor to suggest some kind of speculative correlation between awakenings and church growth, but rather to highlight that the coming of the kingdom of God is not some abstract, theoretical event dragged up out of ancient history to enhance the future of evangelism. To be sure, episodes of this nature pose their own problems and it is tempting to turn aside and discuss the alternative theological and quasi-scientific interpretations they evoke.[6] But we shall resist such overtures and stay with the contention that this episode illustrates that the coming of the rule of God through the work of the Holy Spirit is not confined to Pentecost and the early history of the church but is a dynamic, awesome, mysterious, active reality that sovereignly enters history again and again. It can sweep people along like a flood or fall gently like the morning dew. Either way it transforms human lives, creates a new community of forgive-

6. Classic studies of crucial aspects of the subject are still Jonathan Edwards, *The Great Awakening* (New Haven: Yale University Press, 1972), and *Religious Affections* (New Haven: Yale University Press, 1959). A radically different analysis can be found in Willam Walters Sargant, *Battle for the Mind* (Garden City, N.Y.: Doubleday, 1957).

ness and compassion, brings new hope and joy into the world, and fosters a deep commitment to offer oneself in service to the body of Christ. The church ultimately lives by such power and it ultimately grows by such power.

Evangelism, too, is intimately related to the sweep of God's action in history. It arises out of the inauguration of God's sovereign rule on earth, and its central aim is to see people firmly grounded within that rule so that they can begin a new life as agents of reconciliation, compassion, and peace. Its unique and irreplaceable role in the life of the church is to initiate people into the dynamic rule of God that was ontologically grounded in the work of Jesus Christ in Israel and is continued and sustained by grace through the inimitable activity of the Holy Spirit. Such initiation is *sui generis*. It cannot be collapsed into admittance to some religious institution. It is logically distinct from the kind of psychological and social formation that takes place when one embraces a specific cosmic or historical narrative. It cannot be reduced to the acquisition of some kind of creed or body of knowledge that is intellectually mastered, and it is more than the appropriation of a particular moral vision. It is distinct from the passive endurance of certain rites and ceremonies, it goes far beyond the undergoing of some spiritual or emotional experiences of even the most positive character, and it cannot be drained out into an assiduous activism that seeks to change the world for the better. To be initiated into the rule of God is to encounter a transcendent reality that has entered history and to find oneself drawn up into the ultimate purposes of God for history and creation. Initiation involves most if not all of the processes we have just identified, yet to reduce it to any or all of them is to foment theological folly and spiritual confusion.

The Grammar of Christian Initiation and Its Implications for Evangelism

Having insisted rather strongly that initiation into the reign of God is unique, we can now press home the point that it is not some ahistorical process that fails to touch our lives as we know them. It is no accident that commentators on Christian initiation have focused on admittance to the Christian community as the essence of initiation. They are correctly taking into account the social character of our existence, and they are rightly highlighting one crucial dimension of initiation into the rule of God. One cannot be satisfactorily initiated into the rule of God and remain an isolated spiritual nomad. The kingdom brings with it the Israel of God, that community in which God rules. So to be initiated properly requires that one be joined to that community. Initiation has, therefore, a communal dimension that cannot be set aside as an option to be taken up at will.

The same applies to the other dimensions that constitute part of the kingdom in all its richness and complexity. Thus initiation involves the owning of the intellectual claims without which discourse about the kingdom will be impossible and empty. Initiation is unthinkable without those evangelized coming to believe certain propositions about themselves, about Christ, about God and his kingdom, and so on. The issue here is not the material one of what is to be believed for one to become a Christian (we shall discuss that in the next chapter); rather, the question is the formal one of whether there is a minimal cognitive dimension to Christian initiation. I believe that such a dimension is inescapable. It is true descriptively as a matter of what actually goes on in initiation, and it is true normatively as a matter of what ought to be the case explicitly in initiation. The church, acting through its evangelists, shares with them in handing over an intellectual and theological vision that those initiated into Christianity come to appropriate and believe. Whether this is done intentionally or unintentionally, formally or informally, is strictly irrelevant. Either way, it happens, and we need to be fully open about it.

Initiation also requires the appropriation of a very particular moral vision that serves as the bedrock of moral action in the Christian community and in the world. At the heart of this are the two great commandments to love God and to love one's neighbor as oneself. Moreover, initiation precipitates certain experiences, dispositions, and emotions that naturally arise in one's encounter with the living God revealed in Jesus Christ and made known personally through the Holy Spirit. Thus, for example, those evangelized should come to experience in their inner lives that kind of assurance which only the Holy Spirit can give, which was rediscovered as the birthright of every Christian in the eighteenth-century revival led by the Wesleys and Whitefield. In addition, initiation is marked by the reception and development of particular gifts and capacities that equip one to serve as an agent of God. Initiation is not just a matter of receiving, it is also a matter of learning to give of oneself in the work of the kingdom. To that end, God has given gifts to his church to carry out his work in the world—and initiation is seriously defective if this is overlooked and ignored. Finally, initiation is constituted by the appropriation of certain basic spiritual disciplines that are absolutely essential for the exercise and sustenance of responsible obedience to the joys of the kingdom. At a minimum it involves learning to fast, pray, read the Scriptures, and participate in the eucharist.

In all, initiation involves a complex web of reality that is at once corporate, cognitive, moral, experiential, operational, and disciplinary. Initiation into the kingdom of God is not only one of these; nor is it all of these strung together as a mere human enterprise driven simply by earthly passion and planning; it is all of these set and bounded within the dramatic action of God that is manifest in Christ and fueled by the Holy Spirit.

If we see evangelism as those actions that are governed by the intention to initiate people into the kingdom of God, then several crucial consequences ensue. First, it follows that not just one agent is involved in the process of evangelism but four. The primary agent is the triune God who has created us in his own image, who has acted decisively in Jesus of Nazareth for the liberation of the cosmos, and who has come in the person of the Holy Spirit to make known the work of Christ and to empower God's people to live as his disciples and to participate in his activity in the world. The second agent is the church, which is called to embody the rule of God in its worship, life, and ministries, to identify and to nourish those whom God has specially called to the work of evangelism, and to share with them in their characteristic activity as evangelists. The third agent is the evangelist, whose task is to proclaim the good news of the kingdom and ensure that those who respond are appropriately grounded in the rule of God in history. Finally, the fourth agent is the person or persons evangelized. It is their responsibility to hear the word of truth, respond in faith and repentance, open themselves generously to the work of the Holy Spirit, and gladly own the responsibilities and privileges of the kingdom of God. Evangelism, therefore, calls for the activity of multiple agents; it is never a solo performance. Even when the evangelist may appear to be acting alone, his or her activity depends on the concomitant activity of the Holy Spirit.

Second, it follows from our initial premises that, from the point of view of the agency of the church and the individual evangelist, evangelism is necessarily a polymorphous activity. It is more like farming or educating than like raising one's arm or blowing a kiss. It is done in, with, and through a host of other activities that are intimately related to the specific circumstances in which the evangelist is working. Evangelism will involve such acts as proclamation, basic instruction, prayer, and ensuring that those who respond are brought to baptism or confirmation. It may require acts of mercy, patient conversations, stern rebuke, or the organization of mass meetings. It may depend on the sharing of one's personal spiritual pilgrimage, or on an act of calculated silence, or on the ministering of a special rite of exorcism, or on the provision of catechesis, or on the laying on of hands, or on widespread use of the mass media, or on the development of small groups. No rule exists for setting or limiting the boundaries of action that the responsible evangelist may have to perform in order to carry out fitting and appropriate acts of evangelism. What makes the actions evangelism is that they are part of a process that is governed by the goal of initiating people into the kingdom of God.

Characteristically, of course, we can identify certain central acts that will very naturally crop up again and again. Clearly, evangelism will involve proclamation of the good news of the kingdom; it will generally require the call to repent and come to faith in Jesus Christ; and it will call for the provision of a process of initiation in which the convert to Christianity can be grounded in the theological and moral tradition of the Christian community, be brought into its membership, and be provided with the necessary initial equipment to serve as one of God's agents in the church and in the world. These constitute the meat and marrow of evangelism; the rest are on the menu as occasion requires. The really versatile evangelist will have lots of recipes for action from which to draw.

Put another way, it will be impossible to claim that one act alone is enough to constitute evangelism. Preaching an evangelistic sermon on television is not in itself evangelism; nor is baptizing twenty people on a Sunday morning in church; nor is sending a consignment of Bibles to a tribe that has never seen the Bible before; nor is teaching someone the basic doctrines of the Christian faith; nor is inviting someone to walk the aisle and repent; nor is leading someone in a prayer of personal commitment. Unless such acts are intimately related to a process that intentionally brings people into the kingdom of God, they are something other than or something less than evangelism. To be evangelism they must be causally related to the process of initiation into God's rule, and they must be governed by the intention to achieve this end.

This point is not overturned by considerations drawn from the history of evangelism. Consider the fascinating evangelistic endeavors of Prophet Harris of the Ivory Coast. Called of God, he left his home in Liberia and proceeded to work along the west coast of Africa, preaching the gospel and calling people to commitment. As Neill summarizes his ministry,

> The heart of his simple Gospel concerned belief in one God, the abandoning and destruction of fetishes, the observance of Sunday as a day of rest, and the prohibition of adultery. Those who came under his influence and accepted his teaching were baptised. Harris made them build churches in their villages, stressed the incomparable importance of the word of God, and bade them wait for the teachers who would come later, and give them the fuller instruction which he had no time to give.[7]

7. Stephen Neill, *A History of Christian Missions* (New York: Penguin, 1964), p. 493.

No doubt one could produce other cases to show that evangelistic activity has fallen far short of what I am proposing. But two reasons illustrate why these examples do not overthrow my position. First, they are clearly anomalous, and anomalies should not serve as the warrant for our fundamental principles in evangelism. There are times when God calls his servants to do extraordinary things, when a departure from the usual way of operating is entirely acceptable, and the discerning agent of the kingdom will be open to these moments. But fundamental theory and practice cannot be built on such premises. Second, and more important, what I have argued here is a normative case as to how we should construe evangelism in our present difficulties and crises. This cannot be overturned by marginal historical considerations. To some extent my proposal is a counsel of perfection that cannot always be attained; it is an ideal from which we may often fall; it is a vision that needs to be implemented with sensitivity; it is a revision of conception intended to inform and shape our evangelistic endeavors; but it should not be rejected just because we have failed at times to implement it.

I could summarize my proposal by means of several analogies. To what might we compare the ministry of evangelism? Wesley furnished one interesting image of evangelism when he suggested that we should conceive of the beginnings of the Christian life in terms of entry into a house. The house itself is holiness; it is coming to love God with all one's heart and coming to love one's neighbor as oneself. To get into the house, however, one must go through the porch of repentance and faith. In evangelism I am suggesting that we need to rebuild the porch and make it big enough to contain the basic dimensions of initiation outlined above.

And to what shall we compare the church's evangelists? They need to be shepherds who know where their sheep are and who can find them without driving them further from the fold. They need to be news announcers who get the message straight and who make it known clearly to the nations without resorting to the sensationalism of Madison Avenue advertising techniques. They need to be lawyers who can argue their client's case with integrity, good humor, and grit. They need to be midwives who can help nature and grace bring children of God to birth through the pain of repentance and the joy of faith. They need to be physicians of the soul who can link the lost and weary with the healing medicine of the kingdom. They need to be mothers who bring their little ones to be bathed in the waters of baptism, to be fed by word and creed at the breasts of mother church, to be nourished by the bread of life and wine of heaven, to be drenched in the gifts of the Spirit, and to be equipped with the oil of prayer and fasting.

Clearly, much here cries out for further analysis, defense, and comment. We have furnished enough, however, to respond to some objections that are bound to arise at the outset. It will be profitable to consider these here before I summarize the fundamental reasons for adopting this conception of evangelism as a guide to future action in this domain. Beyond that we can take up various aspects of my proposal at a more leisurely pace in the chapter that follows. At this juncture we will look at five objections.

Objections Considered

An obvious objection that comes to mind is that this way of approaching evangelism sacrifices quantity to quality in the evangelistic ministry of the church. One must maintain a delicate balance between these, and our proposal is far too concerned with the quality of the life produced in the course of evangelism. It is bound to put potential converts off by demanding too much, and it is in the interests of the masses to settle for a more modest start.

While we cannot but have sympathy with this response, it fails on several counts. There need not be any conflict between quantity and quality. This is a bogus contrast. The responsible evangelist will be concerned to win as many converts as possible, but to win them is not just to get them to sign up but to introduce them in a realistic and honest fashion to the reign of God. Moreover, the kingdom of God has its own internal requirements, which are not at our disposal to change at will. Nor is it our prerogative to put one thing in capital letters on the first page of the covenant, liberally filling it up with various blessings, and then to surprise the reader with the demanding details of the small print down the road. In any case, this reading of my suggestion treats the process of initiation as a kind of endurance race or obstacle course that has to be tolerated until better days for the initiate arrive. This view is wide of the mark, for the process is one of receiving and giving, of learning and renewal, and of expanding horizons and deepening commitments. There is no reason why it cannot be one of the most significant and transforming episodes in the life of an individual or group.

Another obvious objection that crops up immediately is that my account confuses evangelism with Christian education or nurture. Or, at the very least, it lets evangelism spill over into areas of the church's life and ministry where it does not really belong. The answer to this is a distinction. We need to distinguish clearly between establishing or grounding people in the kingdom of God and then sustaining and nurturing them in discipleship. Clearly, the Christian life is one of lifelong development and learning; there is always a need for deeper and expanding appropriation of the Christian tradition, for growth in grace, for the development of one's gifts and abilities, and so on. These cannot take place, however, without the kind of fundamental initiation that I am insisting is integral to evangelism. Our present situation is thoroughly unsatisfactory. On the one side, current forms of evangelism tend to offer a reduced version of the gospel and call for very little by way of serious commitment. On the other side, Christian educators tend to shy away from evangelism, trusting that the familial or social environment will supply all that is needed to get Christian nurture on the road to success.[8] The results are predictable: "born again" Christians remain anemic and only marginally, if at all, related to the church catholic; church members remain nominal and barely socialized into the privileges and responsibilities of the kingdom of God. What I am

8. A refreshing comment on the limitations of nurture alone can be found in John Westerhoff III, "A Necessary Paradox: Catechesis and Evangelism, Nurture and Conversion," *Religious Education* 73 (1978): 409-16.

proposing will ensure that there really are foundations from which other ministries of the church can proceed with some hope of success.

A third objection naturally follows. Surely my proposal overloads the young convert with far too much early on in his or her journey of faith. It is much wiser, it will be argued, to preach the gospel and invite people to turn to Christ in repentance and faith, and then give them lots of time and space to work through the implications of their commitment. To take the route I propose is to run the risk of imposing demands that are really only appropriate for those who are mature and who have made some progress in their spiritual journeys.

Paul Hiebert raises this issue in a particularly sharp and forceful way.[9] He asks: Can an illiterate peasant, tired and hungry after a long day's work, become a Christian after hearing the gospel only once? Drawing on modern studies in mathematics, his reply is that one's response to this depends on his or her conception of the set to which Christians belong. Some construe the category "Christian" as a bounded set and insist that certain minimal essentials provide a clear boundary between those who are on the inside and those who are on the outside. Moreover, within a bounded set there is no room for growth and change. If we share this conception of Christianity, then obviously the illiterate peasant cannot become a Christian on hearing the gospel once. Others, however, construe the category "Christian" in terms of a centered set, for which they name a center and then determine the members by finding out who are related in a specified way to that center. This allows for variation in relation to the center; it takes the focus away from the boundaries and relocates it in the relation between member and center; and it allows plenty of room for movement and growth. On this reading of Christianity the illiterate peasant clearly can become a Christian on hearing the gospel only once. Hiebert favors this option.[10] One can become a Christian, he says, so

9. Paul G. Hiebert, "The Category 'Christian' in the Mission Task," *International Review of Missions* 72 (1983): 421-27.
10. Hiebert discusses a third possibility, namely, that of fuzzy set, but this need not concern us here.

long as he or she makes Christ the Lord of his or her life; one can then move on to nurture and growth.

Applying Hiebert's analysis to my proposal, is it not the case, one will ask, that I am working from a wooden and static conception of Christianity that imposes too much on the young Christian and precludes the possibility of further growth and nurture? The answer to this has several parts. First, it is not at all clear that this analogy is as conveniently applicable to Christianity as Hiebert suggests. Certainly, it is illuminating, and Hiebert has exploited it to the full to clarify alternative approaches to evangelism. But it has severe limitations. On the one hand, those committed to even the most rigorous, bounded, set conception of Christianity would not for one moment deny that there is plenty of room for growth. All they are suggesting is that there are indeed minimal and essential commitments at stake in becoming a Christian. On the other side, making Christ Lord of one's life, which is Hiebert's criterion for being a Christian, is not just a change in relationship, although it is, of course, precisely that.[11] It is also the adoption of a particular theological vision and the appropriation of a specific moral orientation. Hiebert misses this because he fails to explore the assumptions built into the act of accepting Christ as Lord, and because he has a common antipathy to knowledge over against obedience as the essence of faith. The analogy with various sets is, therefore, of very limited value in addressing the problem of the illiterate peasant.

Furthermore, this objection fails to acknowledge that the initiation envisaged does need time. Ample space for catechesis and for preliminary participation in the life of faith has to be built into this conception of evangelism, within its logistical developments. We should prefer this to some vague process for which no one is accountable and to which the beginning Christian is accidentally introduced. Finally, this objection evades the fact that Christian existence does have a particular content and structure, and it is psychologically healthy to deal with this at the outset rather than postpone it for greener days. Charles Finney astutely recognized this fact.

11. Ibid., p. 424.

Ordinarily, the Christian character of converts throughout life is moulded and fashioned according to the manner in which they are dealt with when first converted. There are many who have been poorly taught at first, but then afterwards re-converted, and if they are then properly dealt with, they may be made something of. But the proper time to do this is when they are first brought in, when their minds are soft and tender, and easily yield to the truth. Then they may be led by a hair, if they think it is the truth of God.[12]

We can debate just what and how much one should deal with in the foundational phase, but that we need such a phase and that it must have some form and content is incontrovertible. Insisting on a rich process of initiation is one way to address this very difficult problem.

A fourth major objection is the suggestion that reference to initiation as crucial to evangelism takes us in a radically wrong direction by conjuring up images of instruction, of cognitive learning, and of a stuffy, schoolroom approach to the beginnings of the Christian life. We can concede that some will bring these kinds of notions to the idea of initiation; as an objection to the proposal here, however, they are irrelevant. As we saw earlier, initiation is determined by its goal. Entry into the kingdom of God is unique in form. Reducing it to some kind of intellectual process is the last thing I am envisaging. Insisting on the rich, many-sided character of initiation should prevent precisely the kind of atmosphere suggested here.

Finally, some will worry that my approach to evangelism makes evangelism far too complicated as a specific ministry within the church. As a result, they will say, it contributes to the inertia that bedevils so much of the church's evangelistic ministry. It would be more beneficial, therefore, to hone the concept and ministry of evangelism to more manageable proportions, so that there be a fair chance that it will be reinstated as a vital part of the church's overall mission. This is a telling criticism, in the wake of which one is tempted to carve up the process envisaged here

12. Charles G. Finney, *Revival Lectures* (Old Tappan, N.J.: Revell, n.d.), p. 448.

and hand it over to a plurality of ministries. In one sense it is not at all fatal to my proposals if this should happen. From a strictly practical point of view the matter can be seen as simply a question of the division of labor. If we can achieve the same end by dividing evangelism as I conceive it into two or even three logically distinct but integrally related ministries, well and good. This rose by any other name will smell as sweet.

Yet I prefer not to take this route, for the following reasons. There is, first, little guarantee that the kind of unity and coherence needed in the ministries that traditionally border evangelism can be secured without the architectonic horizon furnished by initiation into the kingdom of God. Thus traditional forms of evangelism as applied, say, to mass evangelism usually insist on the absolute necessity of follow-up work of one kind or another. It is one thing to insist on this, but it is another thing entirely to secure it. Our proposal resolves this dilemma by building follow-up into the very definition of evangelism. This is not just a verbal quibble. What we do in our actions is governed in a very fundamental way by our intentions in action, and this principle supports the alternative I am developing. More generally, it is worth pointing out that if evangelism as I conceive it here is more complicated than is normally envisaged, so be it. For too long churches have yearned for a microwave solution to problems in this area. Various schemes, campaigns, programs, and other paraphernalia have been cooked up to save the world, and we have grown weary from the false hopes they have fostered. The time is ripe to set these aside and regain the patience of God in establishing God's love on earth.

Final Comments

In taking the route outlined here we shall be retrieving crucial elements in a pattern of evangelism that worked very effectively in the early centuries of the church's life.[13] And we shall be re-

---

13. Especially notable studies that explore this matter historically are E. Glenn Hinson, *The Evangelization of the Roman Empire* (Macon, Ga.: Mercer University Press, 1981); Ramsay MacMullen, *The Christianising of the Roman Em-*

capturing the breadth of vision that was such an integral part of the ministry of the great evangelists of the past. One can at least hope, in this regard, that figures as far apart in space and time as Paul of Tarsus, St. Patrick, Cyril and Methodius, Francis Xavier, John Wesley, and Catherine Booth might approve in principle my suggestions. We shall have to await a seminar in heaven to resolve this question; in the interim other advantages are worth mentioning briefly.

My approach to evangelism captures most of the insights that have surfaced repeatedly in the debate about how to conceive evangelism. It is no accident that students of evangelism and evangelists have described evangelism in such a variety of ways, such as proclamation, converting people to Christianity, and the planting of local churches. Taken alone, most of these are inadequate and lead to serious problems when implemented. But in their own way they represent crucial facets of initiation into the kingdom of God and the actions needed to bring this about. Our proposal seeks to draw the scattered insights available into a unified, coherent whole, and thus to avoid the reductionism that is such a marked feature of the prevailing options.

Furthermore, by linking together ministries that are at present either nonexistent or fragmented and unrelated, it offers hope for the possibility of genuine renewal in the Christian church at large by calling Christians to first principles and by inviting them to develop ministries of evangelism that have substantial structure and content. One of the truly astonishing features of modern church life is the fact that so many church members need to be evangelized. This judgment is not offered in anger or frustration; it is a fact we record with regret. Renewal can come not by starting from scratch but by clearly understanding that Christian initiation has been partial and incomplete. Perhaps we might say that people in modern Western Christianity have been half-evangelized. They have been

pire (New Haven: Yale University Press, 1984); and Robin Lane Fox, *Pagans and Christians* (London: Viking, Penguin, 1986).

initiated into fragmented bits and pieces of the effects of the rule of God on earth. Crucial in evangelism, as I have presented it, is the need to complete the process, and this can best be done in contemporary circumstances by returning to fundamental principles, assessing what has already been done in evangelism, and then finishing the job.

Moreover, by taking Christian initiation seriously, my proposal puts the evangelization of each new generation on the same footing with those on the distant mission field without ignoring the peculiar position of those who are brought up in a Christian home or in Christian social environment. We need to acknowledge resolutely that God has no grandchildren. Each new generation must find its own way into the kingdom. To be sure, each new generation can adopt this or that civil religion, or it can settle for a nominal relation to its national faith that is satisfied with Christianity as a splendid system of rites adapted to cope with the vicissitudes of birth, marriage, and death. To confuse these with entry into the kingdom of God is ludicrous and self-serving. Yet elements of folk religion are not to be despised. They represent brittle aspects of Christian initiation that have been cut off from their natural home, and given the right handling they can be repaired and renewed in a process of evangelism that sees initiation as central to its goal and execution.

In addition, by insisting on boundaries to the ministry of evangelism my suggestion creates ample room to develop and safeguard accountability and responsibility. And by retaining the need for proclamation as a characteristic activity in evangelism it acknowledges that the gospel is indeed good news that by its very nature must be announced to the nations and the world. Above all, by insisting on the logical primacy of the kingdom of God it puts evangelism intellectually and spiritually in a context where it has a chance to be filled once more with the fresh winds of the Holy Spirit.

My primary concern in pressing my case is to evoke a radical change of vision and orientation. The great need in evangelism is not for some new program, nor for a fresh wave of activism, but for a renewal of theological vision and a reworking of our basic conceptuality.[14] Things cannot, of course, remain on this level. Our visions need to be translated with integrity into fitting forms of ministry that genuinely work in the world. But for most of those engaged in evangelism this is not the problem because the natural commitment to pragmatism more than generously takes care of this issue. To counter this and to draw into evangelism those presently opposed or indifferent to it, we need a recovery of apostolic teaching and spirit. Seeing evangelism as intimately related to the coming reign of God can help us in that recovery. I do not claim that this is the only way to proceed. Nor would I insist that *initiation* is the only term we might use to bridge the gap that currently exists between evangelism and the kingdom of God. It is enough to make this modest claim: our proposal is certainly one way to do this, and it will do until something better comes along.

Charles Wesley nicely expresses the heart of the vision and horizon I am seeking to capture and apply to evangelism:

> All glory to God in the sky,
>   And peace on earth be restored!
> O Jesus, exalted on high,
>   Appear our omnipotent Lord!
> Who meanly in Bethlehem born,
>   Didst stoop to redeem a lost race,
> Once more to thy creatures return,
>   And reign in thy kingdom of grace.
>
> When thou in our flesh did appear,
>   All nature acknowledged your birth;
> Arose the acceptable year,
>   And heaven was opened on earth;
> Receiving its Lord from above,
>   The world was united to bless
> The giver of concord and love,
>   The prince and the author of peace.

---

14. We are in one sense, of course, saying nothing new, for my suggestions seek to implement the full force of the Great Commission.

O wouldst thou again be made known!
   Again in thy Spirit descend,
And set up in each of thine own
   A kingdom that never shall end.
Thou only art able to bless,
   And make the glad nations obey,
And bid the dire enmity cease,
   And bow the whole world to thy sway.

Come then to thy servants again,
   Who long thy appearing to know;
Thy quiet and peaceable reign
   In mercy establish below;
All sorrow before thee shall fly,
   And anger and hatred be o'er,
And envy and malice shall die,
   And discord afflict us no more.

S I X

Conversion, Baptism, and Morality

In 1849 Thomas Carlyle made a visit to Ireland. While there he recorded his impressions of a worship service in a Protestant church. Carlyle was not very happy with what he saw. There were about forty in the congregation, and although the young, red-headed Irish parson who led the worship evidently "performed" the service very decently, something was missing. Carlyle makes this caustic and stinging comment on the whole affair:

> I felt how decent English Protestants, or the sons of such, might with zealous affection like to assemble here once a week, and remind themselves of English purities and decencies and Gospel ordinances, in the midst of a black howling Babel of superstitious savagery—like Hebrews sitting by the streams of Babel: But I feel more clearly than ever how *impossible* it was that an extraneous son of Adam, first seized by the terrible conviction that he had a soul to be saved or damned, that he must rede the riddle of this universe or go to perdition everlastingly, could for a moment think of taking this respectable "performance" as the solution of the mystery for him! Oh, heaven! never in this world! Weep ye by the stream Babel, decent clean English-Irish; weep, for there is cause, till you can do something *better* than weep; but expect no Babylonian or any other mortal to concern himself with that affair of yours![1]

1. Thomas Carlyle, *Reminiscences of my Irish Journey in 1849* (New York: Harper and Brothers, 1882), p. 141.

117

Carlyle captures here what many in the history of modern evangelism have taken for granted. Pietists, Methodists, and Revivalists over the years have given the distinct impression that the heart of evangelism has nothing to do with the rites and ceremonies of the classical liturgies of the church. For them evangelism is centered on new birth and conversion; the individual stands alone before God in need of personal regeneration, which no church can supply; only God through the action of the Holy Spirit can meet this need. The church, rather than helping in this arena, has been at best indifferent and at worst thoroughly hostile. This is the impression one receives from reviewing the history of modern evangelism within the Protestant tradition. What in earlier generations was a mere impression has now become a matter of fixed and absolute principle with the arrival of the television evangelist. The contrast is clear. On the one side is the church with its dead formalism, boring liturgy, and moralistic sermons, which are unlikely to convert anyone. On the other side is the individual soul, stricken in conscience over sin and desperately hoping to find relief in the gospel when called to repentance and faith. The two are set against each other in a relation of mutual hostility.

In this chapter I want to argue that this contrast is artificial and unacceptable. That is, if we are to take initiation into the kingdom of God seriously, then we need in our evangelism to find room for conversion, baptism, and a commitment to love God and neighbor as elements of initiation. In the next chapter, I shall argue that we also need to find room for receiving the Christian creed, for owning the gifts of the Holy Spirit, and for embracing the disciplines of eucharist, prayer, and fasting.

In moving in this direction, I hope to advance the fundamental thesis articulated in the previous chapter, that evangelism should be tied conceptually to Christian initiation. I suggested that evangelism is usefully construed as that set of acts or activities which is governed by the intention to initiate people into the kingdom of God. My aim overall was to argue for this intimate connection between evangelism and initiation and to defend it against certain objections that *prima facie* stand in the way of its adoption. In the nature of the case, the details of the kind of initiation I had in mind had to remain sketchy. Clearly, we now need to expand our proposal so that it can be seen in all its fullness.

We should not underestimate the difficulties that face us. Some will agree formally that evangelism should be related to initiation along the lines I have specified, though they may disagree with the material proposals about initiation that I have already outlined. More particularly, they may want to challenge any of the six aspects of initiation that I have identified. It is important, therefore, that I deal with these concerns directly, and spell out in general terms what initiation involves. In doing so, I hope indirectly to build a stronger case than laid out heretofore for saying that evangelism should be intimately connected to initiation into the kingdom of God.

As we proceed, we must remember that the initiation I have in mind is much more than the execution of certain rites and ceremonies. It refers to those fundamental experiences and processes that take one into the rule of God on earth. Hence it would be a serious misreading of my conception of evangelism to collapse it into the administration of those rites of passage that take one into the church.[2] This has important implications for our account of those actions that are characteristic of evangelism as I see it. In particular I am concerned to keep a crucial place in the economy of evangelism for the proclamation of the gospel.

At this point let us return to Carlyle. He is surely correct to insist that something is missing from the life of the church if it fails to relate the good news of the gospel to those who are desperate to find a gracious God. It is very easy for the church to collapse into an appendage of culture, carried abroad with the rest of the luggage to perform its allotted role as a medium of moral teaching, as an expression of one's national identity, as a meager aesthetic adornment in a barren world, and as a badge of superiority. This has happened repeatedly in the history of

2. This appears to have happened in Robert Webber's attempt to appropriate the forms of initiation developed in the early centuries of the church. See his *Celebrating Our Faith: Evangelism through Worship* (San Francisco: Harper and Row, 1986).

the church. Luther and Wesley amply illustrate the struggles that ensue in such circumstances in their search for an encounter with the living God. When they find what they are seeking, the result is often profound personal and theological upheaval. Both the Reformation and the eighteenth-century evangelical Awakening seek, in their own way, to crystallize the effects of a personal experience of God in their theological emphases and developments. The impact on modern forms of evangelism has been astonishingly pervasive. It finds its most powerful expression in the concern for conversion and new birth.

Conversion

This raises the question of how far evangelism should concern itself with this whole network of experiences and themes. Is conversion an essential part of initiation into the kingdom of God, or is it a passing phase of Western Christianity, a relic of the introspective conscience of the West bequeathed to us by Augustine, a theme that has outlived its usefulness for coherent thinking about evangelism? To answer this we need a richer vision of what is at stake and a clear account of the relation between conversion and the kingdom of God.

There is nothing uniquely Christian about the language of conversion and new birth. The former notion hardly crops up at all in its modern sense in the early church, and the imagery of new birth is very marginal in the New Testament.[3] As developed, say, by Wesley, the idea of a new birth is intimately related to other notions like justification by faith, the witness of the Holy Spirit, and initial sanctification. In broad terms it is very clear that Wesley and others use the language and imagery of the biblical literature as they seek to describe what happens to people when they are confronted with the gospel of Jesus Christ in a personal and existential manner.[4] Through the action of the

3. A useful discussion can be found in Julius Schniewind, "The Biblical Doctrine of Conversion," *Scottish Journal of Theology* 5 (1952): 267-81.
4. He brings this out well in his sermon on the new birth. See Albert Outler, ed., *The Works of John Wesley*, vol. 2, *Sermons II* (Nashville: Abingdon, 1984), pp. 186-201.

Holy Spirit, one is made acutely aware of one's sins, made conscious of the compassion of a holy God, and resolutely faced with the decision to choose either light or darkness, either life or death. To respond in a positive manner is not just one more decision in life, like deciding whether to have jam rather than marmalade on one's toast in the morning. It is to find oneself swept into a new relationship with God where one is acquitted of one's past and enters into a direct and unmediated kind of assurance. In such circumstances the language of new birth is entirely natural and appropriate, for it captures a crucial dimension of what the innocent convert undergoes.

It is extremely difficult to dislodge this kind of discourse from any adequate description of initiation into the reign of God. Nor should we try to do so. It has firm roots in the biblical material, and it has a way of surfacing repeatedly whenever it gets buried beneath the trappings of nominal Christianity and ecclesiastical finery. Furthermore, this language is still present in the classical baptismal liturgies of the church. It did not get there by accident; it stands as lasting testimony to a crucial dimension of Christian initiation. Moreover, it is fueled by the testimonies of hosts of converts who are spread across space and time and who come from all sorts of social and intellectual backgrounds.[5] The danger is that these testimonies represent engaging reading that sometimes threatens to displace the kind of solid reflection without which Christianity is reduced to an esoteric or mystical cult. At its best, this discourse captures in a very provocative way the shattering impact of the gospel on people. Entry into the kingdom of God is not a casual affair. It involves a radical confrontation with God, and it seems impossible that it could happen without a profound self-examination and a penetrating self-knowledge. Given who God is and what human beings are, it is conceptually odd in the extreme to say that one had been confronted with the rule of God but that life could go on as usual. The language of new birth, regeneration, acquittal, conversion, and the like is precisely what

---

5. For a recent anthology, see Hugh T. Kerr and John Mulder, eds., *Conversions: The Christian Experience* (Grand Rapids: Eerdmans, 1983).

we should expect, and it is exactly what we find in the history of religious experience.

Yet such language is now the badge of a party within Christianity; it is under a cloud of suspicion; and it is divorced from the sacramental life of the church.[6] We can easily understand why this has happened. Moreover, it is imperative that we deal with what has happened over the years if we are to have any hope of rehabilitating this important dimension of initiation.

First, the language of conversion and new birth has become buried in a theological underworld that has strained it to the limits. Fruitless debates about the mechanics and logistics of divine grace in the soul have elbowed out the native sense that the language of new birth once transmitted. In addition, attempts to articulate the morphology of conversion have turned much of the theology of evangelism, which this language fosters, into an introspective anthropocentrism that neglects the richer tapestry of Christian theology and encourages the development of a narrow and inadequate piety. This in turn engenders a fierce reaction that seizes on the social and liberating aspects of the kingdom of God and castigates any interest in personal conversion as otherworldly and corrupt. All this is heightened when the advocates of conversion insist on some favored pattern of experience that everyone must undergo if he or she is to be counted among the elect. It is not at all surprising that thoughtful Christians should dismiss the language of conversion, new birth, justification, and the like as the hullabaloo and relic of a bygone age.

Second, the language of new birth has been gradually cut loose from its natural setting in the neighborhood of the coming of the new age of God.[7] It thus has lost its connections with

---

6. Schniewind captures the personal aversion to the notion nicely:

We know from personal experience as well as from the experience of others the feeling of apprehension when someone tries to "convert" us. We may want to avoid a certain house or a particular group of people because we feel: "They want to convert me." Perhaps that feeling is caused by misunderstanding, for turning to God is joy—that is a fact that is often overlooked when we speak of conversion. ("Biblical Doctrine," p. 267)

7. John 3 amply testifies to the connection between new birth and entry into the kingdom of God.

the convert's need to see himself or herself as an agent of the kingdom of God, called by a new birth to participate in the new creation and inspired by the Holy Spirit. It has been cemented into patterns of morality that often neglect the weightier matters of the law and that focus on the peccadillos of individual, personal behavior. In some hands it has been very skillfully used to undergird the foundations of the free-market economy, the fortunes of this or that nation, and the election of conservative politicians. Born-again politics is the ultimate secularization and prostitution of this fragment of the language of Zion and a perfect example of the degeneration of the concept.

Third, the notion of new birth has been separated from baptism and, therefore, finds itself uprooted from that social and ecclesial context, making it an orphan, hopelessly starved of moral and theological content. The story behind this has been repeated often, so we need not do so here. Suffice it to say that the shift from adult baptism to infant baptism ultimately led to a split between new birth and baptism. With adult baptism people could identify relatively naturally with the language of new birth; with infant baptism the language is strained and awkward. To remedy this all sorts of expedients have been attempted, from baptismal regeneration *ex opere operato,* to a covenant theology of grace, to a doctrine of prevenient grace, to pious accounts of the mystery of God's action in the sacraments of the church, and to the invention of a whole new sacrament or quasi-sacrament of confirmation. All these and more have been tried. It would be pretentious to claim that they have all been found equally wanting, but one thing is clear: the comprehensive, unitary conception of initiation that once existed has been lost. This disintegration was aided by the development of a doctrine of original sin and guilt, by the failure on the part of the church after Constantine to deal in depth with initiation, by the careless practice of indiscriminate baptism in modern times, and by absolutist and exclusivist claims about the work of the Holy Spirit.[8] It

8. I have in mind here the tendency on the part of those who stress conversion to ignore the richness of the work of the Holy Spirit outside the experience of conversion.

was further accelerated when pietistic forms of Christianity were hounded from pillar to post, and the whole panoply of church, university, and state were skillfully combined to crush any renewalist movements that made much of conversion and new birth.

I have nothing new to add to the debates concerning the relation between baptism, confirmation, the work of the Holy Spirit, and the like. In their present form, these debates will continue interminably. What we need is a fresh perspective on the whole matter of initiation, one that finds room for an encounter with God, that brings forgiveness of sins and new life, and that also leads to a thorough grounding in the life of the church as represented by baptism.

What the language of conversion and new birth is reaching for is indispensable. If we bury it in the empty formulae of ecclesiastical ceremony, it will creep in through a back door at the first opportunity. Consider Symeon the "New Theologian," one of the jewels in the Eastern Orthodox tradition.[9] Orthodox to the core in his understanding of infant baptism, and despite great opposition, he insisted that every Christian could experience a baptism of the Holy Spirit subsequent to baptism, which was a conscious experience of the Holy Spirit and which brought inexpressible joy and assurance. The whole tenor of Symeon's claims place him clearly within the orbit of the language of conversion and new birth that is the hallmark of classical Methodist theology and of virtually all forms of pietism. Or consider the popular way in which Catholic Christianity copes with the lack of personal experience in infant baptism. Baptism, it is said, involves the planting of the seed of eternal life, which is then nurtured by the Holy Spirit in the life of the church.[10] This is a natural way of preserving the vestiges of the

9. I am indebted to Archbishop Basil Krivocheine, *In the Light of Christ, Saint Symeon the New Theologian (949-1022): Life—Spirituality—Doctrine* (Crestwood, N.Y.: St. Vladimir's Seminary Press, 1986), for basic information on St. Symeon. See esp. chap. 9.

10. I recall this imagery from a written sermon of Austin Farrer, but the source is now forgotten. Bushnell deftly exploits this analogy in his defense of infant baptism. See Horace Bushnell, *Christian Nurture* (New Haven: Yale University Press, 1888), p. 30.

language of conversion when such discourse cannot be applied naturally. Both these cases are a sign that we cannot dispense with the language of conversion and new birth without shedding theological tears. It stands for a crucial, personal, and experiential dimension of entry into the dynamic rule of God. Those who have preserved it have kept alive a vital part of the church's treasure, without which evangelism will be deformed and defaced. Nor is it an accident that whole denominations and evangelistic movements have been initiated and sustained by such discourse and the reality it attempts to describe.

Yet we cannot reinstate such discourse without a fundamental redirecting of its content. José Míguez Bonino is on the right track, therefore, when he suggests that we must attempt a rereading of the concept of conversion.[11] He points out that in Wesley's day conversion was intimately related to particular theological and metaphysical claims that are unsatisfactory today. Thus it was tied to a specific way of conceiving the relation between "being" and "acting" in both God and human beings. For Wesley, "being" comes first, then manifests itself in "acting." In this context, conversion (or regeneration) is seen as taking place in a spiritual or metaphysical realm, which is then reflected in a second movement in history. But this destroys the unity of "being" and "acting" in both humans and God. Those who hold this view tend to see the evangelized person as an individual and self-contained reality, naked and alone before God. Society is then a convenient arrangement brought in to safeguard the growth of the individual as a means to an end. According to Míguez Bonino, this is fiction. Our self-consciousness and our conscience are the focus of a complex process that is embodied in concrete historical relations. Conversion, therefore, does not take place in a vacuum. It is a response to a mediated challenge that already presupposes a certain self-understanding and praxis.[12]

11. José Míguez Bonino, "Conversion, New Creature and Commitment," *International Review of Missions* 72 (1983): 324-32.

12. I leave it to Wesley scholars to sort out whether this is an accurate rendering of Wesley's position.

To take account of this [Wesley] proposes the following understanding of conversion. From a *phenomenological* (phenomenical) point of view I would define conversion as the encounter between a condensation of the Christian message taking the form of a call (an appeal) and a personal, conscious and committed response. Conversion is thus characterised by a consciousness—as the Methodist tradition asserted—both in relation to the contents of the message (*assensus* in traditional terms) and in relation to a new self-understanding, which includes new relations and a new commitment (*fiducia*). Ontologically (if I may use such a term) conversion is the process through which God incorporates the human person, as person, into an active conscious participation in his covenant with humankind, the covenant, which he has attested, renewed and ensured in Jesus Christ.[13]

This requires the call to commitment to relate very specifically to the objective and concrete conditions of those being evangelized. Just as the various authors of the New Testament expressed the call to faith in very different and even contradictory ways (e.g., in their Christologies), so the modern evangelist should trust the Holy Spirit to lead him or her to achieve the same end in the modern world. In so doing, Jesus Christ becomes the Mediator of a truly human life that is both personal and social, and the goal of evangelism becomes not just the formal acceptance of a message or a doctrine but the creation of a new creature.

Early Methodists recognized the significance of this for evangelism by a set of General Rules that spelled out the demands of following Christ in their circumstances.

In contrast our evangelistic appeal is often empty. It has no recognisable face. People fill it, therefore, perhaps unconsciously, with the dominant stereotypes of what it means to be "religious"—the accepted, standard, ideologically loaded images of what "piety" means. Unless the

13. Míguez Bonino, "Conversion," p. 330. The emphasis is as in the original.

evangelizing community confronts people with the challenge of a specific testimony related to the conditions of the time, evangelism can only be an instrument of the continuation and sacralization of the dehumanizing conditions in which people live today. To put it very simply, evangelism must deal with the question: what does it mean, concretely and specifically, in thought and in action, today, to follow Christ?[14]

Míguez Bonino is correct to press for a fresh analysis of conversion that will be purged of inadequate theological and philosophical assumptions. It is crucial, however, that the revisions be as felicitous as we can make them. Two minor points and one major one are worth pursuing here.

First, appealing to the apparent diversity in the New Testament writings on the question of their Christology may not be the best way to underscore the need to couch the call to conversion in concrete, specific terms. This way to read the canonical witness to Christ is contested, and it may not be the best way. I suspect, moreover, that it reflects a classical Protestant account of the canon that is no longer tenable and ultimately undercuts the kind of Christology that is most in keeping with the rule of God in Jesus Christ.[15] It is enough to point out that we need the kind of sensitive and searching analysis of the social situation manifested by Míguez Bonino and that, rather than base this on his account of the New Testament writings, we can trust the Holy Spirit to lead the evangelist to be as alarmingly specific as the prophets, John the Baptist, Martin Luther King, Jr., and the like. This is far from easy to realize in practice, of course, for the history of evangelism is full of evangelists who are only too keen to impose their particular moral agenda on their converts. We shall return to this later.

The second observation is that it is very easy to transform this reconstruction into a particular philosophical and political program whose assumptions and proposals are as all-consum-

---

14. Ibid., pp. 331-32.
15. We shall meet this issue again in the next chapter when we deal with the explicitly cognitive dimension of initiation.

ing and questionable as those they seek to replace. Míguez Bonino does not fall into this trap. Hastier hands can easily fall into it, however, by collapsing the call to conversion into a call to side with certain politically engaged groups who claim a monopoly on moral and philosophical truth.[16] I will not be able to resolve this very delicate issue here, but my concern is simply to draw attention to it. What we need is both a fixed commitment to take on board in our evangelism the concrete demands of the kingdom, as we live in the fabric of history, and also a deeply critical discernment as to what that requires in practice, especially in situations of moral outrage and political oppression. Neither of these is achieved by escaping into a world of inner piety, nor by adopting as our social and political guide the debris of the political wing of the European Enlightenment. Perhaps this is one of the deepest tests of faith in the work of the Holy Spirit that the evangelist and the church encounter.

The third issue Míguez Bonino raises has extremely important implications for evangelism, but it is one that has been insufficiently attended to in the ongoing debate. He correctly insists that human beings are best seen as inescapably social agents who are inextricably shaped and formed by the web of their relationships. While we need not at this stage adopt some doctrine of determinism to acknowledge this point, we should at least recognize the social character of human existence. What does this mean for evangelism? Does it just alter the content of the call to conversion, extending it to include repentance from social as well as personal sin? Is that all that it means? I suggest that it means much more than this. It means that the evangelist must give far more attention to baptism as a means of concrete initiation into the flesh and blood of Christian community than is currently the case. In other words, it highlights the unity of conversion and baptism in ways unheralded in the literature on the subject.

If, in fact, we are shaped and formed by the communities to which we belong, then it is utterly unrealistic to think that

16. Park Hyung Kyu runs this risk in "Conversion as a Pilgrimage to Liberation," *International Review of Missions* 72 (1983): 380-84.

we will be created anew without the support and backing of a community that provides deep sustenance and spiritual nourishment. It is inadequate to think that the new convert can undergo the kind of change envisaged in the coming of the rule of God in isolation, situated alone, so to speak, in a religious cell that is only marginally and accidentally related to the church. The situation becomes even more acute when we build into the foundations of commitment the kind of radical and specific demands envisaged by Míguez Bonino. An obvious principle applies: the higher the initial demands, the greater the need for communal support. It is ludicrous to ask people to commit themselves to a life of costly discipleship, one where their very lives may be in danger, and then leave them high and dry to sustain this on their own.

This explains a salient feature of the history of the evangelist, namely, the pivotal role played by small groups in the assimilation of Christians into the central privileges and responsibilities of the faith. The *collegia pietatis* or *ecclesiola in ecclesia* were vital to the spread of pietism. Wesley's evangelism required and depended upon the development of class meetings and a plethora of other groups.[17] House groups play a significant role both in early Christianity and in modern Pentecostalism.[18] *Comunidades eclesiales de base* are very significant in the re-evangelization of parts of the Roman Catholic Church in Latin America.[19] These groups do not happen out of the blue. They bear witness to the social character of human existence, and they come to our attention because they minister to a vital aspect of persons in transition into the Christian faith. Evangelists and pastors start them and sustain them because they are indispensable to the fostering of deep commitment.

To leave the issue on this level, however, would be in-

17. An important analysis of these groups can be found in David Lowes Watson, *The Early Methodist Class Meeting, its Origins and Significance* (Nashville: Discipleship Resources, 1985).

18. For an example of the use of small groups in Pentecostalism, see Paul Yonggi Cho, *Successful Home Cell Groups* (South Plainfield, N.J.: Bridge, 1981).

19. See Leonardo Boff, *Ecclesiogenesis: The Base Communities Reinvent the Church* (Maryknoll, N.Y.: Orbis, 1986).

adequate and misleading. It tends to construe the matter in crassly utilitarian terms. We need also to see the issue from the point of view of the internal logic of Christian initiation. Becoming a part of the Christian community is not just a utilitarian affair; it constitutes part of initiation. God in his reign has established his eschatological community. It is, therefore, incoherent to say that one can enter that reign but remain outside the church. Baptism is inescapable and essential, once one grasps this point, for it is through baptism that one enters the Israel of God, that body where God rules supreme in worship and praise. To reject this, for whatever reason, is to be selective and self-serving in one's approach to initiation. It is to adopt an attitude of arrogance, willfully separating those things one likes from those things one does not like in the coming of the rule of God. Such an approach bespeaks a failure to comprehend what the kingdom actually is, and it betrays a desire to dictate to God how to run the affairs of his realm.

Baptism

Another way to approach this question is to think of it in terms of the importance of the means of grace in the Christian life. Christian existence is initiated and sustained by grace. We are saved by the action of God; we depend upon grace from the beginning to the end of our spiritual pilgrimage. Grace does not, however, operate in a vacuum. God is free to work as and how he pleases, yet he has covenanted to work generally and regularly through certain means. God works in and through his word, through baptism, through the eucharist, through fellowship, through Scripture, through prayer, and so on. To omit these from initiation is to treat grace as a will-o'-the-wisp unrelated to the concrete, physical character of our existence. The converse of this is obvious: initiation is intrinsically related to physical incorporation into the church through baptism. Initiation without baptism is hopelessly incomplete; to proceed in initiation without baptism is to deprive those evangelized of a vital means of grace.

It is surely no accident, then, that where baptism is ignored in evangelism, as has been the case in most Protestant evangelistic practice over the last three centuries, substitutes have been invented or borrowed to take its place. The obvious example is the development of the public appeal or the altar call, which in some circles is now an indispensable feature. Its adherents marshall arguments to support it that are as passionate as those that might be deployed in defense of a sacrament of the church.[20] Historically, the modern appeal or altar call is a development of the anxious seat, a "new measure," as it was called, that Charles Finney used in his revival meetings in the last century. Not surprisingly, his perceptive eye noticed the clear connection between the anxious seat and baptism. He saw the anxious seat as a means of breaking down pride on the part of the evangelist and an expression of serious commitment on the part of the respondent.

> The Church has always felt it necessary to have something of the kind to answer this very purpose. In the days of the apostles baptism answered this purpose. The gospel was preached to the people, and then all those who were willing to be on the side of Christ were called on to be baptised. *It held the precise place that the anxious seat does now, as a public manifestation of a determination to be a Christian.*[21]

Finney displays here a weak and pragmatic conception of baptism, but his point is extremely significant. Without realizing what is happening, evangelists who neglect baptism have been forced—on psychological and other grounds—to provide an alternative to replace it. In the process these evangelists have lost the richness of grace provided by the sacraments of the church.

We can express this latter point by recognizing the eschatological character of liturgy when it is animated by the pres-

20. See Ian Murray, *The Invitation System* (Edinburgh: The Banner of Truth Trust, 1967); R. Alan Streett, *The Effective Invitation* (Old Tappan, N.J.: Revell, 1984); R. T. Kendall, *Stand Up and Be Counted* (Grand Rapids: Zondervan, 1984); Erroll Hulse, *The Great Invitation: Examining the Use of the Invitation System in Evangelism* (Welwyn, Hertfordshire: Evangelical Press, 1986).

21. Charles G. Finney, *Revivals of Religion* (Old Tappan, N.J.: Revell, n.d.), p. 305. Emphasis mine.

ence of the Holy Spirit. When Christians assemble for worship, or when they gather together for a baptism, it is not just a humanistic exercise or ritual. There is present a mysterious reality that cannot be confined to a mere recital of words, or to the performance of some sign that expresses the faith of those who participate. The invocation of the Holy Spirit involves an epiclectic contemporization of the events inaugurated in the life, death, and resurrection of Jesus of Nazareth. We might say that there is a continuous parousia as the real presence of Christ is made known in the liturgy.[22] To use Paul's language, the kingdom of God is not in word but in power (1 Cor. 4:20), and that power is made present by grace in the liturgical activity of the church. In baptism one is brought into a living encounter with that mysterious, dynamic reality. If we overlook this, we neglect a crucial means of grace and correspondingly impoverish our entry into the kingdom of God.[23]

It is very important that my overall argument here not be misunderstood. My point is that baptism cannot be neglected in initiation, and three main considerations establish this. First, the coming of the rule of God entails the establishing of an Israel of God. The kingdom is embodied in a community that has a determinate and specific character. Since one enters that community by baptism, it cannot be set aside or replaced by

---

22. It should be noted that I am not restricting liturgy merely to the set, formal, written liturgies of the established churches. Liturgy may also be informal and oral, transmitted by custom and word of mouth.

23. The matter is nicely captured in one of Charles Wesley's baptismal hymns:

> Come, Father, Son, and Holy Ghost,
> Honour the means ordain'd by thee;
> Make good our apostolic boast,
> And own thy glorious ministry.

> We now thy promised blessing claim;
> Sent to disciple all mankind,—
> Sent to baptise into thy name,—
> We now thy promised presence find.

> Father, in these reveal thy Son;
> In these, for whom we seek thy face,
> The hidden mystery make known,
> The inward, pure, baptising grace.

substitutes. Therefore, separating conversion from baptism, a practice that is such a marked feature of modern evangelism, is a theological scandal. Second, human existence generally, and Christian existence in particular, is inescapably social in character. We depend crucially on the traditions, the rites, the ethos, the visions, and the conceptuality of a community to shape and sustain our moral and spiritual commitments. It is vital, therefore, that we be initiated into the Christian church if we are to understand and face the full challenge of the kingdom of God on earth. Third, if baptism is a means of grace, then to ignore it in evangelism is to deprive both the convert and the church of an important source of spiritual renewal. It is imperative, then, that the church find a way to reunite conversion and baptism in a coherent, unified process of initiation.[24]

I am not claiming, however, that this displaces in the slightest one's need for a personal, face-to-face encounter with God, naked and alone in his presence. To go that far is unwarranted; it exaggerates the social character of our existence; it confines God's action to the external rites of the church; and it ignores extremely significant empirical evidence that bears noting.

Alexander Veronis has highlighted this evidence by identifying a form of evangelism that he refers to as "passive mission."[25] It involves a heroic commitment to a life of prayer without ceasing and a readiness to let one's light shine before others. It is well illustrated in the lives of those who remain in one place and attempt through prayer and a holy life-style to achieve an advanced state of discipleship and spirituality. "The holy, Spirit-filled life which results not only attracts the attention of many, but brings observers into an acceptance of the Christian Gospel which they credit for producing such holy people."[26] Three men whose lives illustrate this approach to mission are

24. I cannot here pursue the relevance of this for the debate about the timing of baptism for those brought up within a Christian family and community. We can only hope to deal with this, in my judgment, when we put in place an adequate vision of initiation into the rule of God.

25. Alexander Veronis, "Orthodox Concepts of Evangelism and Mission," *The Greek Orthodox Theological Review* 27 (1982): 44-57.

26. Ibid., p. 54.

Anthony the Great, Seraphim of Sarov, and Herman of Alaska. Seraphim, for example, spent years in solitude, including one stretch of silence that lasted thirteen years (1807–1820). In 1825, at the age of sixty-six, he became a starets, or spiritual guide, and streams of people, sometimes thousands in one day, came to see him for spiritual counsel, healings, prophecy, and matters related to the gospel.[27] He summed up his approach in this fashion: "Acquire inward peace, and thousands around you will find their salvation."[28] Of course, these examples do not overturn the fact that our existence is inescapably social, for they stand in a tradition that has always championed the communal character of Christian existence; but they prevent us from overlooking a personal, face-to-face dimension of spirituality, one that can easily be lost when Christians rightly insist on the social demands of the rule of God in politics and history.

The Rule of Life

Another dimension that we must not allow to be lost in thinking through the demands of initiation is the simple and broad command to love God with all one's heart and to love one's neighbor as oneself. This constitutes the third feature of initiation that I want to discuss. My proposal, at this point, is that the commandment to love God and neighbor is the heart of the moral tradition that the new Christian is invited to appropriate and own.

The issue is succinctly joined in an incident in the Gospel of Mark. After a series of controversies with various opponents, a scribe asks Jesus what is the chief of all the commandments. The reply is well known:

> The chief one is: Hear, O Israel, the Lord our God is one Lord, and you must love the Lord your God with your whole heart, with your whole soul, with your whole mind, and with your whole strength. The second is this: You

27. A useful account of Seraphim's life can be found in Valentine Zander, *St. Seraphim of Sarov* (Crestwood, N.Y.: St. Vladimir's Seminary Press, 1975).
28. Quoted in Veronis, "Orthodox Concepts," p. 54.

must love your neighbour as yourself. There is no other command greater than these. (Mark 12:29-31; Moffatt)

After this Jesus commended the scribe for his insightful response to this reply and pronounced that he was not far from the kingdom of God.

The connection between the great commandment and nearness to the kingdom of God is not accidental. Elsewhere in the New Testament the connection between commitment to moral virtue and entry into the kingdom is quite explicit.[29] The eschatological rule of God is a realm of righteousness and love that has a characteristic moral structure. It is in part constituted by that moral structure, the essence of which is to love God with all one's heart and to love one's neighbor as oneself. Just as the identity of a modern American is in part defined by the commitment to life, liberty, and the pursuit of happiness, so the identity of those who have entered into the Israel of God is defined by a commitment to pursue love for God and the neighbor. To enter into the kingdom is to own this moral tradition and to commit oneself to it irrevocably.

This in no way signifies that one deserves to enter into the kingdom because one owns this moral tradition. Entry into the kingdom is a joyous privilege—not a badge of religious merit. Nor does this imply that the ability to love God and the neighbor is somehow self-induced and self-sustained, as if those entering the kingdom were supposed to pull themselves up by their own bootstraps. On the contrary, one turns toward the kingdom and enters into it because one has been intellectually and spiritually won over by its intrinsic beauty and treasure. And once inside it, the ability to live out its precepts, however inadequately, is inspired by the Holy Spirit. What is at issue

---

29. See esp. 2 Pet. 1:11. It is fascinating that John Wesley in a sermon explicitly devoted to entry into the kingdom very quickly links this process to the actual development of love for God and neighbor in the life of the believer. See his "The Way into the Kingdom," in Albert C. Outler, ed., *The Works of John Wesley*, vol. 1, *Sermons I* (Nashville: Abingdon, 1984), pp. 217-32. This whole sermon bears careful scrutiny on the way in which Wesley skillfully interweaves several crucial dimensions of Christian initiation.

here is none of these platitudes of the doctrine of the Christian life but the logically prior point that one cannot enter into the kingdom and repudiate its moral content.

It is illuminating that the Markan pericope that highlights the connection between the commandment to love and entry into the kingdom contrasts the moral content of the kingdom and the purely external adherence to various religious ceremonies. In Mark 12:33, love is set above sacrifices and burnt offerings. Many in the history of evangelism, as we mentioned at the beginning of this chapter, have often made much of this apparent belittling of religious ceremonies. Two standard contrasts are invoked: that mentioned here between moral conduct and external religious behavior, and a more evangelical contrast between personal encounter with God and the passive exercise of religious ritual. It is futile to play these alternatives off against one another. Initiation into the kingdom involves an encounter with God, as described in the language of conversion and new birth, an external religious ceremony, as represented in the sacrament of baptism, and a commitment to a moral tradition, as summed up in the great commandment to love God and neighbor. The crucial distinction to be made is between relying on ceremonies and sacraments as if they were autonomous or even mechanical operations, on the one hand, and using them as the means of grace that God has appointed to mediate his presence and power, on the other. In the latter case there is no necessary tension between undergoing baptism and accepting the substance of the Christian moral heritage for oneself. As many have pointed out, baptism richly symbolizes death to an old life of self-love and rising again with Christ to a new life where one is now under the law of love.[30] The latter must be handed over by the church and the evangelist, and it must be reciprocally received by those baptized as the bedrock of their moral life.

We noted earlier that Míguez Bonino wanted more than this. He drew attention to Wesley's practice of insisting that those who joined the Methodist societies had to assent to the

---

30. This theme is richly explored by Paul in Romans 6 and 7.

General Rules before they could be admitted as regular members. Those General Rules spell out in some detail just what is and is not required of the Christian disciple. Míguez Bonino is not, of course, suggesting that these be wheeled out and used, as they stand, in the modern church. We need, he avers, to find our own, Spirit-inspired, functional equivalents for our modern situation. Actually, when we look at Wesley's practice, he is not that wide of the mark, for the General Rules summarize the marrow of the Christian moral heritage. Aside from a commitment to attend to the ordinances of God, they call for a readiness to abstain from evil and a resolution to do every possible sort of good to everybody.[31] These are then filled out by various illustrations of what they entail in the particular circumstances in which they were written. Moreover, the rules themselves are placed in the context of eschatology, for the fundamental condition of entry is a desire to flee from the wrath to come and to be saved from one's sins.

We need not here debate the merits of Wesley's exact proposals. What matters is that we recognize that the kingdom of God is a new power let loose in the world, and those who enter into it gladly embrace an ethic of active love toward God and neighbor. This will be expressed in specific terms in the varying cultures and circumstances in which the evangelist operates. At times it will demand quite radical and costly action in its concrete manifestation. It may require the resolute rejection of slavery, as it did with Charles Finney in nineteenth-century North America; or it may call for active resistance to political authority, as happened in the days of the Confessing Church in Nazi Germany; or it may demand a sharp repudiation of terrorism, as it does in modern Ireland; or it may call for an overthrow of oppressive government, as it does in various parts of the Third World. Initiation into the Christian community as a sign of the reign of God in history cannot evade the hard decisions that have to be made at this level—and evangelists will need to be on their mettle to meet the demands of their vocation.

---

31. *The Book of Discipline of the United Methodist Church* (Nashville: The United Methodist Publishing House, 1984), pp. 68-71.

Several general points should be borne in mind here. First, not much good is served by those who play the prophet. Christians legitimately differ on how to express their detailed moral commitments; it is self-serving for the evangelist to impose his or her moral agenda on the shoulders of the Christian initiate. It is especially precarious to insist on some particular philosophical or ideological position, whether of the left or the right, as integral to entry into the kingdom of God. Second, to transmit the positive and joyous character of the moral dimension of initiation is vital. Thus Christians love God because God first loved them, and they love the neighbor because God's love has been shed abroad in their hearts. When these factors are neglected, initiation becomes a juridical process that subtly transforms the unique character of the Christian moral tradition. Third, it is important to realize that the Holy Spirit is at work in the church, in the life and mind of the evangelist, and in the conscience of the initiate to convict of sin, of righteousness, and of judgment. A suffocating, fussy moralism of either a personalistic or rigidly political nature is, therefore, a sign of distrust and fear. It is unlikely to be deeply informed by the love and mercy it is seeking to foster. Finally, this is an obvious arena where we need to remember that initiation cannot cope with the full complexity of Christian moral existence and spiritual maturity. There needs to be ample space beyond initiation for development in moral sensitivity, in conceptual dexterity, and in the grasp of morally relevant information. This takes time, and it cannot be produced by moralism or ideological harangue. It is more than enough if the entrant into the kingdom is solidly grounded and established in the substance of the great commandment and gladly commits himself or herself to a life of active love.

Conclusion

In this chapter we have explored three crucial aspects of initiation into the reign of God. As we enter the kingdom of God, we are confronted with a call to conversion and a summons to be reborn into the new age of God's action in the world; we are baptized in water, incorporated into the Israel of God, and joined in a death that unites us to the risen Lord; and we are brought into a moral tradition whose fundamental ethical structure is marked by a single commandment to love God and neighbor. The church through its ministry of evangelism must bear these principles in mind as she seeks to announce the good news and as she invites people across the globe to share in the wonder of God's salvation. As Charles Wesley so beautifully expressed it,

> Lord, if at thy command
>   The word of life we sow,
> Watered by thy almighty hand,
>   The seed shall surely grow;
> The virtue of thy grace
>   A large increase shall give,
> And multiply the faithful race,
>   Who to thy glory live.
>
> Now, then, the ceaseless shower
>   Of gospel blessings send,
> And let the soul-converting power
>   Thy ministers attend.
> On multitudes confer
>   The heart-renewing love,
> And by the joy of grace prepare
>   For fuller joys above.

SEVEN

The Creed, Spiritual Gifts, and Disciplines

Spiritual miscarriages are a common feature of modern evangelism. The evangelist preaches the good news of the salvation of God, the seed is sown and takes root in the womb, significant nourishment is supplied from the bloodstream of mother church, but then the food is cut off or crucial genetic material for the structuring of the new life is not given. The results are predictable: the developing embryo is aborted, or, if it comes to birth, it is weak and malformed.

Consider the following testimony from Peter Mullen, a vicar in the Anglican church.

> I remember going, as a boy, to a radio relay in Leeds Town Hall of one of Billy Graham's sermons and being much moved by what I heard. So at the end, when he appealed to members of the congregation to come to the front and give their lives to Christ, I went forward. Afterwards, sitting at a card table with one of the team of counsellors, I was given a wallet of Bible texts of the "wherewithal shall a young man cleanse his way . . ." variety and told to examine my life for bad habits and to stop doing them. This provoked much guilt and unhappiness in me over the next few months because of course I could not give up all my bad habits. I would try and, after holding out for a while, I would give in—only to be filled with remorse and self hate. It never occurred to me to reflect that the counsellor had asked me to do exactly what I could not do—to save myself by my own moral effort. Whereas, the good

140

news is, of course, that what I cannot do myself, Christ does on my account. God does not condemn but he forgives. All I need to do is to accept his forgiveness. That really is all there is to it.[1]

Mullen's experience may not be typical, and we can be sure that what he went through does not reflect the intentions of those who organized the meetings he attended. But he correctly identifies a salient feature of much modern evangelism: it is satisfied with half-hearted and very limited initiation into the richness of the reign of God. It is satisfied if the person evangelized is "born again," or has "invited Jesus into his heart," or has "said the sinner's prayer," or has "entered into a personal relationship with Jesus Christ," and the like. Those who have gone through this process will be fortunate if they have laid hold of the real meaning of justification by faith. They will be still more fortunate if they have received the fundamental substance of the Christian moral tradition as summarized in the great commandment. And they will be very fortunate indeed if they have been linked in an appropriate fashion with a local body of believers in either baptism or confirmation.

At the very best, most modern evangelism hands over two things: deeply reduced fragments of the Christian message and the personalistic debris of the Christian moral tradition. It does not supply an adequate summary of the Christian intellectual tradition; it does not introduce the new convert to those gifts of the Spirit without which it is impossible to be an adequately equipped agent of the kingdom in the world; and it does not hand over those fundamental spiritual disciplines without which the believer will ultimately suffocate and die. Yet what little it does do is very instructive. It shows that the evangelist is willy-nilly drawn into the process of initiation. As we noted earlier, it is unrealistic and self-defeating to confine evangelism merely to proclamation. The kingdom of God is not talk but power (1 Cor. 4:20); it is not meat and drink, but righteousness, and peace, and joy in the Holy Spirit (Rom. 14:17). As the good news of its

---

1. Peter Mullen, *Being Saved* (London: SCM, 1985), pp. 106-107.

dawning is announced it is accompanied by the work of the Holy Spirit in the depths of the life of the hearer. Thus it is extremely odd that some involved in evangelism pay no attention to the hearer's response, as if it does not need the mediating work of the church acting as an agent of that same Spirit. Hence they find it impossible to avoid the kind of activity that Mullen caustically describes. The fundamental problem in current practice is obvious: only scattered dimensions of Christian initiation are identified, and even then they are given inadequate attention.

This is the problem that I am seeking to remedy in the previous and the present chapters. The hard truth to be driven home is that as bad as current practice may be, it will not be put right by attending simply to conversion, baptism, and the commitment to love God and neighbor. It also requires handing over the substance of the Christian creed, introducing the initiate to the gifts of the Spirit, and providing him or her with the rudiments of the classical spiritual disciplines. In other words, we not only need to attend to the experiential, communal, and moral dimensions of initiation; we also need to deal with its intellectual, operational, and disciplinary aspects. Just as the kingdom irrevocably involves us in an encounter with the living God in new birth, in the joining of the church through baptism, and in the owning of the great commandment, it also involves us in certain specific theological commitments about God, in the exercise of gifts and graces in the body of Christ and in the world, and in the use of fundamental spiritual disciplines. To stop with only three of these, or to add in this one or that one as the mood arises, or to deal with only those aspects that are dictated by traditional practice in evangelism is arbitrary and devoid of theological coherence. If we ignore any of these dimensions, we can be sure that some movement or sect will eventually discover it and proceed to build it into its evangelistic endeavors with understandable enthusiasm.

The Cognitive Side to Initiation

We can begin by noting that initiation has an inescapably cognitive side to it, one that observers of the history of evangelism often have overlooked. In some circles evangelism is believed to be inherently noncognitive, that is, a matter of stimulating certain pious emotions by means of music, personal testimony, hearty preaching about sin, long-drawn-out altar calls, sophisticated crowd control, and the like. There is some truth in this way of interpreting certain kinds of religious meetings. It is clearly possible to use various atmospheres to manipulate people into making certain kinds of religious decisions, and it is also possible to induce certain kinds of experiences that are construed as religious in nature. However, this kind of analysis is often wide of the mark in particular instances.[2] More important, it totally ignores the fact that even in those cases where it does apply it is almost impossible to induce certain decisions or experiences without engaging the mind. Thus, part of what the preacher will do is to attempt to drive home certain truth claims about God, sin, salvation, the last judgment, and so on. If these are omitted, then it would be well-nigh impossible to have much effect on anyone.[3]

It is platitudinous, moreover, to point out that announcing the dawning of the reign of God involves one in making a whole host of truth claims, both explicitly and implicitly. It presupposes, for example, that God exists, that the affairs of this world are seriously out of joint, that God has acted decisively in Jesus Christ to liberate the creation from bondage, that God acts here and now by the Holy Spirit to save, and so forth. To press this point would be to belabor the obvious. What is less obvious is that entering the reign of God commits one to a very particular intellectual heritage. As the kingdom has come in history it has evoked a specific theological tradition that cannot be set aside as secondary to the process of initiation. We will pursue this initially on a purely formal level.

2. Richard Southey's analysis of Wesley's preaching is a good case in point. As is now widely recognized, it is quite impossible to overlook the considerable intellectual horsepower that is evident in Wesley's preaching.
3. We can see this very clearly in Finney's theory and practice of evangelism. He relentlessly drove home certain truths like a trial lawyer and disdained the attempt to make a direct assault on the emotions. One suspects he learned this lesson from Jonathan Edwards.

Let us look again at the pilgrimage of Peter Mullen after his experience at Leeds. Wrestling with the implications of what he encountered did not mean a mere owning of a particular moral position, one which, in this case, he was perfectly right to challenge. It also meant facing up to what God has done, in this case that God had forgiven him unconditionally. Over time it also meant coming to terms with who Jesus Christ is, along with a vast network of related issues. Thus it led into questions about Scripture, about the nature of salvation, about human nature, and about the relation between Christian claims on these issues and opinions developed by such modern psychologists as Jung and Freud. We need not pause here to evaluate Mullen's material account of these issues; the real issue is a general and formal one. Mullen's deliberations represent the efforts of a thoroughly intelligent soul attempting to come to terms with the significance of what God has done in Jesus of Nazareth. The point is that *this is inescapable.* It is not just an atypical, intellectually able individual entering into some kind of esoteric mental exercise. It is what any normal human being would do in the circumstances.

We should note two features of this situation. First, the issues are extraordinarily far-ranging and complicated. They range from historical considerations about Jesus Christ to hermeneutical debates about the meaning of the biblical narratives, to philosophical claims about the relation between religion and culture, to theological proposals about the nature of God, and so on. Talk about the kingdom of God inescapably engenders such topics. As a matter of formal principle, discourse about the dawning of the new age in Christ leads any intelligent person to raise and pursue questions of this character. This is naturally what we would expect, and it is naturally what we find in religious experience from the earliest days of the church to the present. The second feature of this situation follows naturally: it is quite impossible for any human being to resolve these queries. It would take an extraordinarily encyclopedic mind equipped with the profoundest spiritual sensitivity even to lay out clearly and accurately the relevant data and warrants that can be invoked legitimately by the questions these issues pose. Generally, even those who do understand large segments of the terrain are quick to confess their ignorance and inadequacy.

The Rule of Faith

This poses a profound problem for Christian initiation. On the one hand, Christian initiation cannot possibly avoid adopting certain fundamental theological proposals; on the other, the individual cannot possibly work these proposals out for himself or herself either on the spot or over a lifetime of study. In the light of this, what should the church do in its practice of evangelism? My suggestion is a simple one: it is the church's responsibility to hand on the substance of its intellectual heritage in the form of a creed; moreover, the creed to be handed over is that of the councils of the early church. Since this is a controversial proposal, let me spell out why I think that it is by far the best route to take.

At the outset it is vital not to shirk the formal issue at stake here. Some kind of creed is inescapable. Now one could, of course, rebut this by attempting to challenge the theologically prior claim that the intellect is inescapably engaged in religious commitment. Many evangelists have been thoroughly anti-intellectual in their approach to commitment. It is fashionable, especially in fundamentalist circles, to rail against reason, to make fun of serious theology, to castigate the mind as in bondage to sin, to decry the place of "man-made" creeds in religion, and the like. We need not dwell on this attempt to evade the place of the human intellect in commitment. As it stands it is impervious to argument, for it has rejected the use of reason. So there is no point in arguing against it. It also involves a sub-Christian account of salvation by failing to see that salvation affects the whole person, including the person's mind.

A more sophisticated rebuttal is the argument that creeds are secondary in the life of faith. What matters, it will be said, is preconceptual religious experience as evoked by exposure to the symbols, metaphors, and narrative of the gospel; hence, to insist on a creed as essential is otiose and misleading. The only necessity is that the initiate be brought into the Christian community; he or she should be left to work things through as ability and opportunity permit. The fundamental flaw in this view is that it fails to acknowledge that in its own way it is a creed. In reality it proposes the handing over of a metacreed, a creed about creeds. The initiate has a right to know if this is what the faith essentially involves at an intellectual level, and those responsible for initiation have a duty to articulate this claim and defend it as a solution to the problem we identified above. We certainly have not disposed of a creed; we have smuggled one in at the foundation, underneath the back door. Moreover, it is the wrong kind of creed, for it focuses on a complicated and thoroughly questionable account of the relation between religious language and experience.

For the past decade or so the United Methodist Church has tried an interesting proposal relevant to our concerns here. It has construed the fundamental theological heritage of the church to be captured not by a specific creed or confession but by a particular theological method, specifically by what is commonly known as the Wesleyan quadrilateral. Thus the church's theological heritage, it is said, is fundamentally summarized in the commitment to use Scripture, tradition, reason, and experience to address whatever theological problems arise. As an account of the canons of theology this has much to commend it; as a fundamental summary of the faith it is hopelessly inadequate.[4] One might put the issue sharply as follows: we can imagine a spiritual adviser suggesting that the initiate might face martyrdom for belief in the incarnation; it would be ridiculous to suggest that the initiate face death for the Wesleyan quadrilateral.

The real debate, however, is not likely to take place at this formal plane but rather at the material level. Some will very naturally challenge my suggestion that the specific creed to be handed over should be that of the early councils. It is necessary, therefore, to explain why I believe that this suggestion is

4. I discuss the quadrilateral in "The Wesleyan Quadrilateral," in Ted Runyon, ed., *Wesleyan Theology Today: A Bicentennial Theological Consultation* (Nashville: Kingswood Books, 1985), pp. 119-26.

best. I shall argue the case on both negative and positive grounds. On the one hand, the alternatives to the creed of the early councils are not very attractive; on the other hand, there are good reasons why the Nicene Creed should be handed on as a symbol and summary of the faith.[5]

In regard to the former possibility, consider what happens when we do not hand over something akin to the Nicene Creed. Most of the time the initiate is at the mercy of the individual or the local group who happens to have led him or her to faith. In much modern evangelism, especially in North America, what is informally handed over is the fallout of the turn-of-the-century fundamentalist-modernist controversy. The young Christian is initiated into a creed that focuses on Scripture as the inerrant word of God together with a basic narrative of the work of Christ in salvation and his return again after the rapture. Or he or she is left to flounder in the debris of a moralistic liberalism that is ambivalent about its general intellectual content. Neither of these options is satisfactory. The latter is too vague and amorphous while the former is too narrow and complicated. In both cases there is no internal relation to the coming of the rule of God in history. The connection, insofar as there is one at all, is entirely accidental. Moreover, both of them are really only offering a provincial, sectarian rendering of the Christian intellectual heritage. They do not capture the heart of the intellectual implications of the coming of the rule of God in history.

Another alternative would be to hand over some of the landmark Reformation documents or creeds such as Luther's Shorter Catechism, the Westminster Confession of Faith, the Thirty-nine Articles of the Anglican tradition, or the Articles and Confession of Faith of the United Methodist Church. The problem with these alternatives is twofold. First, they are much too long and cumbersome. As foundation documents for a movement or for a church they clearly have merit, and they ob-

---

5. I chose the Nicene Creed over the Apostles' Creed for two reasons. First, it was officially accepted by the early church. Second, it is most likely to receive ecumenical endorsement. Yet we should not make too much of this choice, for the early creeds are so alike that the fundamental issues at stake in the argument do not change with a change of creed.

viously have proven to be powerful expressions of the comprehensive heritage of the Christian faith—else they would not have received the extended support and loyalty that they have evoked. But they do not serve well as a brief, succinct summary of the faith. The initiate needs something of much more modest proportions—which the Nicene Creed supplies. Second, and more important, these alternatives are derivative documents that depend on the fundamental issues that were initially hammered out in the early centuries of the church's existence. The problems these various documents address are important in their own right, for they touch on questions that arise when one seeks to spell out in a comprehensive way the broad outlines of the Christian faith. However, they presuppose and embody the fundamental convictions about God, about Christ, and about the Holy Spirit that are at the heart of the Nicene Creed. Hence we should prefer the more basic and original to the complex and derivative.

Equally unsatisfactory is the attempt to unearth some primitive Christian confession from the biblical traditions and make this the intellectual content of the creed to be handed over. Some might propose a summary of the teaching of Jesus. There are several problems with this option: it is not clear what it would look like in detail; it is likely to be too long; and it will probably be too moralistic in content. The more likely candidate would involve either a selection from or a piecing together of the scattered confessional formulae that are found in the New Testament. A basic problem with this alternative is that, again, it is not clear what this would look like, nor how one might identify and defend the principle of selection used. Furthermore, the formulae invoked would almost certainly be precisely some of the material gathered up and held together in the Nicene Creed. Thus it would be a classical case of reinventing a doctrinal wheel that is already to hand. Most important, those who would advocate this move would generally base their proposal on the assumed canonical status of the New Testament. That is, they would invoke the classical *sola scriptura* rhetoric of the Reformation to undergird their fundamental appeal to the New Testament as the warrant for their "biblical" creed. This, however, is an impossible position, for exactly the same warrants undergird the early creeds of the church as undergird the development of the New Testrament canon. As this argument leads to the positive case to be made for the Nicene Creed, we need here to lay out the basic logic of the argument.

The key point is that for a variety of reasons the early church found it essential to do at least three things to safeguard its intellectual treasures. First, it gathered together the scattered documents that are now enshrined in the New Testament. These were a vital conduit to the foundation events that led to the church's existence in the first place, and they constituted a crucial guide for its reflection and action. Second, it developed a variety of basic summaries of the faith, and these, in turn, provided the fundamental structure and content of the later creeds. In time these became elements of the identity of the Christian community. Finally, it put in place an episcopate whose primary task was to see that the faith would be taught and that Scripture and creed would be maintained as foundational in the intellectual heritage of the community. The process involved in all this is a unified whole. To separate out the Scriptures as isolated and superior to the creed is arbitrary; both represent decisions of the church that were inspired by the Holy Spirit to safeguard the community's heritage and identity across time in the turmoil of history. This in turn required institutional oversight or episcopacy, for there is no point in having a canon and a creed if there is no social mechanism or institution to ensure that they are kept at the heart of the life of the community.

What the classical Protestant tradition has done is to accept the canon along with a revised form of episcopacy. Initially it implicitly took over the creeds of the early church using, as Calvin did, its structure as the fundamental outline of its theology or sometimes insisting, as Luther did, that the church must possess at least one confession that would serve as normative for the community.[6] All the while, however, it has done this in

---

6. According to Cullmann, Luther went so far as to say that this confession by its composition could claim an equal authority with the New Testament. See Oscar Cullmann, *The Earliest Christian Confessions* (London: Lutterworth, 1949), p. 16.

the name of *sola scriptura*, a principle that is utterly at odds with Protestant practice. A community cannot live indefinitely with such fundamental inconsistency. When the implications of this eventually dawned on perceptive intellects, it became normal to set the creed over against the canon. In time substitutes for the creed had to be worked out, ranging from the complicated creeds of Protestant scholasticism, through the simple formulae of nineteenth-century liberalism, through the polemical principles of fundamentalism, to the failed quest of the last generation for a so-called biblical theology.

This is extremely relevant to evangelism. Handing over Scripture as the sole content of the faith is inadequate.[7] The Bible cannot do what a creed does, nor was it ever intended to do so. We might profitably construe Scripture as a handbook of basic theology, moral reflection, piety, intellectual rumination, gospel narrative, and so on. It is much too big and unwieldy as a summary of the faith; it fulfills its function precisely because it is such an astonishing mosaic of poetry, story, proverb, historical narrative, occasional epistle, tracts for the times, and the like. It is inexhaustible; no one can master the richness and diversity that characterizes its form and content; it is as complicated as life itself; and its value in part lies in the kind of spiritual formation that results from persistent wrestling with its claims. It was never meant to stand alone, and when movements try this they end up developing substitutes that fail to exhibit the wisdom manifest in the early creeds. The creed fulfills a different function. It provides a basic summary of the intellectual structure of the Christian mind: it supplies a map that lays out the fundamental contours of how the Christian thinks about God, about Christ, and about the Holy Spirit. As such, it is particularly well suited to meet the needs of the beginner who is seeking to grasp the

---

7. I am implying here that the initiate will be introduced to the sacred Scriptures by being introduced to the Christian community. My concern in what follows is to retrieve the cruciality of the creed as part of the total tradition that is handed over to those entering the reign of God. I have no objection to a formal handing over of both Scripture and creed as a single tradition, for clearly they belong together in unity.

theological essentials of the community that he or she is called to join in baptism.

It is crucial that we grasp the fundamental purpose of the creed at this point. Much confusion and not a little mischief is caused by failing to be clear and resolute on this issue. The function of the creed is not to deal with the host of issues that can be covered only in a full-blown, systematic rendering of the Christian vision of God, creation, human nature, Christ, salvation, the Holy Spirit, the church, the future, and so on. Only a comprehensive, systematic theology can supply this. Nor is the function of the creed to replace Scripture as an absolutely vital and normative source of piety, theological reflection, and moral deliberation. The latter is *sui generis;* it has its own unique place in the total tradition into which the convert is initiated. Nor, finally, is it the function of the creed to replace the gospel announcement of the kingdom of God, which constitutes the church's evangelistic preaching. The latter represents the horizon and basic context of initiation, while the creed represents the intellectual conclusions to which the community of the Messiah was driven when it sought to formulate the implications of the coming of the rule of God for its thinking about God, about Christ, and about the Holy Spirit. In fact, the creed represents an astonishingly fitting summary of the implications of the dawn of God's rule, inaugurated in Christ, and now realized in the Holy Spirit.[8] Nothing in the history of the church can match it in both clarity and reserve. It is unsurpassed as a summary of the intellectual backbone of the Israel of God. Together with its hallowed and sustained role in the history of the

---

8. I am well aware that many are unhappy with the Nicene Creed because they judge it to be too ontological and metaphysical in nature. What I find most striking about the Nicene Creed is its reserve in the area of ontology and metaphysics. I suspect that many philosophers would share this judgment. Moreover, ontology and metaphysics are unavoidable, so there can be no objection in principle to the use of the Nicene Creed in initiation. I am also aware that many theologians are very much opposed to the content of the Nicene Creed and would prefer either to have none at all or a revised substitute. We cannot resolve this issue here. It is worth pointing out, however, that those beginning the journey of faith should surely have access to the classical tradition of the church.

church, these provide the fundamental reasons for the claim that it should be handed over to those entering into the kingdom of God in repentance and baptism. That the creeds of the early church were used extensively in the context of baptism only serves to highlight this point.

Life in the Spirit

So much for the intellectual dimension of initiation into the reign of God. It is a commonplace in piety to note that Christianity is much more than the intellectual believing of certain doctrines or propositions. Thus it has been seen, especially in evangelistic circles, as a religion of the heart, as a faith where the affections are engaged very deeply, and as a transformation of the inner person through new birth to a life of active love in the service of the church and the world. What has not been sufficiently recognized is that both inner transformation and service are to be accompanied by the activity of the Holy Spirit working dynamically through the members of Christ's body in the context of the reign of God. In other words, the Holy Spirit comes not just to make people aware of what God has done in Christ and to woo them to repentance and faith but also to sustain and equip the body of Christ to continue the works of the kingdom today. Where this is ignored the initiate into the kingdom either is left to be a spectator to the work of God or is sent out on missions or service for which he or she is inadequately prepared.

We might illustrate what is at stake here by heeding Ramsay MacMullen's fictional summary of how the Christian gospel took root in the Roman empire.

> Testing to see if I can imagine in some detail a scene that conflicts with no point of the little that is known about conversion in the second and third centuries, I would choose the room of some sick person: there, a servant talking to a mistress, or one spouse to another, saying, perhaps, "Unquestionably they can help, if you believe. And I know, I have seen, I heard, they have related to me, they have books, they have a special person, a sort of officer. It is true. Be-

sides and, anyway, if you don't believe, then you are doomed when a certain time comes, so say the prophecies; whereas, if you do, then they can help even in great sickness. I know people who have seen. And healing is even the least that they tell. Theirs is truly a God all-powerful. He has worked a hundred wonders." So a priest is sent for, or an exorcist; illness is healed; the household after that counts as Christian; it is baptised; and through instruction it comes to accept the first consequences: that all other cults are false and wicked, all seeming gods, the same.[9]

MacMullen draws attention to a very significant feature of the ministry of the early church. The apostolic and postapostolic early church was at ease with a very rich and diverse ministry of the gifts of the Holy Spirit. The community simply expected the Holy Spirit to be present and to operate through the whole body, with each person ideally grafted into a single community of service and love. The Holy Spirit distributed gifts as they were needed, and through time certain individuals became associated with certain manifestations of the Spirit. In due course they may then have developed a specific role or office that identified their particular calling within the body. This might have been the way in which various positions such as pastor, teacher, and evangelist developed. At this point this is a matter of conjecture, but there is no denying that the Holy Spirit was experienced as a dynamic agent of the rule of God empowering and equipping the church to act as an agent of the kingdom in the present. Those brought under the rule of God would have picked this up as a natural element in their experience, and they would have operated as if this was an obvious ingredient in their service of God.

Karl Barth captures what is at stake here by referring to the gifts, lights, and powers of the Holy Spirit.[10] The Christian community, he points out, "can and must be the scene of many

9. Ramsay MacMullen, *Christianizing the Roman Empire*, A.D. *100-400* (New Haven: Yale University Press, 1984), pp. 40-41.
10. Karl Barth, *Church Dogmatics* (Edinburgh: T. &. T. Clark, 1939), IV/3, Sect. 69,4 and Sect. 73.

human activities which are new and supremely astonishing to many of its members as well as to the world because they rest on an endowment with extraordinary capacities."[11] Barth is entirely correct here, and we need to find a way to incorporate this into the process of initiation.

The story of the loss of these capacities from the normal life of the church has not yet been adequately researched and articulated. In most academic circles it is not even on the agenda.[12] It is taken as a mark of the critical historian to dispense with this element of the church's history as myth, legend, exaggeration, hagiography, superstition, and the like. Even in conservative Christian circles where there is, in principle, an openness to the miraculous, talk about the direct intervention of the Holy Spirit in healing or guidance is dismissed as a manifestation of credulity. These events are said to have died out with the apostles, or to be no longer necessary now that we have the New Testament canon, or to be attributable to the demonic, or to be part of the standard trickery of the snake-handling, faith-healing, cultic evangelist, and so on. In suggesting initiation into such activity as an essential dimension of entry into the reign of God, I run, then, the risk of alienating a host of readers who will be deeply sympathetic to my general approach to evangelism. I owe it to them, therefore, to explain why I insist on this as both possible and essential.[13] The crux of the matter is captured in two fundamental points.

First, the operation of the gifts of the Spirit has never

---

11. Ibid., IV/2, p. 828.

12. Gerhard Lohfink makes this point concisely:

Are we even capable of speaking theologically about the deeds of God in history today, and of interpreting a movement which is sweeping through Christianity as "the work of God"? It is to be feared that we are scarcely capable of it. An indication of our inability may be seen in the fact that, in our liturgy and our community assembly, we no longer relate the deeds of God in the present or recent past; we no longer tell of God's leadership, God's signs and wonders. Things like that are embarrassing. We leave them to outsiders or fringe groups. We no longer have even the words to shape such a story. (*The Work of God Goes On* [Philadelphia: Fortress, 1987], p. 20)

13. We cannot deal with the more general philosophical question of the possibility of divine intervention here. I have discussed this issue at length in

completely died out in the history of the church. They have always been associated with the lives of the saints in Latin Christianity. In Eastern Christianity, as represented by the Russian tradition, they have been manifested again and again in the lives of the starets, in the wonder workers, and in the simple fools for Christ. In Protestantism, they have been constantly fomenting beneath the surface in periods of revival and awakening. As Horace Bushnell, a truly unusual witness to their authenticity given the standard account of his views in the history books, has pointed out, direct manifestations of the Spirit were commonplace in the days of the Scottish Reformation.[14] They were accepted as normal and natural for two centuries; then highminded editors felt they knew better about the economy of divine action and carefully naturalized the merest hint of the miraculous.[15] In the eighteenth century, revival manifestations of the Spirit are constantly peeping through like snowflakes in a hard frost of rationalism or like buttercups in a fiery meadow of fanaticism and emotionalism. Wesley, perhaps given to be credulous here and there, took them in his stride. Jonathan Edwards did not. He was forced to develop an elaborate and austere set of arguments to show that what appeared to be the work of the Spirit was a dishonor to God and a wound to true religion.[16] With the development of voluntarism in North America it was only a matter of time before Christians there would have the institutional and intellectual freedom to pursue experimentally this

---

Divine Revelation and the Limits of Historical Criticism (London: Oxford University Press, 1982), and in *An Introduction to the Philosophy of Religion* (Englewood Cliffs, N.J.: Prentice Hall, 1985), chap. 13.

14. See Horace Bushnell, *Nature and the Supernatural as Together Constituting the One System of God* (Edinburgh: Alexander Strachan, 1861), chap. 14.

15. Bushnell draws attention to a fascinating volume where this occurs. It is William McGavin, ed., *The Scots Worthies: Containing a Brief Historical Account of the Most Eminent Noblemen, Gentlemen, Ministers, and Others, Who Testified or Suffered for the Cause of Reformation in Scotland, From the Beginning of the Sixteenth Century, to the Year 1688* (Glasgow and London: W. R. McPhun, 1858). McGavin carefully edits out any supernaturalistic element from the original edition of John Howie.

16. Edwards was very worried about the danger of "enthusiasm." See his discussion of one such case in C. C. Goen, ed., *The Great Awakening* (New Haven and London: Yale University Press, 1972), p. 207.

dimension of the coming of the reign of God. When Pentecostalism arose it was ruthlessly driven out of the established churches, but despite great odds and very meager theological resources it managed to lay hold of this important aspect of apostolic Christianity. It has now returned this gift to mainline Christianity in a variety of theological costumes and movements. It requires an unwarrantable skepticism and a deeply dogmatic spirit to set all this aside as legend, exaggeration, and the like.

Secular historians and their friends in the Christian fold can make of these apparent manifestations of the Spirit what they will. Those who have been immersed in the New Testament and its account of the ministry of Jesus and the apostles will be challenged to take a different view. We have buried in this tangled and complicated history the same manifestations of the kingdom of God that were present in the ministry of Christ and that animated the evangelistic endeavors of the apostles and their successors. The appropriate intellectual response is not to look for some excuse for dismissing such phenomena, such as appealing to the various horror stories, some true and some false, that make the rounds, or pouncing on the abuses of this or that evangelist, or wheeling out the general concerns that every mature theist has about the mystery of God's action in the world. The intelligent thing to do is to think through in a thorough fashion what these phenomena tell us about the total activity of the Holy Spirit. This takes us to our second point.

It is obvious to the fair observer that the recovery of this dimension of the kingdom has had a profound effect for good in the field of evangelism.[17] The spread of indigenous Chris-

17. Emil Brunner's judgment is worth recording at this juncture:

How did the fellowship of Jesus spread? We children of an era that is rationalised through and through always think first and perhaps exclusively in such a matter of what we should call evangelization, or missionary work, in which the stress lies almost wholly upon the proclamation of the Gospel, and this proclamation again is understood in the sense of theological instruction. Of course, teaching and in the broader sense preaching played a decisive part in the spread of the movement. But something at least as important was just that other, that "pneumatic" factor, the non-theological, the purely dynamic. Outsiders were attracted—the story of Pentecost already shows us this quite plainly—not primarily by what was said, but by the element of mystery—what hap-

tianity in Africa, the upsurge of Pentecostalism in modern Latin America and across the world, the renewal of the evangelistic spirit in mainline Protestantism and Roman Catholicism, and the development of the school of Power Evangelism within the Church Growth movement—all these and more are unintelligible without the apparent manifestation of the Holy Spirit acting dynamically and directly in the lives of ordinary Christians. To be sure, we meet here a kind of watershed decision in theology. We are faced with tough alternatives that have a bearing on our fundamental cosmological and metaphysical convictions. In my view the alternatives are clear. Either we follow through on a robust and full account of the gospel, which my earlier proposal on the early creeds already makes manifest, or we adopt one of the revisionist alternatives of the Christian tradition that are currently available. We shall meet this again when we deal with the important issue of secularization. For the present we have come to a fork in the road, and I have no doubt which turn we should take: the mature Christian theist will seek to retrieve the fullness of the work of the Holy Spirit, including that mysterious, dynamic activity represented by direct manifestation both to individuals and to the gathered community. It may well take a full generation for the details of both

---

pened simply. The impression made by the life of believers plays a part of decisive importance in the genesis of faith. People draw near to the Christian community because they are irresistibly attracted by its supernatural power. They would like to share in this new dimension of life and power, they enter the zone in which the Spirit operates before they have heard a word about what lies behind it as its ultimate transcendent-immanent cause. There is a sort of fascination which is exercised mostly without any reference to the Word, comparable rather to the attractive force of a magnet or the spread of an infectious disease. Without knowing how it happened, one is already a carrier of the infection. (*The Misunderstanding of the Church* [Philadelphia: Westminster, 1953], pp. 51-52)

Unfortunately, Brunner goes on to play off the operations of the Holy Spirit against the offices of the institutional church. This is an utterly bogus contrast, for the offices that provide order in the community are themselves a charism of the Holy Spirit without which the other operations of the Spirit are left to flounder and collapse into chaos. The same applies to the doctrinal decisions of the early church in its councils. Following Florovsky, we might call these crucial charismatic events in the life of the church.

faith and practice to be worked out, but the general principle is clear: the kingdom of God is not just talk but power to work as an agent of the rule of God in the world.[18] We cannot omit this from a comprehensive analysis of initiation into the reign of God.

Implicit witness is given to this in the rite of confirmation by the laying on of hands. Sometimes this is construed as a special strengthening given by the Holy Spirit; sometimes it is interpreted as the imparting of the sevenfold gifts of the Spirit.[19] Although confirmation is now under a cloud theologically, it is commonly recognized that it was originally part of a unified rite of initiation in which it was expected that the Holy Spirit would be given to those being baptized. I am suggesting that behind this practice lies the belief that the Christian is ideally called to live a life thoroughly immersed in the Holy Spirit, operating in the Holy Spirit as he or she is led. This should not be taken individualistically. The primary locus of the Holy Spirit's operations is initially in the community as it gathers to worship and

18. We face here a theological dilemma similar to that Wesley and his colleagues faced when they were charged with "enthusiasm." In their day, it took a steady nerve and enormous theological dexterity to ensure that the inward work of the Holy Spirit would be taken seriously by the church at large. The same applies now in the case of the operational gifts of the Spirit. Much academic theology shies away from the topic. In conservative Protestantism, those interested in exploring the issue are sometimes hounded from their teaching positions. In addition, those most committed to this dimension of the work of the Holy Spirit, notably the Pentecostal bodies, are often cut off from the deeper theological riches of the classical Christian tradition. On a popular level, they tend to work with inadequate notions of tradition, to exaggerate the significance of their discoveries, to insist on simplistic and wooden patterns of religious experience, and very easily to fall prey to a ranting fundamentalism in their thinking and preaching. As of yet Pentecostalism has completely failed to face up to the full demands of Christian initiation. It is liable to fall prey to hubris by castigating the great doctrinal heritage of the early church, and it is very prone to turn aside to doctrines of prosperity that make nonsense of discipleship. It is a moot question how far it is prepared to receive from the larger church what it will urgently need to conserve and nourish the lives of its converts against the onslaughts of the world, the flesh, and the devil. A fine treatment of the origins of Pentecostal theology can be found in Donald Dayton, *The Origins Of Pentecostalism* (Grand Rapids: Zondervan, 1987). Walter Hollenweger, *The Pentecostals* (London: SCM, 1975), is indispensable reading.

19. A useful review of the theology of confirmation is found in H. W. Turner, "Confirmation," *Scottish Journal of Theology* 5 (1952): 148-62.

to wait upon God. In this context the Spirit moves within and through those who offer themselves unreservedly in service and who have learned to discern the leading of the Holy Spirit. Initiation into the rule of God, I am suggesting, involves owning this for oneself with gratitude and firmness.[20]

There are two reasons why this is an essential element in initiation. First, the coming of the Holy Spirit to the community of the Messiah was a constitutive part of the fulfillment of the eschatological promises to Israel. To omit this dimension is, therefore, to work with a very reduced analysis of what the kingdom of God involves. This is clearly brought out in the New Testament where it is obvious that the presence and activity of the Holy Spirit is seen as utterly indispensable to its existence and to its spread into the Gentile world. Second, it is extremely odd to think that the kingdom of God can be inaugurated or sustained by mere human means. The reign of God cannot be established by human moralistic endeavor. To believe this is to underestimate the power of evil at work in the world and to prepare the church for ultimate failure in its service as an agent of the kingdom. This is very important in evangelism. Those called to give themselves in active service in the rule of God need some assurance that they do not face the world on their own but that they can face it with hope, knowing that they will be accompanied, led, and used by the Holy Spirit. To omit this is to underestimate the salvation and liberation that God has inaugurated for his people and the world. That salvation is made present in the acts of the Holy Spirit carried out through the agents of the kingdom who are grafted into the body of Christ.

Given this, the challenge to the initiate is high. Meeting it

---

20. This differs drastically from those who see the manifestations of the Holy Spirit as the exercise of supernatural power given to catch the attention of the indifferent or to convince the skeptic. The tradition of Power Evangelism led by John Wimber comes close to this. We touched on Wimber's position above, pp. 86-90. It is worth noting that Wimber is seeking to work through the theology and logic of the work of the Holy Spirit in evangelism with considerable flexibility. For a busy evangelist he shows unusual sensitivity to outside opinion and to theology. In the practice of the gifts of the Holy Spirit he is unusually gifted; I suspect that he is a generation ahead of many in this dimension of ministry.

requires a life of watchfulness and discipline. It cannot be achieved without continuous recourse to the fountains of mercy, love, and grace provided in the church. This is the main reason why initiation must involve a handing over of the fundamental disciplines of the Christian life. Within these a special place should be given to attendance at the eucharist. With this we arrive at the sixth and last dimension of initiation into the reign of God.

Spiritual Disciplines

The bringing of the initiate to communion was one of the major ingredients of the rite of initiation in the early church. Not surprisingly it was interpreted as virtually the climax of the whole process, for here the baptized believer was led into a continuous encounter with the risen Lord that called to mind his passion and resurrection in a unique way. It also called one to identify with the suffering of Christ, offering oneself as a sacrifice of love in the service of God. We need not here resolve the deep theological questions that the eucharist has evoked. What is crucial is that virtually everyone outside those who treat it in strictly memorialist terms find in this sacrament the most profound means of grace that the church knows. It is not too much to claim that in this event there is a fresh entering into the rule of God. The fundamental actions that inaugurated the kingdom in history are relived and represented in the community of the risen Messiah, and the participant is drawn in faith and hope into the kingdom's future consummation. Charles Wesley captures the heart and the complexity of the matter with characteristic power.

> Let all who truly bear
>   The bleeding Saviour's name,
> Their faithful hearts with us prepare,
>   And eat the paschal lamb:
> Our Passover was slain
>   At Salem's hallowed place,
> Yet we who in our tents remain
>   Shall gain his largest grace.

This eucharistic feast
    Our every want supplies,
And still we by his death are blest,
    And share his sacrifice;
By faith his flesh we eat,
    Who here his passion show,
And God, out of his holy seat,
    Shall all his gifts bestow.

Who thus our faith employ
    His sufferings to record,
E'en now we mournfully enjoy
    Communion with our Lord;
As though we every one
    Beneath his cross had stood,
And seen him heave, and heard him groan,
    And felt his gushing blood.

O God! 'tis finished now!
    The mortal pang is past!
By faith his head we see him bow,
    And hear him breathe his last.
We too with him are dead,
    And shall with him arise,
The cross on which he bows his head
    Shall lift us to the skies.

That those entering into the kingdom should be initiated into this experience does not need defense and elaboration.[21] What needs to be stressed in the context of evangelism is that the eucharist introduces one to a whole network of spiritual disciplines without which the initiate will flounder and die. Drawing attention to these is especially important in the wake of our comments on the use of spiritual gifts because discernment in the use of the gifts depends crucially on a sensitivity to the Holy Spirit. Spiritual discernment is in turn nurtured by the exercise of the spiritual disciplines. It is also important because the spir-

21. Geoffrey Wainwright systematically explores the relation between eucharist and eschatology in *Eucharist and Eschatology* (London: Epworth, 1971).

itual disciplines, properly used, are vital in the sustaining of the difficult commitments that both the beginning and the mature disciple have to face in the world as he or she seeks to live a life of active love. It is naive to think that commitment will be easy. The initiate will face opposition and maybe even confrontation and ridicule. It is superficial to think that this can be handled without inward resolution and without a deep sense of the presence of God in one's life. Attending to the fundamental disciplines of piety is by far the best way to cultivate these in the life of the new believer. Any comprehensive approach to initiation cannot, therefore, ignore them.

Attendance at the eucharist will in itself draw one into most of the requisite disciplines. Thus it is appropriate to prepare for the celebration of the eucharist by times of fasting, meditation, and confession. During the eucharist, one will take time to pray, to give thanks to God, to read the Scriptures, to wait in silence before God, to join in fellowship and praise with other Christians, to bring offerings for the poor, to recite the Lord's prayer, and to sing the great hymns of the faith. In time, such basic disciplines as prayer and fasting can become a natural part of the convert's life. What matters in initiation is not that all these disciplines be mastered and understood but rather that they be received as a gift from the church and that they be appreciated as basic to growth in grace. They need to be owned and appropriated as absolutely fundamental to continuing communion with God.

Conclusion

I have sought in this chapter to articulate three elementary dimensions of initiation into the rule of God. First, initiation does not take place in an intellectual vacuum. It requires ultimately a uniquely trinitarian conception of God, one that seeks to hold to the mystery of God's action in Christ and through the Holy Spirit without wandering into a shallow obscurantism. This is represented in the symbol of the Nicene Creed, which articulates the basic form and structure of the Christian intellectual heritage. Second, initiation involves learning to operate in the gifts of the Holy Spirit so that the initiate becomes a participant in the various ministries of the church. Third, initiation entails the handing over and receiving of those spiritual disciplines that alone can foster the kind of spiritual discernment and deep commitment that, in turn, will enable one to use the gifts of the Holy Spirit aright and to endure to the end. Central within this is initiation into the eucharistic tradition of the church where the Holy Spirit is invoked and the parousia is made present afresh among God's people. If any of these elements is ignored or neglected, the church will have failed in its loyalty to the kingdom. Worse still, it will have stored up unnecessary trouble for itself and for those it has sought to bring into the glorious, eschatological rule of the living God.

EIGHT

The Ministry of Evangelism

Our conceptions of evangelism have a profound effect on our evangelistic practices. Fundamentally, they set up the criteria of success or failure, and thus they determine the forms of accountability for our ministry in this area. They also provide the basic starting-point for decisions about evangelistic strategy. For example, if we define evangelism in terms of the proclamation of the gospel, our primary focus in strategy will be to get the word out to as many people as possible, as efficiently as possible. The primary criterion of success will be faithfulness to the content of the gospel message. Proper evaluation will consist of finding out how well the proclamation under review reflects the content of the gospel. Thus, results—as measured in terms of baptisms, conversions, increasing church membership, and the like—will be excluded as a means of evaluation. If, however, we define evangelism in terms of church growth, we shall have an entirely different approach to strategy, and we shall rely on radically different criteria of evaluation. Success in this case will be judged in terms of the gains and losses of church membership, and evangelistic strategy will focus on identifying those measures that will increase the numbers on church records. Developing a definition of evangelism and working out the details of a concept of evangelism are not therefore matters of ivory-tower speculation; they are crucial for the ministry of evangelism, and it is small wonder that they evoke considerable controversy.

My aim in this chapter is to explore the implications of my proposal for the ministry of evangelism. This completed, we

164

can address briefly the place of evangelism in the life of the church as a whole. I begin by reflecting on a pungent comment of Wesley's that takes us into the heart of some of the issues involved. In a letter to his preachers in 1780, he writes:

> The greatest hindrance you are to expect from rich, cowardly, or lazy Methodists. But regard them not, neither stewards, leaders, or people. Whenever the weather permits, go out in God's name into the most public places, and call all to repent and believe in the Gospel: every Sunday in particular: especially where there are old societies, unless they settle upon their lees. The stewards will frequently oppose this, lest they lose their normal collection. But this is not a sufficient reason against it. Shall we barter souls for money?[1]

The immediate context of Wesley's concern was a call to engage in open-air preaching. From past experience, in fact from the day in May 1738 when he had consented to be more servile and had heeded Whitefield's call to take to the fields, Wesley knew that it was crucial to reach the masses where they were, and one of the best ways to do this was to take to the streets and announce the gospel. He had hit on outdoor preaching early on, it had worked, and he was not going to abandon such a useful means of reaching out to the world.

There is more here, however, than just a concern about a particular strategy. Wesley was also worried about societies losing their passion for evangelism, about a loss of nerve, about the growth of sloth within the Christian community, about riches and respectability choking concern for the poor and the outcast, and about opposition from administrators and bureaucrats who are more concerned about numbers and financial figures than they are about reaching out with the good news of the kingdom. We need not here dwell on the realization of Wesley's fears for Methodism; they have all been amply realized. Nothing is to be gained by yet one more lament about the state of the church and its inability to work with integrity, good

1. The "Large Minutes" in the Six Successive Editions, 1780, pp. 451-53.

humor, and diligence in evangelism. We need, instead, to ask how the church might best begin to work again in this field.

The immediate clamor in many quarters will be for a program of evangelism akin to eighteenth-century outdoor preaching that will solve our problems in this domain. Some, of course, will look to television to be this equivalent. Others will look to a program of personal witnessing that will enable the ordinary Christian to share a basic outline of the gospel with his or her friends and neighbors. Some will see the answer in evangelistic crusades of the kind associated with Billy Graham and Louis Palau. Others will look to the annual revival in the local church. Some will pin their hopes on the development of community groups, or of evangelistic Bible study groups, or on an increase of Sunday school classes. Others will look to assimilation programs designed to prevent people slipping away from the church after they have joined it. Some will organize a weekly visitation program to reach out to the unchurched in the neighborhood. Others will organize spot advertising on television and radio. Some will develop a telephone ministry. Others will take to dragging a cross across the world. Yet others will spread the gospel through rock music, throwing Bibles to their audiences. Clearly the quest for some single way, or a combination of ways, to do evangelism is a fervent one.

It is easy to dismiss all this as Western activism and pragmatism at its worst. Many do so eagerly and then return to life as usual in the ministry of the church. Moreover, we might expect that sensitive Christians should recoil from much of what passes as evangelism in the modern world. Some forms of evangelism are so bad that they may dechristianize those subjected to them, or they may inoculate people from the gospel indefinitely. The history of evangelism prior to our own times does not always encourage us, either: we need simply reflect on the forced baptism of many of the tribes of northern Europe and Latin America or on the kind of eighteenth-century revivalism that Horace Bushnell found so offensive.[2] Only the callous and

2. See Horace Bushnell, "Spiritual Economy of Revivals of Religion," in *Building Eras in Religion* (New York: Scribner, Armstrong & Co., 1881), pp. 150-81.

spiritually insensitive could fail to sympathize with the curt dismissal of the quest for a ready-made program of evangelism.

Yet it is premature to dismiss the quest for some kind of program as otiose or out of order. Evangelism is a ministry of the church. It must, therefore, be fleshed out in specific activities that are workable and effective and for which those engaged in them can be held accountable. The passion for action, where it does exist, should be applauded; it should then be channeled into activities that actually embody a responsible ministry of evangelism. Where this passion does not exist, we can be sure that a vital dimension of apostolic Christianity is missing. No amount of protestation in the name of orthodox doctrine, liturgical finesse, administrative maintenance, social action, liberationist fervor, or the like will suffice as an excuse or a rationalization. If the church does not evangelize, it has forfeited the right to be called apostolic, and apostolicity is an ineradicable mark of the church's identity.

I shall not offer here some new program of evangelism that will embody the proposals I have articulated and defended heretofore. This is the wrong way to proceed. Obviously, this whole approach to evangelism is at odds with the basic vision developed above. It bypasses the fundamental claim that evangelism is a polymorphous ministry. Evangelism cannot in principle be captured in some kind of simple program that we can package and take on the road. To perpetuate this kind of thinking is to fall prey to conceptions of evangelism that are unworthy of the Christian gospel. Moreover, this fails to come to grips with the deep problems that the church eventually has to confront in this area. Besides, it tends to suffocate the need for both divine inspiration and human creativity in evangelism. What we need at this juncture are some suggestions concerning the broad, general principles that apply to the ministry of evangelism, together with an illustration here and there to clarify what is at issue.

Evangelism and Worship

The first and most basic principle is that evangelism should begin from a deep sense of the reality of the reign of God within the Christian community. The primary agent in all evangelism is God, and the ultimate objective of evangelism is to see people introduced to and grounded in the kingdom of God as it is manifested in history. If this sense of the reality of God is missing, then all that is done in evangelism will be wide of the mark and inadequate. To be more precise, if God is not allowed to be Lord in the church, then it is unlikely that the church will be very effective in introducing people into the rule of God. The kingdom will be a notional, secondhand theory or concept that is unrelated existentially to life as we know it. The fundamental failures in evangelism flow from the weakness of the church in this area. Hence, if God is not taken seriously; if God's will is marginal; if God's rule is rejected as restrictive; if God's compassion is looked on indifferently; if God's activity in Jesus Christ is dismissed as secondary; if God's presence through the Holy Spirit is merely talked about but not known; if the liturgy, whether formal or informal, is treated as an end in itself, rather than a means to an end—if any or all of these prevail, then evangelism will be deformed and diseased. So one of the primary and irreplaceable ingredients in evangelism is the quality of worship in the Christian community. In this critical area the willingness to acknowledge and celebrate the inauguration of the rule of God is tested in a fundamental way. If God is not celebrated and adored as Lord in worship, it is highly unlikely that God's rule will be celebrated and welcomed anywhere else. Without a deep sense of the reality of God in the regular, liturgical life of the church, talk about initiating people into the rule of God will be vacuous and empty.

The positive reasons for this are obvious. First, only a sense of the numinous reality of God as mediated in worship can provide the sense of wonder, joy, and mercy that can sustain evangelism over the years. Where evangelism is a burden to be borne, or an obligation to be carried out from a sense of mere duty, or a tradition of the elders to be continued for the sake of propriety, there it will invariably become dull and monotonous. The only lasting antidote for this is a continuously renewed wonder and amazement concerning the character, the action, and the graciousness of God. This attitude is fostered by worship and celebration. Furthermore, worship alone inspires that sense of freedom and confidence that is one of the hallmarks of authentic evangelism. Worship releases the church to relax; it makes her aware that God is the primary agent in evangelism; it breaks the temptation to manipulate for worthy ends; and it sets her free to mediate the presence of God and his rule.

To be sure, this is difficult to find in the barrenness and wastelands of much contemporary Christianity. Hence some will be tempted to dismiss my whole approach to the practice of evangelism as romantic and unrealistic. One is reminded of the advice given by the Irishman to the Englishman who was intending to go to Letterfrack in Connemara: "'Tis the devil's own country, sar, to find your way in, but a gentilman with a face like Your Honour's can't miss the road: but if it was m'self that was going to Letterfrack, bedad, I wouldn't start from here." If authentic worship is crucial to evangelism, will the church not have to stop evangelizing until it puts its own house in order first? The answer to this question is a firm No. We could, of course, answer in the affirmative, and take to prayer and fasting until things are put right. Maybe we could do a lot worse.[3] Sometimes, however, we have to act in circumstances that are

---

3. Compare the advice once given by Bushnell:

Instead, therefore, of spending the time, or so great a part of it, in collecting knowledge, trying opinions, and storing the mind with cognitions and judgements, it would often be far better, as a mere point of economy, to occupy many hours in contesting with the sins that make a Saviour necessary, and in those sublime realizations of his power, which reveal him as the inner light and peace of the soul. Nay, it would be better, if necessary to forgoe all instruction, shut up the libraries, give the week to prayer, shave the crown, put on hair girdles, ordain a year of silence — better I would say, to practice any severity, rather than attempt the knowledge of God by the mere natural understanding. Or if it be wise in teaching the military art to spend a full three months each year in the encampment, or service of the field, would it be wider of reason, in the training of a Christian ministry, to spend so long a time, each year, in the holy drill of charity, patience, and devotion. ("A Discourse on Dogma and Spirit; or the True Reviving of Religion: Delivered Before The Porter Rhetorical Society," in *God in Christ* [New York: Scribner, Armstrong & Co., 1877], pp. 332-33)

far from ideal; our contemporary situation is one of these. Furthermore, one way in which the church recovers its first love in worship and celebration is by catching the wonder and joy of those who are newly won to the faith. Reaching out to evangelize may be one way to rekindle a sense of joyous dependence on God. More important, the primary way back to a sense of amazement before God in worship is to retrieve that vision which helped bring the church into existence in the first place. In evangelizing, the church itself is reevangelized; by recovering the gospel of the kingdom and attending to the fundamentals of initiation the church is itself renewed at its foundations. So we have to start from where we are; necessity must be made into a virtue; the church should proceed in this area as she is, warts and all. Besides, God is ingenious enough to work through the church as she is; that is part of the significance of the coming of the kingdom when it was inaugurated initially.

The Place of Proclamation in Evangelism

A second principle worth pondering is that proclaiming the good news of the kingdom is foundational in evangelism. This stems from the very meaning of the gospel. The gospel is constituted by the mighty acts of God in history for the liberation of the cosmos. It is not a set of rickety arguments about the divine order; it is not the expression of some sublime religious experience brought mysteriously to verbal form; it is not a romantic report about awareness of God in nature; it is not a speculative, philosophical theory about the nature of ultimate reality; it is not a set of pious or moral maxims designed to straighten out the world; it is not a legalistic lament about the meanness of human nature; it is not a sentimental journey down memory lane into ancient history. It is the unique narrative of what God has done to inaugurate his kingdom in Jesus of Nazareth, crucified outside Jerusalem, risen from the dead, seated at the right hand of God, and now reigning eternally with the Father, through the activity of the Holy Spirit, in the church and in the world. Where this is not announced, it will not be known. Hence Paul says:

> For whosoever shall call upon the name of the Lord shall
> be saved. How then shall they call on him in whom they
> have not believed? And how shall they believe in him of
> whom they have not heard? And how shall they hear
> without a preacher? And how shall they preach, except
> they be sent? As it is written, How beautiful are the feet
> of them that preach the gospel of peace, and bring glad
> tidings of good things! (Rom. 10:13-15)

In announcing the good news, we need to abandon the
image of proclamation that is so prevalent in the modern Protestant tradition. That image, represented by the solid, tripartite
sermon, usually read from a manuscript, is a culturally relative
phenomenon. What matters is that the good news of the kingdom be transmitted with flair and in culturally fitting forms.
The announcement, furthermore, is to be heralded less in the
church and more in the marketplace and in the world at large.
Moreover, as the gospel is made known formally and informally, the activity of heralding will spill over into other acts of
speech. It will lead into basic instruction, into offering relevant
explanations, into dialogue and conversation, and into offering
a reason for the hope that is within one. It is artificial to limit
proclamation to formal acts alone or to some hygienic act of
preaching, fashioned according to some standard mode, although there is an obvious place for the well-planned, formal
heralding of the good news in appropriate public places.

In addition, the announcing or gossiping of the gospel
should include the invitation to respond in faith and repentance.
The kingdom proclaimed is a present reality, which we are to
enter like little children, open to owning its great joys, suffer-
ings, privileges, and responsibilities. This too needs to be made
known. Otherwise the announcement remains an abstract
"word on high" unrelated to the weal and woe of life in general.
The whole process, moreover, should be soaked in prayer and
sensitivity to the Holy Spirit. Both the word proclaimed and the
invitation to respond are staggering in their proportions and utterly incredible to most people who stop to think about them.
They need, therefore, not just the witness of the speaker as ex-

pressed in his or her sincerity and integrity, for that would be a weak reed to rely on; they need also the inward, mysterious, numinous witness of the Holy Spirit who alone can convict the world of sin, of righteousness, and of judgment. Theodore Stylianopoulos suggestively reminds us of this when he writes,

> the preacher must make up his mind about the Holy Spirit! Paul refers to his apostolic role as one in which he is "taught by the Spirit" so that he may understand God's gifts and proclaim them to others through spiritual, not human, wisdom (1 Cor. 2.12-13). As the preacher identifies himself with the message of the Good News entrusted to him and opens himself constantly to Christ's burning word, he becomes the vehicle of the Spirit and mediates the Spirit's unutterable presence in the congregation. The preacher's deepest act of faith is a humble conviction that preaching is an instrument of the Holy Spirit, that the Lord acts through him, and that what he is doing makes a difference through God's grace.[4]

In taking the gospel to the world one must pay atttention to the context of the hearer, making a careful study of the social and personal circumstances of the hearer or hearers. At times it may require specialist information about the nature of modern cities, or the character of a rural community, or the relation of persons to established Christian communities, and the like. This is especially important when the gospel is taken across significant cultural and linguistic borders. It requires great sensitivity and dexterity to fulfill Paul's policy of being "all things to all men."[5] On the one side, the evangelist must proclaim the gospel with integrity and without compromise; on the other, he or she must be willing and able to meet people where they are, drawing them into the orbit of the kingdom, taking up all that is valid, true, and God-given in the native culture. The history of missionary activity over the last two centuries has made the modern church aware

4. Theodore Stylianopolous, *The Gospel of Christ* (Brookline, Mass.: Hellenic College Press, 1981), pp. 25-26.
5. A delicate treatment of this topic can be found in H. Chadwick, "'All Things to All Men' (1 Cor. ix.22)," *New Testament Studies* 1 (1954): 261-75.

of problems in this domain that earlier generations tended to dismiss as nonexistent or irrelevant. We need all the specialist help we can muster from the social sciences in dealing with the issues raised by cross-cultural evangelism.

Crucial in announcing the coming of the rule of God is the intention expressed in and through such proclamation. As we have developed our definition, proclamation is evangelism only insofar as it is governed by the intention to initiate the hearer into the reign of God—it is not evangelism in itself. This has vital consequences for the tone and character of proclamation. Most contemporary evangelistic preaching is unrelated to the intention to initiate people into the kingdom of God. The intention can be many things: to make people feel bad about themselves, to foster people's self-esteem, to get them to make a decision and come to the altar, or to make them feel favorably disposed to the preacher. Sometimes it is to garner as large a collection as possible or to swell the membership of the congregation; at other times it is an expression of anger, envy, pride, jealousy, and even hatred.

Particular care must be taken to avoid falling into intentions that are fundamentally political and nationalistic in character. Much evangelistic proclamation in the West is tied to attempts to ward off barbarism, to fight communism, and to foster the manifest destiny of North America. Even such an alert theologian as Horace Bushnell was unable to withstand temptation of this kind. Consider his impassioned plea for the support of the evangelistic endeavors of the mission societies that were founded to work on the Western frontier:

> To save this mighty nation; to make it the leading power on earth; to present to mankind the spectacle of a nation stretching from ocean to ocean, across this broad continent; a nation of free men, self-governed, governed by simple law, without soldiers or police; a nation of a hundred millions of people, covering the sea with their fleets, the land with cities, roads and harvests; first in learning and art, and all the fruits of genius, and, what is highest and best of all, a religious nation, blooming in all the Chris-

> tian virtues; the protector of the poor; the scourge of oppression; the dispenser of light, and the symbol to mankind of the ennobling genial power of righteous laws, and a simple Christian faith—this is the charge God lays upon us, this we accept and this, by God's blessing, we mean to perform, with a spirit worthy of its magnitude.[6]

Evangelism for Bushnell was fundamentally a prop to save people from barbarism and an instrument for founding a nation.

In the short term this kind of plea will always be popular among certain groups of Christians, but ultimately it is corrupting. It makes the gospel of the kingdom a means to an end; it cuts proclamation loose from Christian initiation; it makes Christianity an adjunct to a nationalistic ideology that undercuts the transcendence of the kingdom; and it impedes the transformation of culture and politics that the coming of the kingdom should inspire. The only real antidote to this is to insist that proclamation be carried out with the express intention to initiate people into the reign of God. Every other intention should be set aside as sub-Christian and inadequate.

The Need for the Catechumenate

A third principle in the ministry of evangelism is that proclamation must be intimately linked to the grounding of people in the kingdom of God. We shall see shortly that proclamation will in fact be carried over into the actual process of initiation, but this requires that we specify more carefully what we have in mind regarding the concrete particulars of initiation. In essence, what I am suggesting is that the church needs to reinstate the institution of the catechumenate.[7] We need a specific, official, public institution that will ensure that the various dimensions

6. Horace Bushnell, *Barbarism the First Danger: A Discourse for Home Missions* (New York: The American Home Missionary Society, 1847), p. 29.

7. My proposal parallels the move made in recent years within the Roman Catholic Church to reinstate the catechumenate. See, e.g., Patricia Barbernitz, *RCIA: The Rite of Christian Initiation of Adults, What it Is and How it Works* (Ligouri, Mo.: Ligouri Publications, 1983). The Catholic proposal differs in two crucial respects. First, it works out of a primary context that is ecclesiological rather

of initiation we identified earlier are encountered by those who enter into the rule of God.

The precise logistics of this can be worked out in the actual practice of evangelism. It is sufficient here to explain the general character of any specific proposal regarding the catechumenate. First, what matters in the process of initiation is completeness and balance rather than chronological order. Since the six dimensions of initiation are intimately related to one another, it is very difficult to deal with one without reference to the others. Yet all six need to be covered at some point or other; if any are omitted there will be a corresponding price to pay. If we attend only to the experiential dimension, the result will be sickly sentimentalism; we shall have a religion of heat without light, of zeal without knowledge. If we attend only to the commandment to love, the result will be an austere moralism; we shall have a religion of duty without power and joy, of self-righteousness without humility. If we attend only to the creed, the result will be dead orthodoxy; we shall have a religion of light without heat, of knowledge devoid of love and zeal. If we attend only to the gifts of the Holy Spirit, the result will be a frantic activism; we shall have a religion of pentecostal fire without moral content, of pragmatism without intelligent direction. If we attend only to baptism, eucharist, and the spiritual disciplines, the result will be hard ritualism; we shall have a religion of external rite without evangelistic passion, of rigid form without a warm heart. And if we attend to all of these without setting them firmly in the context of the kingdom of God, we shall have only a humanistic religion unrelated to the great sweep of God's action in history for the renewal of creation. All six of the dimensions of initiation must be catered to in the concrete process of initiation.

---

than eschatological. Second, it involves a less comprehensive vision of initiation. Two important historical studies in the literature of initiation in the patristic period are: Edward Yarnold, *The Awe-Inspiring Rites of Initiation: Baptismal Homilies of the Fourth Century* (Slough: St. Paul Publications, 1971); and Hugh M. Riley, *Christian Initiation* (Washington, D.C.: The Catholic University Press of America, 1974).

Of secondary importance is the order in which we deal with each of these. Consider, for example, the place of baptism in the process of initiation. Should baptism take place in infancy or should it be postponed until the child is aware of what is happening? Arguments of a cogent nature have been marshaled on both sides. What is important in the present context is that both alternatives have advantages and disadvantages. If we take the second option and insist on believers' baptism, then it is likely that the experiential dimensions of conversion will be given thorough consideration in the total process of initiation. However, those who hold this view tend to treat infants and children as little pagans who are partially locked out of the household of faith until they have sinned enough to repent and have faith.[8] If we take the former option and insist on infant baptism, then it is likely that the communal dimensions of initiation will be given thorough consideration. Yet this view tends to shun and treat suspiciously the experiential side. My own preference on balance would be to have an immediate rite of entry into the church in infancy, expressed in baptism and admission to the eucharist. This would then be followed at an appropriate time with a period of intense catechesis dealing with the creed and the fundamentals of the Christian moral tradition. Alongside this there would be a series of retreats and workshops dealing with one's personal relationship with God, with the operations of the Holy Spirit in the ministry of the church, and with the fundamental features of prayer, Scripture study, and fasting. This would be brought to a climactic conclusion with a covenant service in which the eucharist would be celebrated and in which there would be the laying on of hands signifying the setting apart of the candidate for Christian ministry

8. Bushnell makes the point nicely:

There could not be a worse or more baleful implication given to a child, than that he is to reject God and all holy principle, till he has come to a mature age. . . . Wherein would it be less incongruous for you to teach your child that he is to lie and steal, and go the whole round of vices, and then, after he comes to mature age, reform his conduct by the rules of virtue? (*Christian Nurture* [New Haven: Yale University Press, 1888], pp. 8-9)

and the invocation of the Holy Spirit to empower and equip for such service. Adults entering the Christian community would join in much the same process as those baptized in infancy; after appropriate baptismal and eucharistic instruction, they would be baptized and admitted to the eucharist; they would then enter into the same catechesis and experiences as those baptized in infancy.

It is very important that we not reduce this process to a purely intellectual operation. The rich ceremonial treasures and symbolism of the church should be used to the full. If need be, we should develop new rites or retrieve and adapt old ones. Local circumstances may require unique local practices or unique features of more general practices. Careful attention should be given to the use of appropriate hymns; some of these should become a fixed feature of the process. Churches should find space for the ministry of a spiritual director, although it is crucial that this should not become a mechanical affair; decisions on this matter should be taken only after prayer and consultation. It might be appropriate to appoint sponsors from within the church to encourage and support those entering the kingdom. The whole process of initiation should be conducted in a spirit of firmness and celebration; to this end it should be steeped in prayer—if need be, enlisting the support of a group of saints who would covenant to pray for the constant presence of the Holy Spirit in the activities related to initiation.

In initiation the kingdom will be announced afresh. This will happen in two ways. First, it will be essential to repeat the good news of the gospel in order to foster an accurate understanding of the whole process of initiation. Christian initiation is first and foremost initiation into the kingdom of God; hence there needs to be a clear grasp of what the kingdom is and how it has been inaugurated in the life, death, and resurrection of Jesus of Nazareth. This good news must be repeated again and again in the acts of initiation to ensure that they are placed in their appropriate context. Second, the actual dimensions of initiation require reference back to God's action in inaugurating his rule if they are to be explicated adequately. For example, the creed is hopelessly misunderstood if it is presented as an ahistorical set of doctrines rather than as the fundamental working through on a theological and intellectual level of the consequences of the inauguration of the kingdom of God. Likewise, conversion, or the new birth, will be distorted if it is not seen as a helpful way of signaling the consequences for the individual of the dawning of the new age. Hence the various phases, rites, and particulars of initiation furnish a fresh opportunity for the sharing of the gospel of the kingdom of God. Moreover, proclamation and the act of initiation are held together in unity; both of them are elements of evangelism; the one illuminates the other.

It may take time for the local church to accept this kind of process. This is a matter for prudent judgment. Actually, various elements of initiation are currently in place in most local churches. Confirmation classes, membership classes, regular Sunday school classes, covenant groups, weekend retreats, and the like all perform some of the functions identified in our account of initiation. Thus, it would not be a radical step to incorporate these into a comprehensive approach to initiation. It is vital, however, that we avoid a juridical cast of mind when reinstituting the catechumenate or in establishing it for the first time. No good is served by laying down the law and insisting on some strict set of procedures. This is liable to engender a spirit of arrogance or alienation on the part of the potential candidates, depending on whether they are for or against it. Yet the process of initiation does need to have precise boundaries. It must have a clear beginning and ending and a solid content, and those who refuse to own the full privileges and responsibilities of the kingdom of God must be confronted with the implications of their choices. The church must be prepared at times to say No to those who deliberately reject the path of discipleship. Pastors and priests will need to be wise as serpents and innocent as doves as they meet their responsibilities in this domain.

Initiation itself is no absolute guarantee of sanctity or of entry into the kingdom of God. In these matters judgment remains forever in the hands of God. The church will always be a mixed body of saints and sinners; there is no need to pretend otherwise. Yet the church has a duty to lead the candidate for its membership into a full encounter with the dawning of the rule of God. When it refuses to do this, it ultimately erodes and loses its profound and rich heritage of reflection, spiritual experience, and action. Much of Western Christianity is in a perilous state because of a deep neglect of the full contours of initiation. In addition, those seeking to enter the kingdom of God deserve more than superficial and perfunctory initiation from that community which seeks to embody the rule of God in history. They deserve to receive the full riches of the gospel of Jesus Christ. Whether or not those churches that take this route will grow is a matter of opinion at present. If we can rely on history, then the prospects are far from bleak. Both the early church and early Methodism grew beyond all expectations, despite (or perhaps because of) the fact that they took initiation with the kind of seriousness that I am recommending here. We can leave such matters in the hands of God. Our task is to be faithful to the full implications of the dawning of the reign of God.

The Urgency of the Evangelistic Mandate

A further factor we must bear in mind is that the coming of the kingdom is ultimately God's affair, and we can be sure that God is more committed to it than we are. It is a sad feature of the church's life that commitment to evangelism is often a sporadic and half-hearted affair. Some churches with fine ecclesiastical pedigrees are embarrassed by evangelism. Sometimes this is entirely understandable, for much that passes for evangelism is a scandal. Yet the issue cuts much deeper. A church can easily invest all its energies in institutional maintenance, or in social and moral programs, or in educational projects. In time it can lose all interest in evangelism; it can forget how evangelism used to be done in its own tradition; it can refuse to explore how it might usefully be carried on in the present; it can develop a distaste for this vital ministry of the gospel; and it can set itself to ridicule those who press for its rightful place in the economy of the church's actions. Again and again evangelism

has been driven to an underground group or even driven outside the church to a new movement or ecclesiastical body. When
this happens it is a tragedy for all concerned. The church is then
no longer apostolic, for it has ceased to repeat the works of the
apostles. Those driven underground or driven out are cut off
from the full life of faith, and they invariably end up reinventing
the wheels of ancient ecclesiology or falling into superficial conceptions of faith or into outright nonsense and heresy. In the
meantime the world fails to be encountered by the full signs of
the coming kingdom of God.

This is not a new problem in the Israel of God. The prophet
Ezekiel addressed the issue in an indictment of the shepherds
and sheep of his day that has burning relevance to our contemporary circumstances. The heart of Ezekiel's denunciation of the
shepherds of Israel was that they had settled into an institutional pattern of maintenance that catered to their own interests. They neglected the basic work of caring for the sheep. Essential to caring for the sheep was the seeking out and finding
of those that had been scattered and lost; yet the shepherds of
Israel had failed to do this. Consequently, God was going to remove the sheep from their care; God was going to see to it that
they were given proper pasture and feeding. Especially vivid is
Ezekiel's indictment of the sheep who had aided and abetted
the shepherds in their neglect.

> As for you, my flock, thus says the Lord God: Behold, I
> judge between sheep and sheep, rams and he-goats. Is it
> not enough for you to feed on the good pasture, that you
> must tread down with your feet the rest of the pasture;
> and to drink of clear water, that you must foul the rest
> with your feet? And must my sheep eat what you have
> trodden with your feet, and drink what you have fouled
> with your feet?
>
> Therefore, thus says the Lord God to them: Behold, I, I
> myself will judge between the fat sheep and the lean
> sheep. Because you push with side and shoulder, and
> thrust at all the weak with your horns, till you have scat-
> tered them abroad, I will save my flock, they shall no
> longer be a prey; and I will judge between sheep and

sheep. And I will set over them one shepherd, my servant David, and he shall feed them: he shall feed them and be their shepherd. And I, the Lord, will be their God, and my servant David shall be prince among them: I, the Lord, have spoken. (Ezek. 34:17-24)

It is not fanciful to apply this prophecy to the history of the church in the field of evangelism. The general picture that emerges of most of the mainline churches in the Western democracies is one of a church that has lost any deep interest in the finding and healing of the sheep and that settles instead for a ministry focusing exclusively on social action or on maintenance or on social aggrandizement. In such circumstances God may set aside these institutions as agents of evangelism and raise up others that will heed his will in this area. Many of those chosen are far from perfect or complete, for God works through whomever he can find to go among the poor and the dispossessed; fortunately, God does not ask anyone's permission as to how and where he will act, and the very stones will cry out if none can be found to share in this work. In short, God is irrevocably committed to achieving his purposes for creation, and he is ingenious enough to find some way to gather the sheep into his kingdom.

The Place of Evangelism in the Life of the Church

We are now in a position to address the question of the place of evangelism in the life of the church as a whole. If we understand the ministry of evangelism along the lines laid out above, should it be a primary or secondary activity in the comprehensive ministry of the church? Is it on a par with activity such as Christian education, social action, acts of healing, and the like? This issue is important, for many still see evangelism as in competition with other activities, such as social action. I have two things to say in response. First, evangelism, like all else the church does in her ministry, is a subordinate activity. Second, evangelism has a unique relation to everything else that the church does, which at once makes it more important and less important than the church's other ministries depending on the angle of vision adopted.

Evangelism cannot be the primary activity and preoccupation of the church as if everything revolved around it like the earth revolves around the sun. This coveted position belongs to the kingdom of God. The kingdom of God must be the primary, unconditional priority of the church, which exists in and for the coming of the rule of God in history. Only as she exists in and for that kingdom is she authentic and valid. Evangelism is important only because the kingdom is important; it is subordinate to the kingdom. Only because evangelism involves initiating people into the kingdom of God does it deserve our attention, our allegiance, and our very best endeavors. And only as we keep evangelism utterly subordinate to the dynamic rule of God are we liberated to participate in it with appropriate joy and confidence. To make evangelism the primary concern of the church is to give it a misplaced and exaggerated position in our lives. The first task of the church is to worship: to bow down before the Lord of glory, to celebrate God's love and majesty, and to invite God to rule over the length and breadth of all creation.

We should pause at this point to note that we can understand and sympathize with those who want to make evangelism the primary concern of the church. Evangelism is hard work; it is difficult to keep Christians motivated in this area; it repeatedly falls into disfavor so that prophets have to arise and call the church back to the task. It is only reasonable, therefore, that in frustration and eagerness some should seek to foster its significance by insisting that it be absolutely primary. In the long run, however, the consequences of this course will catch up with us. It will lead to an unhealthy situation where worship will be utilitarian, where converts will be anemic and unbalanced, and where the sheep will look up and not be fed. History shows that a church that focuses exclusively on evangelism will either breed a reaction where evangelism falls into abject neglect, or it will operate as a doorway to other ecclesiastical bodies. Hence we must resist the temptation to overreact to past mistakes and make evangelism the primary task of the church.

That task is to open itself in joyful obedience to God, to wait quietly before God, and let God's rule come in all its fullness this side of eternity. Evangelism, like all else the church does, must be secondary to that primary task.

Moreover, evangelism enjoys a unique relation to the other ministries of the church, such as social action, acts of healing, educational activity, and the like. It is not just one ministry alongside others; these latter ministries are all dependent on the ministry of evangelism. If there were no evangelism, there would be no intentional agents of the kingdom, and without agents of the kingdom there are no ministries of the church. Evangelism, therefore, is essential if there are to be ministries such as social action. If there is no evangelism, there will be no church; if there is no church, there will be no ministries of the church; and if there are no ministries of the church, there will be no social action. From this perspective evangelism is more important than anything else the church does in other areas.

The relation is not, however, reciprocal or symmetrical. There can be a ministry of social action without that having to lead to evangelism. The poor, for example, can be fed, housed, healed, and educated in the name of Christ; and this can legitimately and properly be done without any intention to initiate them into the kingdom of God. Such social action should be done because of its intrinsic nature and out of love for the neighbor. By contrast, one cannot initiate people into the kingdom of God without entrusting to them the commandment to love the neighbor, which cannot be expressed fully without ultimately engaging in works of mercy and love.

Another way to make this point is to say that one of the goals of evangelism is to establish agents of the kingdom who are irrevocably committed to doing the works of the kingdom. Insofar as these works involve social action, evangelism must lead to social action. Evangelism and social action would then be causally and conceptually related. The reverse does not hold. Social action can stand on its own feet without leading to evangelism; it is done out of love for the neighbor and not as a mechanism for enticing people into the kingdom of God. Evangelism, by contrast, is incomplete if it does not lead to the creation of agents of the kingdom who, in appropriate circumstances, express their love for the neighbor through social action.

From this angle of vision evangelism is subordinate to social action. It is like a means to an end. Just as the point of boot camp is to break in the new recruit and initiate him or her into the art of soldiering, so the point of evangelism is to break in the new convert and initiate him or her into the art of being an agent of the rule of God. Just as the point of a door or a porch is to lead people into the building of which they are a part, so the point of evangelism is to lead people into an edifice of works of love and mercy. Boot camp cannot be put on the same level as soldiering; doors and porches cannot be put on the same level as houses; evangelism cannot be put on the same level as the works of the kingdom of God. We can turn this around, too. Without boot camps and recruiting officers there would be no armies to liberate the oppressed; without doors and porches, there would be no houses or buildings worthy of occupation; without evangelism there would be no community that lives in and for the kingdom of God.

So evangelism is essential; it is an enduring obligation of the church in every culture and every generation; yet it exists only to gather, to establish, and to ground people in a kingdom marked by acts of love and mercy. There is, then, no necessary conflict between evangelism and other ministries of the church, especially if we relate evangelism to initiation into God's reign of justice and mercy.

Evangelism and Modernity

Not all students of evangelism will welcome the kind of robust, classical expression of the gospel that I have adopted heretofore as the best way forward in evangelism. Some, for example, will question the general content of the theology embraced. Others might agree with the general direction and challenge specific details. In either case there will be plenty of room for disagreement on the various theological elements that are brought together to underwrite my central suggestions. Thus, one could very legitimately challenge the way in which I have assembled and brought together, for example, the eschatological, ecclesiological, and pneumatological considerations. I welcome this challenge. We need a thorough conversation on these issues and their relation to evangelism. Clearly, much remains to be done to articulate and defend the data and warrants I have deployed at key points in my analysis. It would be pretentious to claim that I have done anything more than lay out the basic contours of a particular vision of evangelism in an exploratory fashion.

It is in order, however, to go one step further and respond to two fundamental concerns that the alert student of evangelism will have naturally voiced long before now. The first is whether my whole approach to evangelism is viable in the wake of modernity. The second is whether it can be sustained in the light of the wider ecumenism that is currently underway between the great religious traditions of the world. In the next two chapters I shall address both these concerns. As might be expected, I shall argue that neither modernity nor the wider ecumenism should inhibit our commitment to evangelism as I have described it.

The Concept of Modernity

It is important that we begin with a clear understanding of what we mean by modernity. This is not a temporal concept; if it were, we would not need to deal with the issue at all, for my proposals are modern in the sense that they are written in the twentieth century, and not, for example, in the thirteenth century. This is not what is commonly meant by modernity. Rather, the concept is a normative or persuasive one. It is usually deployed to distinguish certain features of the temporally modern world that have a status or privilege not shared by other features, which are construed as ancient, or traditional, or premodern, and the like.

Consider John Shelby Spong's comment in this regard:

> Evangelism is an intriguing word. It captures in its nuances the battle that is being waged between those whose minds are basically premodern in their thought form and those whose minds are postmodern. To look at this word helps us to examine the emerging new consciousness that will finally deliver us from regional and provincial thinking, which is a necessary transition before we can embrace the frontiers of the world where tribalism is now dying. If one cannot move out of a local and provincial mindset, the wider questions will never be raised.[1]

Clearly much hangs for Spong on the words *premodern* and *postmodern*. They open up for him two fundamental ways of approaching evangelism. The one is traditional in its thought forms, as well as regional, provincial, local, and tribal. The other is open to the new consciousness, as well as liberating, universal, and inclusive. It is not difficult to expand the list of adjec-

---

1. John Shelby Spong, "Evangelism and Mission Strategy in a Posttribal World," in *Into the Whirlwind: The Future of the Church* (Minneapolis: Seabury, 1983), p. 160.

tives. One approach to evangelism is closed, plodding, propositional, simplistic, barren, static, dogmatic, superior, absolute, derivative, metaphysical, mechanical, traditional, imperialistic, manipulative, dishonest, and exclusivist. The other is vulnerable, creative, poetic, subtle, fertile, dynamic, insightful, humble, relative, original, intuitive, imaginative, new, sensitive, loving, honest, and pluralist. One is delivered from a cistern of authoritarian dogmas; the other is birthed in a fountain of fresh insights. One is hurriedly taken from the microwave; the other is carefully cooked from a well-stocked larder.

The concept of modernity, as Spong uses it and I have extended it, is not just normative; it is loaded in a particular direction. It is used to outlaw as immoral, insensitive, and un-Christian a carefully crafted stereotype of evangelism. With this in place it is then easy to gain acceptance for a rival account with a minimum of argument.[2] Clearly, we need to walk warily when we deal with the concept of modernity; it can be unpacked in several radically different directions. Two main possibilities come quickly to the fore.

One usage of the term is sociological in nature. For some, to say that we live in the modern world is to claim that the West has seen the gradual erosion of the influence of religion on the central institutions, activities, and consciousness of society. Religion has been privatized and relegated to the fringe of the public arena. The evidence for this is cumulative and, as David Martin summarizes one prevailing account, is documented in the facts

> that ecclesiastics less and less play a political role, that political parties are less and less organised around Christian labels and norms; that fewer resources are dedicated to religious purposes and buildings; that the intellectual writ of priests has ceased to run; that law, social control and economic activity pay little deference to religious institutions and concepts; that social legitimation no longer requires a divine accolade, vox populi, vox Dei; that ed-

2. It is perhaps too generous to suggest that Spong offers a rival account, but it would be a distraction to decide that issue here.

ucation is increasingly a state responsibility, without doctrinal content.[3]

Behind this process of secularization lies a rich network of change. Western society has become so complex that it has become customary to differentiate between various spheres of activity. Science and technology have become more and more predominant. The fundamental ethos of society at large is now generally directed to working out means-ends relationships; hence it has become increasingly impersonal in orientation. Religion, no longer the center of life, has been driven to the margins; values are utilitarian in character or are seen as subjective in nature, and they are systematically cut loose from religious concepts and themes. In such circumstances the chances are very slim for a religion of a classical nature to flourish. At best it will remain as a leisure activity chosen by the select few on subjective grounds. Moreover, the pattern of decline in religion manifested in Europe is likely to spread eventually to the rest of the world.

A second conception of modernity is intellectual in character. In this case to live in the modern world is to adopt a set of philosophical assumptions, assumptions that render obsolete any kind of classical vision of evangelism. The crucial element in this vision is the development of the natural sciences and their application initially to particular religious doctrines and then to the whole field of religion in general. At first the issue was joined with the shift to a Copernican view of the universe; at this stage the doctrine of creation had to be jettisoned and reworked. Then historical criticism appeared and called into question not just the reading of this or that text of Scripture but the whole conception of divine agency, which was tied up with the inspiration of the Bible and the prevailing attitude toward the person of Jesus Christ recorded in the classical creeds. This was accompanied by Darwin's revolutionary account of the origin of human beings; subsequently the

3. David Martin, "The Secularisation Thesis and the Decline of Particular Religions," forthcoming. Martin is a persistent critic of the prevailing account of secularization.

doctrine of the fall and related notions of sin were untenable. Meanwhile, with the development of the new sciences of psychology and sociology, particular religions were viewed as entirely natural phenomena that could be accounted for on the basis of the standard type of causal explanations that were so successful in the natural sciences.

These developments have had a profound impact on Christian theology. Our interest with them here is their impact on evangelism. What effect have these conceptions of modernity had on evangelism? Since the matter is tangled and complicated, there is no agreed answer to this question.

One plausible way to read the impact of modernity on evangelism is to interpret it as eroding the commitment to evangelism so that it has withered and died in many quarters. Taking modernity as a change in the intellectual map of the West, the process of erosion has proceeded both directly and indirectly. Directly it has undermined the kind of basic theological agenda out of which evangelism most naturally arises. It rendered obsolete the supernaturalism behind classical thinking about evangelism by calling into question the doctrines of sin, of Christ, of the work of the Holy Spirit, and the like, which had been assumed in the proclamation of the gospel and the initiation of people into the church. To be sure, not everyone committed to evangelism faced the full impact of this. Some attempted to marry evangelism to a vision of the Christian faith that was built on personal religious experience, so it was possible for a time to avoid the substantial implications of modernity.[4] This sounded good rhetorically, especially among preachers, but it did not really carry the day intellectually. The direct assault was ultimately devastating, for it has created a climate in which evangelism receives next to no critical attention.

Indirectly the impact of modernity had to do with the energy and resources of the modern theologian. So much attention was given to the redirecting and revising of the Christian tradition that little time was left for thinking through a new conception of evan-

---

4. See, e.g., Robert Ferguson, *The Meaning of Evangelism for Today: Our New Approach to the Old Task* (London: Holborn Publishing House, 1930).

gelism that would be serviceable in the modern world. This has, of course, been the case for centuries, for theologians find themselves spending so much time on prolegomena or on their doctrines of God, Christ, and the like that they have little time available to take up questions about the church's mission and ministry. It is noteworthy, in this respect, that Barth's theology did not lead to the revitalization of evangelism despite the fact that it radically altered the theological landscape across the globe. Perhaps some Barthians will yet explore the richness of Barth's theology for the ministry of the church and for evangelism, but only time will tell whether there shall be fruit in this domain.

Modernity as a sociological phenomenon aided and abetted in this process. Once laid hold of by theologians, it heightened the sense that the gospel as traditionally conceived was meaningless. It provoked a deep alienation from the life of the church, and it fostered a sense of radical anxiety about the future of Christianity in the world. This took various and curious forms. On the one hand, it provoked a despondency about the church's faith that bordered at times on a collapse of nerve and a refusal to work through the issues. On the other hand, the decline of Christianity or of Christendom has been greeted with great excitement, for it posed a crisis that called for the restructuring of religious life and thought along entirely new and radical lines. Either way evangelism has not been taken very seriously.

It is arguable, of course, that the quest for a new expression of the Christian faith was itself inspired in an indirect way by the evangelistic thrust of Protestantism in its classical expressions. From this perspective, Bultmann's proposals on demythologizing are at once remarkably evangelistic and remarkably conservative. They have a pivotal place for preaching in the ministry of the church; they embody a direct encounter with God in the hearing of the kerygma; they express in a radical way Luther's doctrine of justification by faith, a theme endemic to Protestant forms of evangelism; and, above all, they represent a quest for a conceptuality that will speak to modern human beings without sacrificing either the scandal of the cross or the life of the mind. Moreover, it was common in this period of revision to appeal to the diversity of the theologies of the New

Testament as a warrant for casting the gospel in terms intelligible to the modern person. Hence it was possible to combine a deep commitment to critical work in biblical studies with an intense longing to reach out with the gospel to the modern world. It is rare, however, to find all this translated into terms that made contact with the ministry of evangelism. It is doubtful even if there were any promissory notes about how it might be worked out in detail.

Secular Evangelism

A fascinating exception to this general trend can be found in the proposals of Fred Brown, an officer in the Salvation Army in London.[5] Brown makes no claim to being either a biblical scholar or a theologian, but his views deserve to be taken with the utmost sympathy not only because they represent one of the very few attempts to grapple with the problem of modernity in relation to evangelism but also because they represent a profound *crie de coeur* from someone who had given his life to the ministry of evangelism.

Brown's diagnosis of the problems of and solutions to modern evangelism in a secular world operate at several levels. At one level he is deeply uneasy with traditional ways of thinking about evangelism: the language is archaic; the approach to the outsider is superior and condescending; there is too much chronic introspection; the focus is too much on converts rather than on people; Christian caring is treated as an evangelical tactic; there is no real identification with people in their needs; God is depicted as a vindictive bully; there is no room for the action of grace outside the channels of dogmatic orthodoxy; the spirituality to which the convert is introduced is narrow and restrictive; and little attention is given to the importance of community. This is familiar territory, and Brown's indictment of much traditional evangelism is close to the standard, informal orthodoxy on the subject in most theological circles.

The solution to the ills of evangelism that Brown offers is

5. Fred Brown, *Secular Evangelism* (London: SCM, 1970).

clear. The way forward is to be found in the development of a new Christian community that is tolerant in character, open to new ideas, and integrated into existing structures. In this new community, for example, there would be no common program of worship. Small groups within the community would be free to experiment as they desired with the full support of the whole community. The result would be a blend of traditional activities and new alternatives.

> The Christian community I have in mind will allow its members to work out their affinities within the smaller groups; it will foster relationships of loving mutuality, and by its very nature, the nature of its basic evaluations and aims, widen the possibility of personal fulfilment; its activities, many of them apparently secular and beyond the usual interest of church organization, will serve creative ends and thereby clarify the essential requirements of fulfilment; it will provide traditional forms of worship without making them obligatory, and welcome new expressions of worship without imposing them on all and sundry. Its spirit of tolerance will be tested as experiments are shared in the overlap.[6]

Crucial to the creation of this new community is the realization that worship is not confined to church buildings. Reality can be found outside the church. Indeed, this is precisely what the younger generation of secularists have discovered. They do not, of course, use religious language to describe their encounter with God, but God is there nevertheless. This generation has encountered the divine reality in their quest for a just community, in their compassion, in their zest for living, in their search for love, peace, responsibility, and truth, in their rejection of materialism, and the like. As a result, there is more Christianity in Britain than ever before. Observers miss this point because they forget that God is already at work in the world. As Harvey Cox has explained it, our task is to discern where God is working in the world and then join enthusiastically in that

6. Ibid., p. 112.

work. Drawing on the great diversity of gifts within the community, Christians in their local situations should do two things. First, they should step out and get involved in their local contexts to meet the needs that they, aided by relevant professionals, have identified. Second, they should become a Christian presence in small cells at the grass roots of community life.

One should not give too much attention to creedal commitments in this process, according to Brown. Certainly there is no hope of reaching the modern secular person if acceptance of the orthodox creeds is made a condition of being religious. This is asking the impossible, for it will mean a sacrifice of intellectual integrity, or it will involve the kind of absolute commitment that the secular person is either not ready or not willing to make. Yet we cannot reject the modern secular person as a pagan. Rather, we need to see that Christian belief is sometimes confirmed and clarified by Christian action. Thus, the church should invite such people to become unconscious "doers of the word" and to move in the direction of practical Christian service. The creed can take care of itself in the light of experience. This, to be sure, requires a spirit of adventure on the part of the church, but such an attitude should be embraced in faith. The church needs to meet the secular person where he or she is, and be fully prepared to learn the truth that sets humankind free.

What are we to make of this account of evangelism? It would be very unwise to dismiss Brown's proposals summarily as a cheap accommodation to secularism. He is wrestling with some crucial issues in evangelism that have to be addressed. On one level he is attempting to find points of contact with a whole generation of people who find religious language unintelligible. Quite naturally he wants, therefore, to cut evangelism loose from the language of Zion and to find a vocabulary that will communicate to those who are alienated and distanced from the church. His strategy is to appeal to values embedded in the secular culture that parallel those he finds in the Christian gospel. Overall he is not too concerned to communicate a particular message; his tactic is to invite the secular person to join in the kind of social transformation that Brown believes is integral to the Christian faith. We should applaud both these moves.

Clearly, Christian discipleship has a moral structure that we need to identify and cultivate. Indeed, it would be astonishing if vestiges of the Christian moral tradition were not to be found in a culture that is itself deeply influenced by the Christian faith; thus, it would be insensitive and odd not to incorporate these into Christian commitment. Moreover, from the beginning Christians have been quite daring in their use of language. The way in which John's Gospel, for example, uses the language of eternal life rather than the language of the kingdom of God illustrates this admirably.[7] So one of the marks of the mature evangelist will be an ability to speak naturally in the language of those he or she is seeking to initiate into the reign of God.[8]

Furthermore, we should heartily welcome Brown's concern to cultivate a vibrant Christian community. In this respect he differs very markedly from others influenced by secularism who prefer to bypass the church entirely except insofar as the church is Christians in action, joining in the work of God in the world.[9]

---

7. G. R. Beasley-Murray nicely summarizes this issue in a comment on John 3:3:

> . . . it is surprising that the Evangelist has chosen to avoid the expression kingdom of God in the rest of his gospel. But the reality of the kingdom without the term dominates the Fourth Gospel. If the kingdom of God is God's sovereign action bringing judgement and salvation to man, as modern research believes, that characterizes the entire activity of the Son of God in this Gospel. And if the supreme gift of the divine sovereignty is acquittal in the judgement and life in the new age, that is exactly the theme of the discourse in chapter 3. Eternal life is not to be used as a synonym for the kingdom of God; it is rather the individual's existence under the divine sovereignty, with all that that entails of the blessings of divine grace in the new age. ("John 3:3, 5: Baptism, Spirit and the Kingdom," *The Expository Times* 97 [1986]: 168)

8. On the contemporary scene one of the challenges facing the evangelist is the use of the language of the kingdom in a situation where this is often perceived as oppressive, especially by women. This delicate matter cannot be resolved by a footnote or an aside in a few paragraphs. I hope to give this issue the attention it deserves on another occasion. Suffice it to say here that what matters is theological substance rather than verbal continuity or dexterity.

9. A good example of this can be found in the influential suggestions of J. C. Hoekendijk, in *The Church Inside Out* (Philadelphia: Westminster, 1966). Hoekendijk is keen to set evangelism in an eschatological context. For him this means that evangelism will involve kerygma, koinonia, and diakonia. Koinonia could provide room for an emphasis on community, but Hoekendijk is so con-

As we argued above, it is very difficult to see how Christians will be able to sustain the costly commitments that the gospel inaugurates without the nurture of a supportive social environment. This aspect of traditional forms of evangelism within Protestantism is greatly neglected, and Brown rightly excoriates it.

Yet Brown is asking for much more than a new theological language or for a greater acknowledgment of the work of God outside the church or for a deeper commitment to community. He is also looking for a whole new way of thinking about God's action in the world and a corresponding reconceiving of the evangelistic ministry of the church. At this level there is an important ambivalence in his suggestions. On the one hand, he desires to maintain a commitment to much of the traditional Christian message, at least for himself. On the other hand, he wants to treat most of the commitments of the secular saint as the equivalent of that language expressed in action. No comprehensive response to modernity can avoid this crucial issue. Brown highlights the dilemma of the modern evangelist in a very interesting way.

He knows that it is not possible to collapse the Christian faith into a fully materialist account of reality. He is, in fact, quite hostile to a throughly materialist view of the world.[10] Yet he does not want to dismiss the concerns of the secularist as irrelevant or immature. So he seeks to find a middle way between rejection and hostility, and he does this in part by extending the activity of God in two different directions at once. He sees God at work in the strivings of modern people seeking for community, authenticity, and the like. He also sees God at work in social transformations and in the meeting of human needs. By construing these as the equivalents of the work of God made manifest in Christ he is able to interpret those who participate

---

cerned to offset the danger of a return to Christendom that he does not pursue it in an ecclesiological direction.

10. Brown accuses the materialist of neglecting emotion and of insisting on an exclusively scientific approach to reality. This scarcely does justice to the intellectual attraction of modern materialism. See his comments in *Secular Evangelism*, p. 46.

in these strivings and goals as already Christian and, therefore, as no longer in need of the gospel as generally understood. As a result, the primary task of the evangelist is to extend the boundaries of the church to receive the secular person as a Christian. It is not, then, surprising that he does not discuss the place of proclamation in evangelism. He drops this from the agenda without a whisper. Nor is it surprising that he ends up by collapsing the Christian faith into a moralism defined by a commitment to authenticity, respect for individual choice, zest for community, active involvement to relieve the needs of the world, and the like.[11] Brown designates these as the heart of Christian commitment. Nor is it odd that he dismisses creeds as secondary, for they are accretions that are liable to get in the way of true commitment as Brown understands it.

Problems in Secular Evangelism

Articulating Brown's proposals in this fashion reveals some serious difficulties in the whole structure of his response to modernity. First, his position is inconsistent in that it trades on the classical tradition of the church while at the same time rejecting it. Brown needs this tradition, for without it he has no way of identifying God's action in the contemporary world. For Brown, Christ is clearly the touchstone of God's action in the world — the lens through which he discerns God's actions in history.[12] This is not, however, a self-supporting platitude; it rests on the classical conviction that in Christ God is uniquely at work in history. Yet it is exactly this language that the modern secularist finds meaningless and irrelevant. So Brown either jettisons it, or he turns it into a private preference for those inclined to use it for devotional purposes. Eventually one must choose between these two options: to abandon fully the classical position (but if this happens, talk of discerning God's action in the world loses

11. Formally, Brown wants to avoid falling into moralism but materially he does not fulfill his intentions in this regard.

12. There are other ways of articulating criteria for divine action in the world than relying on the paradigm supplied by the classical tradition, but Brown does not consider such an alternative.

its Christian character), or to take more seriously the classical position (but if this happens, then it can no longer be jettisoned or treated as a private preference, and the formal position concerning the creeds will have to be reworked).[13]

Second, Brown's suggestions contain a serious lack of realism. It is simply impossible to reconcile the Christian gospel with the modern world as conceived by Brown. This constitutes the crisis that his work quite correctly seeks to address. In our present situation a choice has to be made between several competing visions of the world, some secular and some theistic and Christian. Or, more accurately, we find ourselves believing in one vision of reality rather than another one. Brown himself expresses this when he rejects modern metaphysical materialism. He has no room for accommodation here. Yet he generally operates on a principle of accommodation. For example, he thinks that the Christian community and tradition should include those who reject basic Christian claims about God, human nature, Christ, the church, and so on, simply because the modern secularist cannot accept them. He resolves the resulting crisis by siding with the secularist and treating the great themes of the gospel as redundant or optional. There is an air of dishonesty here. At best it involves the pretense that those who have deliberately set themselves outside the Christian community are really some kind of anonymous Christian or hidden believer. At worst it involves a fundamental lack of respect for those who reject the Christian faith, for it refuses to take seriously their explicit commitments. In addition, it entails a cavalier attitude toward the great themes of the Christian heritage, for the Christian faith is much more than the modern moral platitudes Brown identifies. Any account of evangelism that confuses the two will be defective.

Third, Brown's account of community is inadequate. The crucial issue at stake here is how to identify the community he envisages. Obviously, a community is not just a list of names on a membership role; nor is it an organization formed to ful-

13. Brown could turn to a third alternative should he so desire, but he does not discuss any other options.

fill certain programs of social reform; nor is it a particular group that happens to occupy space in certain specified buildings on a Sunday morning; nor is it a gathering of people bonded together by certain feelings of belonging. A community is a group of people held together in a common history, sharing certain ideals, and formed by certain specific convictions about ultimate reality. All of these are missing from Brown's analysis. What we have is a rhetoric of inclusiveness, activism, and freedom without any substantial content. To be sure, there is more here than general goodwill, but it is difficult to see how the rudiments of a genuine community could be created and sustained over time. It might work for those already formed in certain ways, such as those brought up in a Christian environment, as is the case with many of the examples Brown cites as model participants. It is difficult, however, to see how such a community could be created from scratch. Brown simply creates it by extending the boundaries of the church to embrace those who share his strivings for spiritual reality and his moral commitments.

This leads very naturally into our final comment on Brown's position. In the end the most striking feature of his proposals is the extent to which they represent the manifestation of modernity within the church itself. We can see this in several areas. First, it is clear that the fundamental contours of Christian theism have been abandoned within the life of faith. Theism is taken no more seriously here than in politics, law, economic institutions, education, and the like. At best it is seen as a private option for those who need a source of personal motivation. At worst it is construed as a form of intellectual bondage that inhibits proper moral development. The general impression one receives is that Christian theism is an embarrassment. Second, the key values to be communicated are personal freedom, authenticity, human fulfillment, community, and supportive relationships—precisely the kind of values that one associates with secularism. They are the leftovers in the Western moral tradition when some version of utilitarianism has occupied the public arena. Individualism reigns supreme; community is lauded so long as it does little to interfere with personal freedom and the quest for creative authenticity. Finally, there is a thoroughly utilitarian attitude toward worship, piety, creeds, liturgy, and the like, which are guided by a technical rationality that evaluates them on the basis of how far they contribute to goals that are tangentially related to substantial theological themes or doctrines. In the light of these considerations one can conclude only that they represent a further manifestation of the problem of modernity in the field of evangelism rather than a solution to it.

In this respect Brown's proposals are much closer than he realizes to the traditionalism in evangelism that he repudiates. Traditionalists will, of course, be quick to applaud my criticism of Brown's position; they should walk warily as they do so, however, for one of the marked features of modern evangelism is precisely the extent to which it is deeply influenced by secularism. This goes unnoticed because on the surface modern evangelists set themselves forth as bastions of orthodoxy and as noisy assailants of modernity. We cannot take this self-description at its face value. Fundamentalism and modern evangelicalism, the appointed guardians of traditional evangelism, are unintelligible when they are separated from modernity in both its intellectual and sociological senses. Intellectually the theology behind most popular evangelism is a reaction against modern theology since Schleiermacher. It is very uneasy, for example, with the theory of evolution, and it is deeply opposed to historical criticism. In fact, it is deeply reactionary and defensive at heart. Its fundamental response to the modern world is to retreat to a slim and reduced outline of the Christian faith that focuses on biblical inspiration and miracles as the essential substance of the Christian tradition. These act as substitutes for the great classical heritage of the faith as enshrined in the Scriptures, creeds, and early tradition. In more recent years much of the focus has shifted to the servicing of the individual psyche with self-esteem and self-actualization, or to rescuing the family from the ravages of permissivism and from the effects of the modern quest for money and happiness, or to providing apocalyptic hope in the midst of international despair or of Middle Eastern wars.

Sociologically, modern evangelism is deeply infected by secularism. Decisions are generally made on a technical and pragmatic basis. There is a heavy emphasis on organization over against genuine community. Much attention and money is given to public relations, advertising, and commercial enterprises like tapes, records, and books. Evangelists offer friendship and love for sale through radio and television, and educational credentials are used as passwords into the lives of the gullible. The whole operation depends on a personality rather than on serious preaching. Ministry is reduced to messages and miracles transmitted through the airwaves on the latest technology from Japan. In all, modern evangelism has become a kind of entrepreneurial industry organized, funded, and run like a modern corporation.[14]

The Prospects for Authentic Evangelism

If my analysis is correct, the prospects for evangelism in the West may seem to be rather bleak. On the one side, modern culture appears to be deeply opposed to the intellectual content of the Christian gospel and tends to dismiss it as meaningless and irrelevant. On the other side, those who are most resolute in their championing of the cause of evangelism are liable to be reactionary or they have themselves succumbed to the acids of modernity. We seem to find ourselves in a profoundly pagan situation where the church itself needs to be evangelized before it can have much hope of evangelizing the modern world. Those mainline denominations that might have some of the theological resources to deal with the situation have only a superficial interest in evangelism.[15] Their intellectual leaders are

14. This description is deliberately overdrawn to make the point. What I have in mind is best instantiated in much modern television evangelism. A good analysis of this is provided in Razelle Frankl, *Televangelism: The Marketing of Popular Religion* (Carbondale: Southern Illinois University Press, 1987).

15. It would seem that every thirty years or so the cry goes up to take evangelism seriously, but little progress has been made. In this connection it is fascinating to read Charles B. Templeton, *Evangelism For Tomorrow* (New York: Harper and Brothers, 1957). Much of this book rings remarkably true thirty years later.

torn internally by disputes about sexism, race, modernity, institutional maintenance, and the vast social and political problems
that face them. At the same time, those committed to evangelism are cut off from the classical tradition of the church; they
are quick to take conservative political action when they have
the opportunity to do so; and, insofar as they are committed to
the life of the mind, they generally work with a reduced and
polemical version of the Christian gospel.

Of course, we can read the situation in other ways. Things
may not be as grim as they appear. It can be argued that there
is an ineradicable quest for spiritual reality in the human heart;
that modern human beings have not rejected religion since they
are still committed to civil religion,[16] or they have simply embraced alternatives to the faith that has shaped and given birth
to the modern world; that signs indicate that modernity in all its
forms has contributed to an impoverishment of the human spirit
rather than to its enlightenment and liberation;[17] that Christianity is spreading rapidly outside the West and that the predictions
that secularism will inevitably spread from Europe via North
America to the rest of the world are premature; that there is a
profound spiritual renewal of the Christian faith currently under
way in the Pentecostal and charismatic movements; and that
there is a deep renaissance of Christian belief in philosophical
circles.[18] All of these propositions can be argued persuasively.
They can also be contested all along the line.

The crucial point to be made about evangelism in this situation is essentially negative in character. Yet we should not
allow too much to hang on these propositions either way. The

16. Robert Bellah's essay on civil religion is a powerful statement to this
effect. See "Civil Religion in America," in his *Beyond Belief: Essays in a Post-
traditional World* (New York: Harper and Row, 1970), pp. 168-89.

17. Alexander Solzhenitsyn pursues this theme with characteristic power
in *Warning to the West* (New York: Farrar, Straus and Giroux, 1975), and in *A
World Split Apart* (New York: Harper and Row, 1978). Also significant is Alasdair
MacIntyre's *After Virtue: A Study in Moral Theory* (Notre Dame: University of
Notre Dame Press, 1981).

18. Keith Ward documents some of this in *The Turn of the Tide: Christian
Belief in Britain Today* (London: BBC, 1986). Philosophical circles in Britain and
North America have experienced a remarkable renaissance of Christian belief.

development of a healthy and robust ministry of evangelism does not depend on writing history before it has happened. Evangelism has never depended on a sunny analysis of the culture it is seeking to christianize; if that were the case, the West would never have been evangelized in the first place. The mature evangelist will be able to take a worst case scenario and set about the work with enthusiasm. This does not mean that the evangelist will be diffident about analyzing the current situation in the West or that he or she will eschew the development of an accurate map of modernity and of the prospects for evangelism in the light of it. Rather, the fundamental sources of inspiration do not rest on empirical or quasi-empirical accounts of the modern world. Hence there is no good reason why the evangelist should be intimidated by prophets of doom who argue that the prospects for evangelism are bleak in the extreme.

Theories of the state of modern culture will always be complex and contested. They trade on sophisticated bodies of analytical evidence that are difficult to collect and collate; they depend also to a great extent on metaphysical visions of human history and destiny that are thoroughly underdetermined by evidence.[19] A third conception of the contemporary world, which is currently gaining attention in theological circles, illustrates this. In this view, the concept of modernity should be read in a fundamentally political or sociopolitical fashion. To live in the modern world is to live in a world where the fundamental horizon of existence is oppression. The key issue is the distribution of power, and power is unfortunately restricted to certain groups, such as the owners of the means of production or a certain class, sex, or race. This has a determining ef-

19. This applies not just to the kinds of analysis mentioned above but also to those accounts that focus either on postmodernist, deconstructionist accounts of our current situation, or on liberationist themes that emphasize oppression, sexism, and racism. It is not sufficiently recognized that all of these depend on complex sociological and philosophical claims that invariably trade on metaphysical and epistemological premises that are very difficult to establish conclusively. It is easy to prevent radical examination of these proposals by retreating to an engaged standpoint or by working from a naively realist account of our social and intellectual world.

fect on every other aspect of culture—on its literature, religion, customs, mores, superstitions, and political ideologies. The exercise of power especially determines the system of beliefs that render intelligible the social order as a manifestation of the drama of human destiny. Such an analysis calls for an engaged intellectual commitment and evokes a spirit of radical criticism of the status quo and a thrust forward toward liberation as expressed in solidarity with the poor and the oppressed. Crucial to this is a hermeneutic of suspicion that unmasks the rhetoric of normality and probes beneath the surface of belief in order to expose the true forces at work in the world. Crucial also is a call to engagement and radical transformation. We face here a conception of modernity very different from the two encountered above, although it is always possible to blend all three into a single vision of the modern world.[20]

In the light of these shifts we ought to think and walk cautiously. Formally, there is a limit to the flexibility that the evangelist can exercise. If we move in one direction to accommodate one form of modernity we shall find ourselves at odds with another form. To say that we are to be all things to all people is a counsel of perfection; it is not a call to adjust the gospel to every wind of secular doctrine. Moreover, it is odd to approach the issue in this fashion, as if we were free to believe one thing about the gospel today and something else about it tomorrow on a purely voluntary basis. The gospel is not like a car that can be redesigned at will to suit the buyer, and the evangelist does not have the requisite personal control over his or her beliefs to provide the required realignments. What we can legitimately expect is that the mature evangelist be deeply informed by the convictions and sensibilities of those he or she is seeking to address in the name of the gospel, and that he or she be able to relate the faith in a realistic fashion to those convictions and sensibilities. There are no guarantees of success in this endeavor, for the

20. We should note also that there are those who see all talk of modernity as itself outdated for, it is said, we have now moved into a postmodernist era in which the old readings of the world are replaced by deconstructionist accounts that leave behind the austere canons of rationality associated with the hard sciences and even with modern sociology.

gospel itself, as the Word of God, stands in judgment over all secular ideologies. Some of these ideologies are not just false but intellectually and spiritually corrupting; where this is the case the word of the evangelist comes as one of searching judgment and examination. After all, we cannot always satisfy the intellectual or political Pharaohs and Pilates of this world.

More positively, we can insist that the evangelist can face the modern world in all its shapes and forms with integrity and equanimity. He or she can even begin from the premise that it is not irrational to read the contemporary scene as one that is deeply hostile to the Christian gospel,[21] so long as one bears the following general principles in mind.

First, the fundamental, determining factors in our thinking about evangelism do not rest on an analysis of the modern world but on the internal logic of the Christian gospel. It begins from the apostolic witness to the coming of the rule of God in Christ.[22] The events related to this signify that God has acted decisively for the liberation of the cosmos. If the modern world rejects this, it does not render inoperative God's action in salvation; it simply means that the rejection will be taken up into God's providential action in history. Nothing is gained, therefore, by some kind of bargain with the world that will offer it a reduced faith in return for assent and service. To adopt such a strategy ultimately makes Christianity a maidservant to modern culture. This is not the kingdom of God; nor can it become the kingdom by theological finesse. Evangelism is constituted by

21. This is the assumption behind Lesslie Newbigin's reflections on evangelism in the West in *Foolishness to the Greeks: The Gospel and Western Culture* (Grand Rapids: Eerdmans, 1986). See also Alfred Krass, *Evangelizing Neopagan North America: The Word that Frees* (Scottdale, Pa.: Herald Press, 1982).

22. Cf. Letty M. Russell:

There are many perspectives from which to approach our subject and each is colored by our own context, our own life story, and the ways in which we struggle together with others to live out the gospel message. The ultimate meaning of liberation or evangelization is not determined, however, by our perspective, be it feminist, black, Third World, or whatever. The meaning comes from the biblical story of what God is doing in bringing about the New Creation in Jesus Christ. ("Liberation and Evangelization—A Feminist Perspective," *Occasional Bulletin of Missionary Research* 2 [1978]: 128)

the coming of the rule of God—and if this means anything it means that the gospel is not at our disposal to manipulate so that we can coax the modern person into believing that the kingdom has come in Jesus of Nazareth or that he or she should take steps to become initiated into the Christian community.

Furthermore, a profound intellectual conversion constitutes entry into the kingdom of God. From the beginning the gospel has appeared as foolishness. Belief entails a spiritual appreciation for certain events in history that lie way beyond the plausibility structures of the modern mindset insofar as these structures rule out talk about the agency of human persons and of the supreme agent of all, the Lord God.[23] It engenders a comprehensive and searching understanding of oneself as a child of God who has fallen into sin and rebellion, and into corruption and self-delusion. It calls for a radical reversal of one's vision and values as evoked by a narrative of mercy and love that will forever appear astonishing and incredible. And it evokes a longing for fellowship and community that can be satisfied only by worship and adoration among the saints and martyrs. These beliefs cannot be packaged and marketed like soap and cornflakes. We should be astonished if they are embraced quickly without struggle and without intellectual sweat. Moreover, one can appreciate and accept them only in the light of divine grace, and their intellectual articulation and defense depend upon the restoration and redemption of reason itself.[24] The mature evan-

---

23. Whether it is plausible to believe that God is an agent who has acted in history is a philosophical and theological issue that we cannot pursue here. It is enough to claim that this is an entirely legitimate option for the contemporary Christian.

24. Consider in this respect a prayer used by John Wesley in his devotions on Wednesdays:

> O God, whose grace it is that mightily rescues our reason from the desperate rebellion of our passions; grant, we beseech thee, that the experience of the miserable effects of yielding to their allurements may make us warier in observing and severer in repressing their first motions; and let thy grace so strongly mortify us against all their assaults that reason may more and more recover its due force and calmly join with faith to secure and exalt in our hearts the blissful throne of thy love, through our Lord Jesus Christ, Thy Son, who liveth and reigneth with thee and the Holy Ghost, one God, blessed for ever.

gelist will not, therefore, be taken by surprise if what he or she proclaims is rejected as meaningless and irrelevant. What is needed is fortitude, patience, modesty, and a deep faith in the Holy Spirit. The gospel itself liberates us from bondage to reactionary and defensive attempts either to make the scandal of the kingdom acceptable or to erect fences to safeguard the unsearchable riches of Christ. The faithful evangelist is freed to live out of a context that is open to whatever the future may hold in the purposes of God. In the end the kingdom will come; in the meantime let us prepare the world to receive its Lord and Savior.

Within this preparation there will be a place for apologetics in evangelism. All sorts of intellectual issues need to be addressed. Misunderstandings and confusion need to be cleared up; points of contact should be established; the intellectual content of the gospel must be expressed clearly and concisely; past errors have to be acknowledged and due repentance performed; and nothing should be spared in the effort to give a reason for the hope that is within one. There are, in fact, considerable prospects for the renewal of an apologetics that would be of great service to the evangelist. Moreover, it is surely astonishing how many people in the West actually believe tattered elements of the Christian faith. So there is no need for despair and depression. Yet this avenue of communication has its limitations. It can easily put the gospel in a procrustean intellectual bed that does not permit the full mystery of the faith to be expressed and thus reduces the gospel to proportions that are cramped and restrictive.[25] More important, apologetics cannot act as a substitute for a deep personal encounter with the living God. Christian commitment to the kingdom is not fully or finally grounded on inferential considerations, nor is it evoked by simply clearing

25. This is often what happens when attempts have been made to establish the secular meaning of the gospel, or to demythologize its content in order to make it credible to so-called modern persons. The intention is entirely understandable from an evangelistic point of view, but the effect is usually counterproductive. The real test of this would be the requirement that such exercises be put to work in a pure form in local missionary situations where the classical content of the gospel is eliminated from the liturgy, prayer, teaching, and preaching.

obstacles in the way of belief; it depends in part on the internal witness of the Holy Spirit, on direct encounter with God in the inner person.[26] If this is ignored, the place of apologetics in evangelism is either corrupted or exaggerated.

Finally, if the modern situation is as bleak as many postulate, initiation in all its fullness is as crucial as I have described it above. There will be no advance against the acids of modernity if Christians simply proclaim the good news of the kingdom, or invite people to a personal decision, and leave it at that. To proceed in this fashion is both unworkable and cruel. It is unworkable because it does not equip the Christian to lay hold of the significance of the coming of the new age of God. It is cruel because it offers people light and hope in the midst of darkness and despair and then leaves them to continue their journey in the wastelands of superficial religion, greed, and idolatry. Extensive catechesis or instruction, incorporation into the body of Christ, the handing over of basic spiritual disciplines, participation in the works of the Holy Spirit—all these are minimum equipment to enable the convert to stand up to the ravages of the world. One suspects that Christianity has lost ground in the West precisely because it has neglected these matters for so long. It cannot hope to regain it if these continue to be neglected or if they are treated haphazardly in the work of evangelism. So an analysis of modernity reinforces the approach we have taken to evangelism on independent grounds.

Concluding Comment

When all is said and done, it is extremely important to avoid taking modernity too seriously. This is not a call to be insensitive or reactionary; nor is it an invitation to close one's ears and eyes to the oppression and bondage in which so many are enmeshed. There is much in the modern Western world that the

---

26. The witness of the Holy Spirit should not, of course, be confused with some particular pattern of spiritual experience. The Spirit blows where and how God wills, as the diverse phenomenology of Christian experience amply testifies.

Christian community can welcome and applaud; there is much also to drive it to prayer and fasting. Our catalogues of weal and woe should be assembled with ruthless honesty and exemplary thoroughness. Yet to be preoccupied with the conversion of the West is likely to be self-defeating. The reason for this judgment is deeply theological. To be preoccupied with the conversion of the West is to perpetuate the anthropocentrism that has corrupted so much evangelism since the eighteenth century. It puts ourselves and our conversion rather than God at the center of the world. Such a posture is at best sub-Christian and at worst idolatrous. The coming of the rule of God, however minutely and weakly it comes, is to be preferred to such a state of affairs. In the end, even modernity will become obsolete in the wake of the final fulfillment of the good purposes of God for creation and history. The future has already dawned; we should live in fear and trembling in the interim. God's compassion ultimately will be established at the heart of the universe; we should strive with all our being to let God reign in justice and mercy.

As Charles Wesley so powerfully expressed it,

> See how great a flame aspires,
>   Kindled by a spark of grace!
> Jesu's love the kingdom fires,
>   Sets the kingdoms on a blaze.
> To bring fire on earth He came;
>   Kindled in some hearts it is:
> O that all might catch the flame,
>   All partake the glorious bliss!
>
> Saw ye not the cloud arise,
>   Little as a human hand?
> Now it spreads across the skies,
>   Hangs o'er all the thirsty land:
> Lo! the promise of a shower
>   Drops already from above;
> But the Lord will shortly pour
>   All the Spirit of His love!

T E N

The Wider Ecumenism

While evangelists and students of evangelism have attended to the relation between Christianity and other religions, they have paid little attention to the more recent challenge facing them from the wider ecumenism. To be sure, evangelists and strategists of world mission have always been acutely aware of the existence and challenge of other religious traditions. This was true in the early church as well as throughout the history of evangelism. However, this challenge has done more to spur them on to new developments in methodology rather than to invite them to review in any fundamental way the whole question of evangelism to those of other faiths. Proposed new developments have themselves been a matter of deep controversy. The debate between the Jesuits and Franciscans in the attempt to evangelize China in the sixteenth century comes immediately to mind. The primary issue then was, as it is now in most circles, the question of how far the evangelist should go to accommodate the beliefs and customs of the evangelized. In the contemporary debate, however, the issues cut much deeper and precipitate not just disputes about strategy but fundamental questions about the legitimacy of the ministry of evangelism itself. What makes the contemporary discussion particularly interesting is that influential and serious theologians within the Christian tradition insist that we can no longer defend evangelism as a legitimate expression of Christian obedience.

The Challenge of Pluralism

Those interested in the logic of evangelism should heed the challenge that the wider ecumenism presents. In this chapter I want to examine in schematic form some of the prevailing arguments that call evangelism into question as a legitimate ministry of the church directed to the adherents of other religions. We need to begin, however, by dismissing two ways of dealing with the challenge of the wider ecumenism.

One way to deal with the issue is to say that Christianity itself allows for the possibility of many ways to God. Some come to God through suffering, some come through the influence of a godly home, and some come through a dramatic religious experience that radically alters their life-style and outlook. There is no single psychological process on the human side that everyone must follow to reach God. The same is true sociologically. Some are like Tatiana Goricheva, a recent Russian convert from atheism who encountered God in a recital of the Lord's Prayer during a yoga exercise.[1] Others, like many in the mass movements in India that were much discussed in the literature at the turn of the century, come as part of a caste or clan or wider social group. Diversity of pathways to God is what we expect and diversity is what we find.

This argument, however, will not begin to satisfy those concerned about the implications of the wider ecumenism. It leaves intact the fundamental Christian claim that the only way to God is through Jesus Christ. The variety of psychological and sociological pathways alluded to here assume that Christ is in fact the only way to God, and it is precisely this claim that has come under scrutiny and strain in the contemporary situation. Those who think that there are many ways to ultimate reality usually hold that God or the divine order can be reached equally well through the different religious traditions that exist in the world. This is the whole point of using the phrase "the wider ecumenism." The intention behind this use of the language of ecumenism is very clear: just as it is unacceptable in the wake

1. See Tatiana Goricheva, *Talking About God is Dangerous* (New York: Seabury, 1985).

of Christian ecumenism for any single Christian denomination to claim a monopoly on the means of salvation, so it is now unacceptable in the wake of the wider ecumenism developing between the world religions for the Christian religion to claim such a monopoly. Brief surveys of the diverse morphologies of conversion to Christianity do not begin to do justice to this issue, so we can dismiss them as strictly irrelevant.

A second possible solution to the problem is to focus on the concept of evangelism. Suppose we confine evangelism to acts of mercy, justice, and peace. The conceptual warrant for making this adjustment is perfectly honorable and legitimate. It stems from that tradition which construes evangelism fundamentally as acts of witness. Evangelism and witness are basically the same activities; any act of witness is also an act of evangelism. Clearly acts of mercy, justice, and peace constitute acts of witness, hence it is natural to read the latter as perfectly acceptable forms of evangelism. The rise of the wider ecumenism does not call such evangelism into question. On the contrary, it will encourage it. Since the motivation for the wider ecumenism is in part to alleviate human suffering, acts of justice, mercy, and peace will be welcomed and supported. Furthermore, the more widely this conception of evangelism is accepted within Christianity the less likely it will be that other forms of evangelism will be practiced. It is the other conceptions of evangelism that are so troublesome to the universal ecumenist.

What are those other conceptions? As we noted earlier, there are at least four. First, we can think of evangelism as the proclamation of the good news about the grace of God in Jesus Christ. Here the focus is on the communication of a message, irrespective of results. Second, we can construe evangelism as converting people to the Christian faith. Here the emphasis is on certain religious experiences or intellectual operations that end in a personal commitment to Jesus Christ as Savior and Lord. Third, we can define evangelism as the planting of local churches of this or that denomination across the world. The primary concern here is the incorporation of converts into local fellowships of believers. Finally, we can interpret evangelism as the initiation of people into the eschatological rule of God inaugurated in Jesus of Nazareth. Here evangelism is understood polymorphously as any activity governed by the intention to initiate people into the reign of God.

The fact that these alternative conceptions of evangelism exist at all is enough to put tremendous strain on the attempt to confine evangelism to acts of humanitarian witness. Indeed, few substantive arguments in the literature articulate this option. One meets it fairly frequently in the mainline denominations, but here it bears all the marks of an *ad hoc* invention deployed to keep ecclesiastical bureaucrats self-satisfied and to keep critics at a healthy distance. One has to develop an intellectual pedigree for it in order to keep it alive as a possible alternative. For this reason alone it is not likely to satisfy anyone interested in the deeper questions raised by the wider ecumenism. I shall therefore ignore it in what follows. I shall not worry too much, moreover, about the genuine differences between the four other conceptions; it is not clear to me that they make a whit of difference to the issue of whether Christians should evangelize those of other faiths. Hence for the purposes of this chapter we can define evangelism very broadly as any attempt to win others to allegiance to the Christian faith. This evangelism has come into question in the wake of the wider ecumenism and is the issue under discussion here. What I want to argue is that there is a very close connection between our commitments in Christology and our commitments about the wider ecumenism and about evangelism. More specifically, I shall suggest that a classical or high Christology mandates both an openness to other religious traditions and a responsible ministry of evangelism on a worldwide scale.

From the beginning Christians have claimed that the only way to God is through Jesus. In Acts Luke reports that Peter brought an exclusive message about Jesus to his fellow Jews when he insisted that there was no other name under heaven given among men by which they must be saved (4:12). John records a similar claim:

> Thomas said to him: "Lord, we do not know where you are going; how can we know the way?" Jesus said to him:

"I am the way, and the truth, and the life; no one comes to the Father, but by me. If you had known me, you would have known my Father also; henceforth you know him and have seen him." (14:6)

Here we have exclusivism at its purest, it would seem, and it is held in the teeth of both the Judaistic and the Samaritan traditions of the time.

Taken in a *prima facie* manner and in isolation, this claim is absurd. It is surely extraordinary to insist that people can come to God only through a first-century Jewish day-laborer who was sentenced to death and crucified by the conventional legal processes of the Roman judiciary in Palestine. The claim is an obvious scandal, and Christians who make it without reflecting on this can scarcely profess to understand in any deep sense what they are saying. Consider a contrary claim to the effect that the world can be saved only through Johnny Megaw, an Irish house-decorator who was killed by terrorists in Enniskillen on November 8, 1987. No one would take this seriously, yet, stated in a bald fashion, this is what classical Christianity wants to uphold. Moreover, many Christians cling to this ferociously; when it is challenged they are apt to blow up in your face—figuratively speaking, of course.

The Revisionist Impulse

Revisionist and enlightenment versions of the Christian tradition have been so scandalized by such talk that they have sought to find a way either out of it or around it. The central revisionist line is to make the Christian position concerning Jesus and his place in salvation more palatable by means of a vision of revelation. Revelation, it will be said, should be understood not from above as something that breaks into human life and history but more as something that naturally develops from below as religious believers seek to make intelligible sense of their developing journeys. Revelation is really a code word for significance. To say that Jesus is revelatory is to say that he is uniquely significant for Christians in their experience of God.

Indeed, Jesus is revelatory because he is significant; it is not that he is significant because he is revelatory. This reminds me of the witty comment of an Oxford friend after a tour of houses in Dallas. Outside Dallas, he averred, houses are expensive because they are valuable; in Dallas, houses are valuable because they are expensive. In the classical view Jesus is significant because he is revelatory. Certain features of his person and work are seen as warrants for interpreting him as having a crucial role in the process of universal salvation. In the revisionist view this is reversed. Jesus is revelatory because he is significant. Certain features of the response that people make to Jesus, such as its moral depth and spiritual overtones, are seen as warrants for construing him as revelatory of the character of ultimate reality. The intelligent Christian needs to single out this really critical factor from the tangled options available in the modern debates in Christology.

Consider now two interesting consequences that follow if we take the revisionist position. First, we need not reject other claims to revelation provided we construe revelation in such cases along the lines applied here. Other events, experiences, persons, and sacred texts may also legitimately be read as revelation. Indeed they demand to be interpreted in this fashion. What makes them revelatory is the response they have evoked and the traditions they have inspired. Clearly the major religious traditions of humankind satisfy this condition perfectly happily. Second, it would be natural not to seek to evangelize persons in other religious traditions. Each tradition has its own way to God; each has its own means of salvation or authentic existence; and each has its own sources of divine revelation. To evangelize in such circumstances would be otiose and inconsistent with one's primary theological principles. The appropriate attitude to adopt is that of mutual tolerance, shared service, and cross-cultural enrichment.

Of course, a person could engage in evangelism under these circumstances provided he or she paid a price for it. If one held that Jesus was uniquely revelatory of God then it might be possible to argue for evangelism on the grounds that he was the highest revelation of God and that, therefore, everyone had a right of access to that revelation. Yet I do not see how one can sustain this argument with any degree of credibility. Under this conception of revelation Jesus will be seen as uniquely revelatory because he is uniquely significant, but it is hard to see how one could provide adequate warrants for the unique significance of Jesus in this context. Significance here is a matter of response, and it is impossible to see how a set of responses in one religious tradition is more significant than the responses in another tradition. One might stand fast and simply state fideistically that Jesus is uniquely significant as a source of religious response, but very few will be prepared to go this far. Hence it is not at all surprising that those who construe the major religious traditions as revelatory and salvific avoid graded judgments on their efficacy and treat them as essentially equal as bearers of revelation and salvation.

Many Christians, both at the grass roots and at highly sophisticated levels, resist this way of responding to the new consciousness concerning the world religions. Their revisionist opponents, however, immediately explain this resistance as a continued expression of the imperialism that dogged the missionary ventures of the nineteenth century. Missionary work in the great drives of the last century was essentially an attempt to evangelize the world in a generation or two and was intimately related to the expansion of the exploitative empires of the West. To continue working for world evangelization at the end of the twentieth century is to perpetuate in more subtle forms the imperialistic endeavors of an earlier age.

There is undoubtedly some truth in this argument. How much truth can be determined only by careful historical analysis of the history of missions. Suffice it to say that the history of missions is a very complex affair.[2] Thus the missionary thrust of the nineteenth century as initiated by the Pietists was built very fundamentally on a desire to see individuals converted and brought into Christian communities. Some of the pioneering

---

2. Hints of a revisionist account of the history of missions can be found in Lamin Sanneh, "Christian Mission in the Pluralist Milieu: The African Experience," *International Review of Missions* 74 (1985): 199-211.

missionaries, like the hard-pressed Moravians, were themselves victims of oppression. Moreover, some, like the philosopher Gottfried Leibniz, who had a minimal but surprising hand in helping to shape the character of missionary endeavor, argued for a broader conception of missions by insisting that missionaries should take the benefits of the European Enlightenment across the globe.[3] Hence he wished to see the benefits of science and education shared for the glory of God and the good of the commonweal. He also hoped that missionary work would significantly enhance the scientific study of linguistics, of ancient history, and of the chronology, geography, and ethnography of foreign lands and civilizations. Furthermore, there is no doubt that early-twentieth-century missionaries were profoundly concerned about questions of race, health, education, poverty, national identity, social justice, and the like. John R. Mott coined the phrase "the larger evangelism" to capture this broadening of interest,[4] and some observers were very worried indeed that the development of such concerns could lead to a lack of balance in the commitments of missionaries.[5] All this does not, of course, settle in any final way the question of the exact relation between evangelism and imperialism, but it certainly calls into question any simplistic account of the relation between them.

There is another reason for challenging the appeal to imperialism as an explanation of continued evangelistic activity. Clearly, evangelistic activity is motivated and directed by a whole host of considerations. The appeal to imperialism implies a single set of reasons why people engage in evangelism, but this is not the case. For some the issue is one of personal vocation and calling; for others it is a matter of attention to the Great Commission as found in the Synoptic Gospels in one form or another; for some it is a natural expression of joyful exuberance as they seek to give freely that which they have freely received;

3. See Francis M. Merkel, "The Missionary Attitude of the Philosopher G. W. Von Leibniz," *International Review of Missions* 9 (1920): 399-410.
4. See John R. Mott, *The Larger Evangelism* (New York: Abingdon-Cokesbury, 1944).
5. See Sidney W. Clark, "Is Foreign Mission Work out of Balance?" *International Review of Missions* 3 (1914): 683-95.

for others it is a question of sharing in the rich heritage of evangelism that has been central to most denominations at some time or other; for some it is a burden laid upon them as they seek to stem the tide of secularism that has hit the West and threatens to spread elsewhere; for others it is a response of fear as they attempt to save the world from the demons of secular humanism, state socialism, or atheistic communism; for some it is a participation in the last great events of history before the final apocalypse; for others it is a commitment to rescue souls from eternal perdition. In the light of this it is unconvincing to lump all evangelistic activity to other cultures as the expression or fruit of imperialism.

The Finality of Jesus Christ and Its Evangelistic Implications

Among Christians, however, the most important reason for rejecting the proposed revisionist account of revelation, salvation, and evangelism lies neither in history, nor in psychology, nor in sociology, but in theology—that is, in the internal logic of the classical Christian tradition. In other words, resistance stems as much from a high Christology as it does from anything else. Briefly stated, Jesus is seen as the only way to God because he is believed to be the eternal Son of God through whom God acts in creation and redemption. Given the perceived relation between the agency of God and the activity of Jesus Christ, the claim that Jesus is the only way to salvation is analytic. It is not surprising, therefore, that those who want to undermine the ministry of evangelism engage in a profound revision of the Christian tradition. What is at stake is not just a reworking of the concept of revelation but a fundamental rejection of divine intervention in the world, of the classical version of Christology, and of its attendant trinitarian doctrine of God. John Hick's theological pilgrimage illustrates this admirably. His encounter with other faiths has led him to reject the incarnation and to adopt a radically revised doctrine of ultimate reality.

It is worth dwelling on this alternative account of the emergence and continuation of the evangelistic passion within Christianity. Charles Wesley captures quite splendidly its crucial ingredients in one of his lesser-known Christmas hymns.

> Let earth and heaven combine,
>   Angels and men agree,
> To praise in songs divine
>   The incarnate deity,
> Our God contracted to a span,
>   Incomprehensively made man.
>
> He laid His glory by,
>   He wrapped him in our clay,
> Unmarked by human eye,
>   The latent Godhead lay;
> Infant of days He here became,
>   And bore the mild Immanuel's name.
>
> Unsearchable the love
>   That hath the Saviour brought;
> The grace is far above
>   Or man or angels' thought:
> Suffice for us that God we know,
>   Our God, is manifest below.
>
> He deigns in flesh to appear,
>   Widest extremes to join;
> To bring our vileness near,
>   And make us all divine:
> And we the life of God shall know,
>   For God is manifest below.
>
> Made perfect first in love,
>   And sanctified by grace,
> We shall from earth remove,
>   And see his glorious face:
> Then shall his love be fully showed,
>   And man shall then be lost in God.

Three separate but closely related elements deserve mention as we reflect on this classical expression of the Christian gospel. There is, first, a strong, substantial conception of revelation. God has revealed himself in an amazing act of humility and manifested himself from within history. This act constitutes the second element, namely, a high Christology in which Christ is conceived as God "contracted to a span, incomprehensively made man." Wesley captures quite brilliantly here the shock and paradox of the incarnation. Finally, there is a reference to the work of Christ. His life and ministry are formed by the goal of joining humankind to God and making human life divine.

We now need to explore some of the ramifications of these and related themes for our understanding of other religious traditions. It is commonly thought that they prevent any degree of openness to competing accounts of reality. There is merit in this perception, for a degree of exclusivism follows logically from the high Christology embraced. The situation, however, is far more subtle than initial reactions generally permit. Moreover, it does not in the least sanction intolerance or other morally unacceptable attitudes, although, as we shall see, the whole question of tolerance is far more complicated than most observers realize.

It is important to grasp at the outset the full implications of the high Christology the classical tradition represents. In this view the activity of Christ, although crucially related to the events of his life, ministry, and death in Palestine, is not confined to that short segment of history. Jesus is the incarnate embodiment of the cosmic Christ who is at work enlightening all people (John 1:9). John, whom we quoted earlier as a thoroughgoing exclusivist, is here a universal inclusivist. Christ was also at work in Israel, so much so that one canonical witness, the author of Hebrews, says that Moses unwittingly considered abuse suffered for Christ greater wealth than the treasures of Egypt (11:26). Surely this implies that it is perfectly consistent to hold both that Jesus is the exclusive path to God and that people may genuinely encounter God outside the Christian church without explicitly knowing about Jesus of Nazareth.

This posture is substantiated by the Christian adoption of the Hebrew Bible, which was designated in an interesting fashion as their Old Testament. By doing so, Christians were insisting that God was genuinely known, loved, and worshiped in Israel prior to the coming of Jesus. Paul is absolutely secure in this thought, for his model of the justified believer is Abraham, a man who had never heard the gospel about Jesus (Rom. 4). If one has to know about Jesus of Nazareth to be saved, then Abraham could not have been saved. Abraham did not have such knowledge, yet he was saved; hence it must be possible to be saved without knowing about Jesus. This does not entail, however, that one is saved apart from the activity of God's Son. For the eternal Son is not swallowed up ontologically in the life of Jesus; the eternal Son who is fully manifest in Jesus of Nazareth is actively at work in all creation and history. It is precisely this that the high Christology of the classical tradition has sought to capture. Moreover, it is a conceptual truth in this tradition that salvation was wrought in us and for us by Christ. In other words, the relation with Christ is not straightforwardly contingent. Wherever there is salvation, it is intimately connected to the work of Christ, the eternal Son of God.

We can press this further. If Christ's activity extends through all creation, and if it is possible in principle to be saved without hearing of Jesus, then it is reasonable to infer that people outside the biblical traditions may also be saved and acquitted. Clearly such people will not know that their salvation has come to them through the work of Christ, but then Abraham did not know that either and this does not at all disqualify him from salvation. Nor is this a mere hypothetical possibility dreamed up to fit a favored theory. Cornelius is a good example of such a case from the biblical traditions. In the Lucan account of the incident involving Cornelius, Peter confesses that God shows no partiality, and proceeds to insist that in every nation everyone who fears God and does what is right is acceptable to God (Acts 10:34). So a high Christology creates space for openness and generosity to other religious traditions. As a corollary to this Christology we might say that the church should be seen not so much as the ark of salvation but as the locus of witness to and experience of the fullness of the work of Christ, which is made manifest in Jesus of Nazareth.

It does not follow from this that Christians should in any way or to any degree slacken in their efforts to take the gospel to everyone. Paul sets the pace in this matter. He argues, as we have seen, for Abraham as a model of the justified believer, yet he is so keen to see Abraham's descendants become followers of Jesus Christ that he is prepared to be accursed and cut off from Christ for their sake (Rom. 9:1-3). His untiring efforts in evangelism and missionary zeal confirm this commitment to take the gospel everywhere.

It is not difficult to see why this should be so. First, it is vitally important from within this perspective that everyone know of the fullness of what God has done in Christ. In Christ God has acted not exclusively but uniquely. God has summed up and concentrated the vastness of his grace in creation and Israel in his action in Jesus of Nazareth, and the whole world has a right of access to such grace. So generosity and love compel Christians to share the unsearchable riches of Christ. The history of evangelism is laden with this kind of commitment, but perhaps it is best illustrated in the action of the early Moravian missionaries to the West Indies who were prepared to become actual slaves in order to share the gospel with the slaves of that region. Second, it is only right that those who have already responded to the light of God that they have received outside the gospel should know of the true source of that light. Third, they should also have access to the full measure of God's grace and power, which is made available in Jesus Christ. In this domain attention will need to be given to the fullness of initiation into the kingdom of God. It is perfectly coherent to construe such initiation as a journey or set of stages, as the literature on spirituality and piety makes abundantly clear; just as one might minimally or maximally appropriate the action of God outside of Jesus of Nazareth, so might one appropriate the action of God *in* Jesus. Lastly, it is entirely appropriate that those who have rejected God be given the opportunity to respond to him afresh. If God has come to us uniquely in Jesus Christ, then the fullness of God's grace in Jesus may awaken them from sin and bring them to eternal life.

We should note in this context that one of the marks of those who have already responded to God without hearing of Jesus Christ is that they actually commit themselves to the gospel and become part of the body of Christ. In coming to Christ they are more explicitly and more fully meeting one whom they already know and love to some degree. Expressed in more traditional language, we might say that the hands they see in the cross are the full embodiment of those hands that they have already discerned in creation and in their own experience of the divine. Indeed, they recognize God's action in Jesus of Nazareth because through grace and faith they have already learned to recognize God's action outside of Jesus. It is worth repeating that this move in no way undermines the Christian claim that all of God's work in the world is ultimately wrought exclusively through Jesus. That is a matter of election on God's part; all we can do is accept or reject this as either a theological truth or a falsehood. God is sovereign over all his works and the fact that he has chosen to act through the Son is not something we can alter at will.

What I am proposing here in very embryonic terms is the beginnings of a Christian theology of the world religions. We are laying out some of the crucial premises that should inform a Christian understanding of other faiths. In itself this is nothing new. From the beginning Christianity had to develop its own vision of Judaism, signaled by the designation of the Hebrew Scriptures as the Old Testament. As we now know from contact with modern Jewish scholars, this is not an innocent, casual affair; it is a cryptic but very significant way of insisting on the finality of God's revelation in Jesus Christ. No serious Jew would be satisfied with this description of the Jewish canonical literature. Moreover, from the beginning the preachers and theologians of the Christian tradition were forced to articulate the relation between God's action in Israel and his action in Jesus of Nazareth. So what we have sketched here is simply an extension of what has been carried out in Christianity from the outset. Where there is a difference, it is one of degree and not of substance, for informed readers will have noted that the roots of the position we have expounded lie, at the very least, as far back as the second century in the work of Justin Martyr. They will also have noted that this position is deeply contested within the history of Christian debate on this subject.

What this shows afresh is that we are dealing with a project whose primary intent is to make theological sense of the history of religion. If this is so, it must be evaluated fundamentally on theological grounds. It must be resolved by the application of appropriate philosophical, historical, and theological criteria just like the evaluation of any other theological proposal.

We can also describe this as a metareligious claim, and thus may summon other criteria for and against it. By a metareligious claim I mean a claim about how to make the best sense of the more general metaphysical, moral, and spiritual space occupied by the world religions. Some refer to such proposals as world hypotheses. These two ways of describing the issue, the theological and the metareligious, are in fact logically related. Just as one's position on the truth or falsehood of Christianity has a bearing on the position one takes up on metareligious questions, the position one embraces on the metareligious issues has a bearing on the line adopted on the truth or falsehood of Christianity. In fact, one cannot resolve the metareligious question of how to construe the relation between the world religions without coming to a decision on the nature of ultimate reality.[6] This explains in part why it is no accident that adherents of most versions of inclusive reconstructionism are in general aggressively opposed to classical Christianity. They are evangelists for a new metareligious order even though they confine their evangelistic activity to very modest proportions by restricting it to publishing books and articles on the subject. Their evangelistic fervor leads them as a matter of logic to seek to displace its rivals at both the metareligious and the theological level.

Global Unity, Tolerance, and Dialogue

At the metareligious level more general criteria may be brought to bear on my claims. Thus they can be judged on the basis of

6. I discuss some of the philosophical issues arising from the existence of the world religions in *An Introduction to the Philosophy of Religion* (Englewood Cliffs, N.J.: Prentice Hall, 1985), chap. 18.

rational coherence or logical consistency, as well as on the basis of moral considerations. These moral concerns are expressed for two reasons. First, some believe that some kind of unity between the world religions is essential for the welfare of the human community given the breakdown of the old tribalisms and the emergence of a global village. This becomes particularly acute for those who insist on either a logical or psychological connection between religion and morality. Second, some invoke moral considerations in cases where it is thought that the particular theology of the world religions under review involves intolerance. Thus it is sometimes suggested that those who hold, say, to the finality of Jesus Christ will necessarily be intolerant of those who do not share this claim. They will, therefore, be opposed to any kind of genuine dialogue between the great religious traditions of the world.

Concerning the first of these problems, we should note that the fact of global unity was not lost on those committed to the task of world evangelization. Part of the argument for worldwide missionary activity was precisely that such activity provided the kind of universal faith that would be needed in the modern world to give it unity and moral coherence. Many believed that Christianity could provide exactly this service to the modern world.[7] I doubt, however, if this was a very significant factor in missionary motivation. Even if it was, it was deeply intertwined with the conviction that Christianity was true, that God had commissioned the missionary task of the church, and so on. So this solution to the problem of global unity has no attractions to those who think that classical Christianity is a relic from the past whose adherents have failed to come to terms with the new consciousness about pluralism. In recent times any attempt to see Christianity as the world religion of the future tends to be replaced by the insistence that the only religion that could provide coherence is one that embraces all the major religious traditions in an inclusivist mode.

Neither of these proposals is at all convincing as a solu-

7. A clear hint of this can be found in J. S. B. Brough, "Missionary Apologetics," *International Review of Missions* 8 (1919): 393.

tion to the problem at hand. Both rest on questionable assumptions about the relation between religion and morality. Certainly, it is not at all obvious that the whole of morality, including its social and political dimensions, depends on some logically prior religious base. We shall touch on this again later, but, at the very least, we note here that this is far too murky an area to provide warrants for any claim about the necessity of any religion or configuration of religions as the foundation of the moral, social, and political order.[8] In addition, both proposals involve fanciful judgments about the nature of the unity of the modern world, as if unity depended necessarily upon some agreed-upon religious cement to hold society together. Indeed, it is not at all clear what unity means in this context. It surely cannot be some world government, for all attempts to bring this about founder on the deep attachment to nation and soil that is such a marked feature of human existence. In fact, religious commitment is taken up and used quite ferociously in the national interest, as a host of examples from Dallas to Durban to Dublin makes clear. Nor would such a world government necessarily be a good thing, morally and politically. It conjures up images of dominion and dictatorship that may harbor more than a grain of truth. And even if it were a goal to be desired, one suspects that any world religion brought into being to undergird its moral structure would be as servile and cumbersome as most forms of state and civil religion have been. It is difficult in these circumstances to take these positions very seriously. At the very least they need to be laid out far more extensively than is currently the case.

We can resolve the second concern without too much difficulty. Is it true that those who believe in the finality of Jesus Christ are necessarily intolerant? On the surface it seems to many that if one believes that God is revealed uniquely in Jesus Christ then one must reject other religious positions as inevitably incomplete; therefore one is bound to be narrow if not

8. Basil Mitchell explores this matter very sensitively in *Law, Morality and Religion in a Secular Society* (London: Oxford University Press, 1967) and *Morality, Religious and Secular* (Oxford: Clarendon Press, 1980).

225

bigoted in one's allegiance. Some form of this argument undoubtedly lies behind the desire of many to adopt an inclusivist
attitude toward the religious systems of the world. Such a posture seems *prima facie* more loving and Christian.

We cannot resolve this matter by appealing to history. That
is, we cannot point to past instances of intolerance on the part
of the Christian community to settle the matter. Clearly, Christian individuals and communities have been intolerant in the
sense that they have displayed a lack of respect for practices
and beliefs other than their own. They have conducted crusades
against those whom they believed to be their enemies both
within and without Christianity. They have at times been
thoroughly unpleasant in their attitudes and actions against
other religions. All this is beside the point. The heart of the
issue is whether belief in Jesus as a unique revelation of God
necessarily leads to intolerance. Finding a correlation of sorts
between some who believe in Jesus as uniquely revelatory and
some who practice intolerance does not establish either a causal
or logical link between the two. Intolerance has been fueled by
many convictions and motives that have little to do with belief
in the uniqueness of Jesus, and, even if it has been initiated by
such belief, there is no reason why it may not be purged and
overcome.

The crux of the matter, then, is semantic. We use the word
intolerance loosely to cover a variety of actions and attitudes.
Strictly speaking, it means a lack of respect for the beliefs and
practices of others.[9] Used loosely, it is extended to cover bigotry,
narrow-mindedness, sectarianism, persecuting zeal, obstinacy,
fanaticism, and the like. Understandably it also gets stretched
to cover straightforward disagreement on important issues that
are self-involving. This is the usage that is invoked when one
applies it to those who hold to the finality of Jesus Christ.
Clearly, those who believe that Jesus uniquely reveals God will
disagree with the adherents of other religions who do not
believe this. It is simply a matter of logic. One cannot believe
two contradictory statements at the same time unless one is

9. *Oxford English Dictionary* (Oxford: Clarendon Press, 1932), XI, 12.

blind, muddled, or inconsistent. So if one believes that Jesus uniquely reveals God, one cannot simultaneously believe that he does not uniquely reveal God. To turn this kind of intellectual competence into a species of intolerance is odd in the extreme, for it cannot be a moral fault to be consistent in one's beliefs. Nor can the abandoning of such consistency be made into a prerequisite of genuine dialogue with those of another religious tradition, for such a posture invites participants in dialogue to be insincere and dishonest. On the contrary, dialogue requires a frank exchange of convictions, and mature believers of incompatible traditions will take deep disagreement on fundamental issues in their stride. Moreover, they will bring to dialogue a commitment to respect the religious beliefs and practices of others. This is the essence of tolerance, and the thoughtful evangelist should have no more difficulty in exercising this virtue than other mortals. So there is no reason why the Christian evangelist cannot enter genuine discussion with others to explore fully and sincerely incompatible convictions.

Religious reconstructionists and radical inclusivists run the grave risk of falling into precisely the moral fault that they lay at the feet of metareligious exclusivists. There is a real temptation to play down as secondary or as insignificant those beliefs that are at the core of the great religious traditions. Those who hold to these core beliefs are castigated for clinging to outworn myths or for believing due to psychological or sociological causes. What this means is that the exclusivist is being interpreted and treated as a patient undergoing certain deterministic-like processes rather than as a rational agent weighing arguments and seeking to arrive at the truth. This comes perilously close to a lack of respect for the partner in dialogue at the metareligious level. We might justly say that it is a form of intolerance.

We need to note that dialogue itself differs categorically from evangelism. It is governed by its own intentions and conventions. Strictly speaking, "dialogue" is just another word for conversation.[10] This very easily gets lost because persuasively

---

10. *Oxford English Dictionary,* III, 312.

defined conceptions of dialogue are smuggled into the discussion. If we stick to its common meaning we can be on guard against such ploys, especially in circumstances where sophisticated ideological moves of a religious or quasi-religious character are being pursued. If we do so, we can also quickly separate dialogue from other notions that are in the neighborhood. Thus dialogue not only differs from evangelism, it also differs from debate and negotiation.

What is absolutely crucial to dialogue is that those engaged in it respect the beliefs of those who share in the process, and that they be prepared to follow the conversation and the evidence wherever they lead them. The latter claim is implicit in the act of dialogue, for if one is not prepared to change one's mind in the light of what is presented in conversation, then one is not really taking the partner in conversation seriously. This extends to inclusivists and exclusivists, to orthodox and heretical, to liberal, radical, and conservative. That many people, including metareligious reconstructionists, have difficulty achieving this only goes to show that we all fear risk and that dialogue may be more demanding than we at first realized. Beyond this all we need to note is that dialogue may serve all sorts of laudable purposes. It may be used to banish ignorance and increase understanding, to broaden one's horizons, to deepen one's awareness of one's own religious commitments, to help clear up various kinds of conflict, to explore common moral problems, and so on. It is not too highbrow to add that it is worth pursuing for its own sake.

It follows from this that dialogue should not be used as a covert form of evangelism. This sours the atmosphere, and it undercuts the intentions that constitute genuine dialogue. Once we turn dialogue into an attempt to advance some particular religious position or to implement a specific metareligious agenda we are changing the rules of the game in midstream. If they avoid this, there is no reason why Christians who are also committed to the task of evangelism may not engage in dialogue with integrity. If they are also by training and temperament evangelists, they may not, of course, be the best people to delegate as participants in official dialogue between the world religions. Evangelists are given to winning people to a cause, which is liable to spill through in their conversations. On the other hand, evangelists have at least this in their favor: they understand from within what it is to be passionately committed to a particular faith, and should, therefore, be able to understand this when they meet the same in others. They should also be skilled in explaining to others what their faith means. In the end these are empirical matters that can be resolved only in the light of the relevant evidence. In principle there is no reason why the Christian cannot be as tolerant as others in dialogue.

Evangelism and Tolerance

Even when acting as an evangelist the Christian is bound by the constraints of the Christian tradition to be committed to tolerance and freedom. To put it negatively, Christians have several reasons why they should reject intolerance. First, they believe that God has made everyone in his own image and that Christ has died for all. This has profound implications for relations with others. At the least it means that the evangelist must allow those being evangelized the freedom to respond as agents who are to be persuaded by divine love rather than coerced by emotional or intellectual gymnastics. Evangelism must be carried out in a spirit of love, showing the same kind of compassion, patience, humility, and boldness that was manifest in the incarnation.[11]

In addition, in sharing the gospel and in seeking to initiate others into the kingdom of God, the evangelist has nothing to give that has not first been received. It is not a matter of offering the superior riches of one culture or imperialistically imposing them on another, as if the evangelist were the source of the

11. Timothy Gorringe usefully explores the relation between the incarnation and the character of evangelism in "Evangelism and Incarnation," *Indian Journal of Theology* 30 (1981): 69-77. As our discussion here is devoted to the legitimacy of evangelism in the wake of the discovery of religious pluralism, we cannot take up the question of how to evangelize those of other religious traditions. One lesson to be stressed, were we to do so, would be the cruciality of respecting the specificity and particularity of the various religious traditions. Attending to these is a mark of both love and respect.

reign of God. Rather, the evangelist seeks to participate in humility and hope in the prevenient work of the Holy Spirit as God extends his gracious rule across the face of the earth. From within this horizon it is otiose to engage in acts of evangelism that fail to respect the judgment of those who are offered the benefits of God's grace.

Further, the evangelist must believe that everyone has to come to see the truth for himself or for herself. People cannot be coerced into the kingdom of God, for conversion always involves divine grace at work in the human heart. Where this is forgotten evangelism can easily degenerate into manipulation and shallow forms of initiation. Also, Christians are commanded to love their enemies, leaving God to execute judgment as and when it is appropriate. Besides, it is common sense to recognize that intolerance creates an atmosphere where other evils, such as bigotry and sectarianism, can grow like a cancer. Every effort should therefore be made to ensure that affection, esteem, and goodwill prevail within the church and within society. All are called to provoke one another to love and good works.

This is easier said than done. Every society is built on a measure of consensus; it cannot exist without the cultivation of that consensus across the generations. Neither a religion nor a nation can exist without agreement on certain beliefs and principles. Of necessity these must be articulated, defended, and handed down in the form of tradition. Otherwise the society or religion concerned will be replaced by an alien or different set of ideals that undermine its general character, or it will lose its integrity and disintegrate from within. This is perhaps the grain of truth that lies behind the desire to cultivate as much agreement as possible across the religious traditions of the world. However, this grain of truth in no way sanctions some grandiose quest for an inclusivist religion that might serve as the basis of society. To follow this route is to make religion a means to an end, and it is likely to ignore the extent to which society may be undergirded by moral and rational principles that are not necessarily grounded in religion at all.

In any case it is utopian to think that religion can overcome the divisions that seem at times to constitute the human condition. We can expect profound conflict between people of contrary metaphysical and religious visions. Formally, religions have much in common. Thus they characteristically offer a network of proposals on creation, on the uniqueness of human nature within creation, on what has gone wrong with the world, on how to put it right, on how things are going to turn out in the future, and the like. Materially, however, they differ profoundly on the particulars of their claims in each of these areas. In fact, they enter into aggressive competition in the marketplace of ideas on these matters. Commitment on these issues is unavoidable in life. How one decides has profound consequences for one's identity, one's sense of community, one's moral ideals, one's political aspirations, and one's hopes for the future. It would be more astonishing if there was no deep disagreement in this domain. Moreover, it is natural, given the human propensity for fanaticism and for zeal without knowledge, that disagreement will at times spill over into intense conflict. It requires great wisdom, discernment, and political dexterity to deal with this. In society we are invariably entangled in messy compromises and untidy solutions that not even the common North American rhetoric about the separation between church and state can eliminate. It surely requires heroic faith to think that the development of some kind of global theology of the world religions will solve the problems that we have to face at this level. Perhaps it is more realistic to settle for as much tolerance as we can muster.

Christians can contribute to this by cultivating a catholic spirit within their own ranks, by entering into dialogue with other religious traditions, and by seeking the maximum liberty that is compatible with the public good within society as a whole. This demands strength of character and a lack of sentimentality about human nature. The fact is, we must withstand vigilantly the dark and corrupt forms of the Christian religion. We should confront them with the full challenge of the coming of the reign of God. Given the grimmer side of human nature, we might also expect that there will at times be serious conflict. The best that we can sometimes hope for, as Schlatter once shrewdly observed, is that our battles be fought with clean and honorable weapons. Unfortunately not all Christians have learned this lesson. Some sentimentally and naively think that the battles can be avoided. Some, unable to find a fray, will invent one so that they can have a good fight. The path of wisdom is to avoid such options and seek at all times to love our neighbors as ourselves. Insofar as evangelism is conceived as initiation into the rule of God in history, it has a clear contribution to make to this end.

Conclusion

We can bring this chapter to a close by commenting on the relevance of our arguments for the wider ecumenism. Perceptive readers will notice that we have not used the phrase at all extensively. Ecumenism has been for the most part a Christian concept. In recent discussions it has been extended to cover the developing dialogue between the world religions. In this context it is far from being an innocent or innocuous notion. Remember, ecumenism began because of attempts by Christians to evangelize the world in the last century. It was argued very forcefully that the unity of the church was essential for the credibility and completion of the worldwide missionary task that faced the churches.[12] Considerable progress has been made in joint projects, in the development of common statements, and in other areas. It is far from clear, however, whether the organic unity of the church is any nearer now than it was a century ago. The reason for this is clear: there cannot be unity without agreement in belief, which is extraordinarily difficult to achieve. It is not surprising, then, that in the moves to develop a global unity across the religious traditions of the world aggressive efforts are being made to press for the adoption of a new metareligious or metatheological vision that seeks to convert others to an inclusive reconstruction of one kind or another. Given the original connection between ecumenism and evangelism, it should not surprise us that the wider ecumenism championed among us

---

12. William Richey Hogg explores the beginnings of the modern ecumenical movement in *Ecumenical Foundations* (New York: Harper, 1952).

produces its own forms of evangelism. The wary will be on the watch for those metareligious evangelists who are keen to initiate us into a new-world theology and the institutions and practices related thereto. Nor should it surprise us if at times evangelism at this level degenerates into popular propaganda; we can expect this given what we know of the history of Christian evangelism. Nor should we be taken unaware if the results of these efforts are as bleak as those that confront us on the Christian ecumenical landscape.

Index

Altar calls: and baptism, 55, 131; and evangelism, 55
Anabaptist tradition, 97
Anthony the Great, 134
Anthropocentrism: in conversion, 122-23; in evangelism, 58-59, 69, 208; *see also* Individualism
Apocalyptic writers, 23-24, 28; eschatological language of, 30; and Peter's prophecy, 31; *see also* Eschatology; Kingdom of God
Apologetics in evangelism, 11, 63, 206-7, 206-7 nn. 25-26
Apostles: and baptism, 131; and early evangelism, 50-51; and gifts of the Holy Spirit, 156; and Jesus, 52; and the proclamation of the good news, 52
Apostles' Creed, 147 n. 5
Articles and Confession of Faith of the United Methodist Church, 147
Augustine, 18, 120
the Awakening: example of, 99-100; and personal experience of God, 120

Baptism: adult vs. infant, 176-77, 176 n. 8, 123; and altar calls, 55,

131; and Christian initiation, 97-98; and confirmation, 98; and conversion, 123-35, 133 n. 24, 176-77; and Eastern Orthodox Church, 124; vs. evangelization, 52; forced baptism, 166; and grace, 130, 133; and the Great Commission, 53; and the Holy Spirit, 98; the issue of evangelism, 11; and kingdom of God initiation, 14, 99, 123-24, 130-34, 136, 138-39, 142, 175-77, 176 n. 8; and original sin, 123; and the proclamation of the gospel, 44; and rebirth imagery, 121; and Roman Catholicism, 124-25
Barrett, David, 52
Barth, Karl: and the Christian theological position, 6; and evangelism, 190; and the power of the Holy Spirit, 153-54
Beatitudes, 27
Bohr, David, 4
Bonino, José Míguez, 125-29, 136-37
Booth, Catherine, 113
Born-again politics, 123
Brown, Fred: and Christian communities, 192-95, 197-98; and

234

mensions of, 102-3; and communion, 160; and conversion, 138-39, 178; and the development of gifts, 103; and the eucharist, 160-62, 176-77; and evangelism, 103-5, 211-12; and fasting, 176; and the gifts of the Holy Spirit, 163; and God's action, 175, 230; and the catechumenate, 174-78, 174 n. 7; and the power of the Holy Spirit, 114, 141-42, 159 n. 20, 163, 230; and prayer, 176-77; the process of, 98-101, 119; and the proclamation of the gospel, 173; and Scripture, 176; spiritual disciplines of, 103; theocentric vs. individualistic focus of, 98-99; and tolerance, 229-30; *see also* Christian initiation; Kingdom of God; Kingdom of God initiation theory (of evangelism)

Kingdom of God initiation theory (of evangelism): and accountability, responsibility, 114; advantages of, 113-15; and baptism, 130-34, 142, 175-77, 176 n. 8; cognitive learning in, 111; and conversion, 142; and the creed, 142, 175, 177-78; definition of, 95-98, 96 n. 3; division of ministries within, 111-12; and ecumenism, 14; and the eucharist, 175-77; and evangelism, 118-19; and folk religion, 114; and the gifts of the Holy Spirit, 114, 142, 163, 175; implications, 164-65; intellectual component of, 142-45, 143 nn. 2-3, 162, 175; and love of God and neighbor, 175; and modernity, 14; and morality, 134-38, 175; and the power of the Holy Spirit, 152-60, 154 n. 12, 156 n. 17, 159 n. 20;

and the proclamation of the gospel, 114, 119; the rule of faith in, 145-52, 147 n. 5, 150-51 nn. 7-8; and spiritual discipline, 142, 160-63, 175; support of, 13-16; *see also* Christian initiation; Kingdom of God; Kingdom of God initiation

King, Martin Luther, Jr., 127

Lausanne Covenant, 42, 46
Laying on of hands, 158-59, 176
Leibniz, Gottfried, 216
Liberation theology, 12
Luke, 25
Luther, Martin: and early church creed, 149, 149 n. 6; and personal experience of God, 120; and Luther's Shorter Catechism, 147

McGavran, Donald, 3; background of, 93; and church growth through evangelism, 71-72, 74-75; and evangelicalism, 80; and theological issues, 79-80, 79 n. 13
MacMullen, Ramsay, 152-53
Mark, 24
Martin, David, 187-88
The Master Plan (Coleman), 3
Methodism: class meeting system of, 66; and conversion, 124, 126-27, 136-37; and God's action, 179; and the Wesleyan quadrilateral theological method, 146
Methodius and Cyril, 113
Meyer, Ben F., 36
Mission: church growth, 70; and evangelism, 42, 133-34; and revisionist position of Christian tradition, 215-16
Modernity: concept of, 186-91; conflicts in secular evangelism,